The Political Is Political

Essex Studies in Contemporary Critical Theory

Series editors: Peter Dews, Professor of Philosophy at the University of Essex; Fabian Freyenhagen, Reader in Moral and Political Philosophy at the University of Essex; Steven Gormley, Lecturer in Philosophy at the University of Essex; Timo Jütten, Lecturer in Philosophy at the University of Essex; and Jörg Schaub, Lecturer in Philosophy at the University of Essex

The Essex Studies in Contemporary Critical Theory series aims to develop the critical analysis of contemporary societies. The series publishes both substantive critical analyses of recent and current developments in society and culture and studies dealing with methodological/conceptual problems in the Critical Theory tradition, intended to further enhance its ability to address the problems of contemporary society.

Titles in the Series

The Political Is Political

*Conformity and the Illusion of
Dissent in Contemporary
Political Philosophy*

Lorna Finlayson

ROWMAN &
LITTLEFIELD
————————INTERNATIONAL

London • New York

Published by Rowman & Littlefield International, Ltd.
Unit A, Whitacre Mews, 26-34 Stannary Street, London SE11 4AB
www.rowmaninternational.com

Rowman & Littlefield International, Ltd. is an affiliate of Rowman & Littlefield
4501 Forbes Boulevard, Suite 200, Lanham, Maryland 20706, USA
With additional offices in Boulder, New York, Toronto (Canada), and London (UK)
www.rowman.com

British Library Cataloguing in Publication Information Available
A catalogue record for this book is available from the British Library

ISBN: HB 978-1-7834-8049-4
ISBN: PB 978-1-7834-8050-0

Library of Congress Cataloging-in-Publication Data

Finlayson, Lorna, 1986–
The political is political : conformity and the illusion of dissent in contemporary political philosophy
/ Lorna Finlayson.
pages cm.—(Essex studies in contemporary critical theory)
Includes bibliographical references and index.
ISBN 978-1-78348-286-3 (cloth : alk. paper)—ISBN 978-1-78348-287-0 (pbk. : alk. paper)—ISBN
978-1-78348-288-7 (electronic) 1. Opposition (Political science) 2. Dissenters. 3. Political science—
Philosophy. I. Title.
JC328.3.F56 2015
320.01—dc23

2015001366

∞™ The paper used in this publication meets the minimum requirements of American
National Standard for Information Sciences Permanence of Paper for Printed Library
Materials, ANSI/NISO Z39.48-1992.

Printed in the United States of America

Police kettle protestors against tuition fees on Westminster Bridge, December 9, 2010. Photo: Jon Cartwright.

Contents

Acknowledgements

I am greatly indebted to the following people who read drafts of all or part of this book and gave me useful feedback and discussion: Natalia Baeza, Duncan Bell, Nick Bruton, Tim Button, Christina Cameron, Ben Colburn, John Dunn, Koshka Duff, Katharine Jenkins, Steven Methven, Basim Musallam, Sebastian Nye, Janosch Prinz, Richard Raatzsch, Diana Siclovan, Dan Swain, and the editorial board of Essex Studies in Contemporary Critical theory (especially Fabian Freyenhagen and Jörg Schaub).

Special thanks are also due to the supervisors of the dissertation which eventually turned into this book, Raymond Geuss and Hallvard Lillehammer.

A number of people have contributed support in forms intellectual, moral and alcoholic. In addition to several of the above, I would particularly like to thank Tessa Frost, Amelia Horgan, André Hough, Pauline and Peter Jackson, Orlando Lazar-Gillard, Louise and Steve Lock, Lucy McMahon, Clément Mouhot, Eva Nanopoulos, Remi Oriogun-Williams, Usch and William Spettigue, Wesley Wrigley, and my family: Jerry Finlayson, Caroline Wheeler, Baz Wolfram-Wheeler, Mr Finlay T. L. Wolfram and Gordon Finlayson.

Introduction

Nothing could be more at odds with our stage technique than the prologue of the Euripidean drama. Having a character at the beginning of the play tell us who he is, what has preceded the action, what will happen in the course of the play—a modern stage-writer would describe this as a wilful and unforgivable repudiation of the effect of suspense. We know what is going to happen, so why should we wait until it actually does?

—Nietzsche[1]

Nobody should really have to point out that political philosophy is political.[2] What this book tries to do, nonetheless, is to point out precisely that, and to describe the conditions that make it necessary to do so.

The discipline of political philosophy is (or rather, has become) a peculiar one. Insofar as it differs from related subjects, such as political science or sociology or political theory, the difference conventionally lies in the expectation that at least part of what interests political philosophers will be the explicitly evaluative projects of prescription, recommendation, condemnation, demand and critique. But political philosophy is not just this abstractly defined activity of enquiry. It is also an institution, with its own culture, publications and community of paid professionals—and like any community, it goes through phases and fashions. This book is about the contemporary institution of political philosophy. In particular, it is about the institution of political philosophy in the Anglo-American world. It is concerned above all

1

to expose that institution's peculiarities and to ask what they tell us: both about the parochial realm of academic political philosophy and about the wider world which (albeit increasingly halfheartedly) produces and fosters it.

This might seem already to raise a problem. This book, I've just admitted, has as its object of study a peculiar and parochial discipline: a particular form of political philosophy, which has taken hold in a particular time and in particular places. So it seems that either I must admit that the study of this phenomenon is of very limited relevance, or else I am at risk of that much more culpable parochialism which mistakes a backwater for the whole ocean, claiming a broad or universal significance for something that is of strictly local interest.

There is a big difference, however, between the assumption that the rest of the world must be just the same as your own particular village, and on the other hand, thinking that the world is a sufficiently interconnected place that in-depth local studies may tell us something about the surrounding environment. The tradition of 'critical theory', to which this book is fairly heavily indebted, has as one of its characteristic features an emphasis on the interconnectedness of the social world, and the commitment to the idea that a lot can be gained from careful scrutiny of small and apparently insignificant details. My project in this book is in the same spirit: it is not that I think that a particular kind of political philosophy is the whole world, or that I think that the whole world (or even the whole of academia, or even of political philosophy) is just like it; but what I do think, and will suggest throughout, is that political philosophy is not an isolated field having nothing to do with anything else around it, but a human institution, overlapping with other human institutions—all of which inevitably bear traces of the social world in which they are embedded. If I didn't think that, I would not have bothered to write about it.

Political philosophy, by definition, must be in some way concerned with or directed at matters political. What the trivial formulation of the title of this book is meant to convey is that the ways in which political philosophy is political *would* seem obvious to us, were it not for the various deceptive mechanisms which, I'll suggest, are at work throughout that discipline's characteristic discourse. These mechanisms are the ideological overgrowth concealing the true political character of this institution.[3]

The point I make in stressing the political nature of political philosophy is parallel to that of the slogan on which my title plays: 'the personal is political.' For feminists of the 1960s and 1970s, this highlighted the fact that crucial aspects of women's oppression were rendered invisible by a construal of 'the political' which excluded from its scope such phenomena as marriage, the family, beauty norms, and so on.[4] Like the personal, I want to say, the political-philosophical is political in a double sense. First, it has its own internal politics, just as there is an internal politics of (for example) the family. I'll suggest, in particular, that a major theme of the politics of political philosophy is the deployment of methodological norms covertly rigged so as to maintain the dominance of a particular (liberal) framework. The second and related point is that political philosophy has to be understood as a form of human activity which is part of a wider political reality. In other words, political philosophy is political inside and out.

Then there is a further sense to my title, which might be termed the 'aspirational' sense: political philosophy should *strive to be* political—in the same sort of sense in which an individual might decide to think of herself and act as a 'political' rather than an 'apolitical' person. Political philosophy should be informed by political reality and embrace and seek to understand its own political significance.[5] As it stands, of course, few political philosophers would openly disown this ideal—the important question is what the ideal should actually involve. The answer implicit in the chapters that follow is that it must involve, at the very least, abandoning the attempt to uphold a 'trichotomy' between the following:

a. 'politics',
b. 'political philosophy' and
c. the 'methodology of political philosophy'.

One problem, then, is the gulf that opens up between (a) and (b). Contemporary political philosophy seeks to make itself in various ways independent of politics: 'ideal theory' tries to describe what *ought* to be the case politically, regardless of what is;[6] the later Rawls tries to transcend the reality of deep political disagreement through the chimera of a 'political conception of justice', grounded in the 'reasonableness' of citizens.[7] But in addition—and this is in fact no more than an extra-complicated way of maintaining the dichotomy between (a) and (b)—a separate *third* realm is conjured: that of the 'methodology' of political philosophy. The function of this, I'll claim, is to push politics still further away from political philosophy, by sustaining the false impression that 'methodological' considerations (e.g., prized philosophical values such as 'charity', 'clarity' and 'rigour', or competing models of the relationship between philosophy and politics) can somehow be evaluated without presupposing positions on what might be called 'first-order' political-philosophical questions—that is, questions about the sort of place the world is, could be, or should be. Just as the political-philosophical is political, *the methodological is political-philosophical.*[8]

My main focus will be on collapsing the second gulf of the trichotomy: that is, collapsing the methodological into the first-order political-philosophical—or rather, showing how it already invariably does collapse (although many theorists don't seem to notice it). But it's worth noting that, from the point of view of having already envisaged the closure of the first gulf—the one between politics and political philosophy—this second collapse should come as no surprise. If political philosophy is a species of politics, then the methodology of political philosophy is the activity of reflecting on a species of politics, which is just to say that it is itself a species of political philosophy (and hence of politics too). And this relationship also obtains in reverse: the manner in which the 'methodology' of political philosophy collapses into first-order political philosophy helps us to close the gap between the unity that is political-philosophy-and-its-methodology, on the one hand, and politics—what we might normally think of as political philosophy's object of study—on the other. The point here is not as elaborate as it sounds. The fact that it sounds so off-putting is partly the result of the unnaturalness that often comes with the attempt to describe the structure of arguments in advance of making them—an overrated practice, as I'll suggest shortly. But it is worth briefly explaining two main *ways* in which my effort to close the gap between political philosophy and its methodology may serve, at the same time, to narrow the gap between political philosophy and politics.

First, the account I give of the *function* of the attempt to treat methodological questions as independent of political-philosophical ones produces, in the end, a picture of political philosophy and its methodology as an 'ideological' phenomenon, in something like the Marxist sense of that term—that is, a distortion of reality which occurs because of its tendency to reinforce certain interests. As already noted, political philosophy is itself a piece of politics, inside *and* out: its regulative norms are subservient to a form of liberal theory, which might in turn be seen as subservient to a predominantly liberal political status quo.

Second, it is significant that a central characteristic of that status quo is an apparent 'depoliticization' of life and even of politics itself. The wider social context in which the depoliticization of political philosophy takes place ex-

hibits a more *general* depoliticization which is, if anything, even more palpa-
bly absurd than its local manifestation in academia. In the wake of the 'end of
ideology' and 'end of history' theses,[9] we are confronted with a world in
which student unions are expected to be 'apolitical', environmental and economic crises are regarded as issues that require us to 'transcend' political
disagreements (if we are to do justice either to the seriousness of those
problems or to the demands of 'practicality') and in which politicians say
things like this:

> Stick resolutely to the centre ground. In an era where people no longer see
> politics through an ideological prism, that is where they want their politicians
> to be.[10]

Meanwhile, old-fashioned political language finds an unlikely sanctuary in
marketing: 'Stand up to split ends!', 'A revolution in eyelash technology'.[11]
The depoliticization of political philosophy, in that case, is just more of the
same, right down to the technique of breaking the world up into apparently
independent fragments: compare the holding apart of politics, political philosophy and methodology with, for example, the disconnect between the
university and the rest of society that is presupposed by the contemporary
rhetoric of 'representing students *as students*'. To find in political philosophy
trends which mirror the trends of politics more broadly is grist to the mill of
anyone inclined to cast doubt on the clean detachability of the two.

From its own perspective, then, what I am writing now is a piece of
political philosophy *and* a piece of methodology of political philosophy, and
even a piece of politics (albeit a very, very puny one).[12] This need not be
incompatible with my complaints about all three categories. These complaints are not in the first instance against politics or political philosophy or
methodology per se, but against ways of doing them that I allege are currently dominant. Of the three, 'methodology' is perhaps the category most frequently declared inadequate *as such*, on the grounds that it is a self-indulgent
diversion of resources from the supposedly more urgent business of getting
on and doing some actual political philosophy.[13] Since this is the category to
which the contents of this book would most likely be assigned (within the
schema that I ultimately want to reject), it's worth saying something now in
reply to this kind of anti-methodology sentiment. The first thing to say is that
it only really makes sense to dismiss methodological reflection as an unwel-
come frivolity if it is assumed that political philosophy is going along sufficiently well. The more derelict or corrupt or decadent political philosophy is

thought to be, the more the charge that the study of *methodology* is decadent loses its bite. Plus, of course, to come to a judgement about whether political philosophy is 'working' is already to take a methodological stance (what does it *mean* for political philosophy to be 'doing its job'?).

Manifestly enough, I don't think that political philosophy is 'working'—not relative to any very admirable ends, anyway. This is not a premise of this book, however, but a case which it tries to make. If it succeeds, it retrospectively justifies the decision to embark on a 'methodological' project in the first place. [14]

The root of at least some anti-methodology sentiment is perhaps just a thoroughly inculcated aversion to behaviour that is deemed disruptive—a word most closely associated with the castigation of naughty schoolchildren. From the vantage point of a school and its teachers trying to discharge their usual functions, having pupils trying to question, criticize, reform or sabotage those functions is at best an irritation, and at worst a serious threat. But that is just to say that many of the normal functions of a school are non- and even anti-educational—and certainly, anti-philosophical. [15] It may be that the closest we can get to an 'essence' of philosophy is a kind of restless and insatiable troublemaking—a disruptiveness that extends to ourselves, our activities and the institutions to which we belong. [16] Since troublemaking is never going to be much appreciated by those on the receiving end of it, it makes some sense to think that if philosophy is not hated or feared, then something has gone wrong.

✳✳✳

That's about as much of an 'introduction', in the normal sense of the term, as this book is going to have, and this is related to the fact that the book is in some respects an eccentric one. I've allowed its form and style, as well as its content, to deviate at times from what will be considered normal or appropriate. This runs the risk of being looked upon as affectation but is on the contrary dictated by sincerity, given the view I put forward as to the current state of political philosophy. It is not just that I have no reason to ape the characteristics of the kind of philosophy I reject—sometimes, in fact, I think it *is* appropriate to do this, for example, in order to make internal criticisms, for example, or just to make points more palatable to one's opponents. The point is that, if I actually mean what I say about the continuity between the philosophical and the methodological (and do not for any reason regard myself as a special case), then I have no choice but to philosophize not only with the explicit claims I make but also with the way in which I make them.

Often, the most effective way to bring a previously unconscious or invisible norm into clear view is (wittingly or unwittingly) to break it. One of the aims of this book is to draw attention to norms of philosophical discourse that might otherwise be taken for granted or go unnoticed. So to the extent that my own violation of norms—like those demanding polite and formal language, helpful introductory sections, impersonal examples, and so on—is deliberate, it is 'attention-seeking behaviour' only in this sense (doubling as a self-defence strategy against the sheer boredom that the diligent application of these norms will produce, boredom of the extreme kind that in any case tends to destroy inhibitions).

Anyway, setting out to write the introduction for this book, I found that I could not really bring myself to write the sort of thing that is customarily provided at the start of philosophy books, but that it might be interesting to say something instead about why that is—about what it means to introduce something, about the way in which philosophy texts in particular tend to be introduced, and about what this might tell us about those texts. What I'm going to say about this here will be sketchy and provisional, but so what?[17] I don't see any reason, in philosophy, to abide by the principle of not starting what we cannot finish—a principle which would probably preclude ever starting anything[18]—and anyway, part of the point I want to press, incompletely and open-endedly, is that philosophical projects are necessarily incomplete and open-ended.

Etymologically, to 'introduce' just means to 'lead [something] into [something else]' (Latin: *introducere*), which looks like a pretty straightforward and promising metaphor for what the opening section of a book does to a reader—as well as for other common uses of the term; for example, to refer to the initiation of an acquaintance between two or more persons. But it's also clear that, notwithstanding the superficial unity of the concept, what an introduction actually *involves*—or what it should preferably or ideally involve—is subject to potentially enormous variation, depending on (at least):

a. the *kind of thing* to be introduced and its properties (e.g., book, city or person? If person: casual acquaintance, close relative or oneself? How predictable or volatile, normal or idiosyncratic, is the person in question?); and

b. the particular *purposes* of the person doing the introducing (do I want
the person or thing that I introduce to be of use to someone—and if so,
how?—or, first and foremost, for it to be *understood*, or to have a
more or less drastic transformative effect on something, or for it to be
liked, or for it to make *me* liked, or respected, or feared, or rich, etc.
etc.?).

We might therefore be able to discover something about the nature and state
of political philosophy by looking at the way in which its authors introduce
their texts. Every introduction is different, of course. One of the main concerns of this book, though, is to look not for the ways in which contemporary
political philosophy varies, but for the *samenesses* it exhibits. By identifying
the common themes of the introduction, we may get an insight into the
commonalities of political-philosophical texts and of the purposes of their
authors.[19]

In the present case, it's not difficult to start to identify generalities, as the
philosophical introduction seems to be a prime breeding ground for clichés
and telling stylistic tics. You might be forgiven for inferring that the authors
purchase their introductions in kit form, expressing their 'individuality' by
assembling the components in subtly different ways: there are the expressions of humility, the hand-wringing as to whether the book should have
been written at all, given the magnitude of the task and its woeful inadequacy
in the face of it (for which the author takes full responsibility, and which can
only be put down to his pigheadedness in the face of the wise advice of a
great long list of White Male European Names, who have generously de-
voted their time to combing over clumsy drafts of the present unworthy
manuscript); then there is the equally inevitable statement of self-justification
(appealing to the *modest contribution* that the text may yet make, or the
avenues it may open to the enquiries of the bright minds of posterity); then
comes the courteous preview of topics to be covered and conclusions to be
established; and lastly, the touching words of inexpressible-yet-apparently-
all-too-easily-expressible gratitude to a long-suffering Female Name for
making it all worthwhile (this Female Name will be one of relatively few
women to make it into this exclusive section,[20] alongside the equally long-
suffering but not so quite so highly prized Ms. Cheerful Typist—because
typists, for some reason, are always cheerful).

Beyond their relative homogeneity, two features of the philosophical
introduction are perhaps the most striking. One is the sense that a main

purpose of the introduction is to make the author *liked* by the reader. The second is that the other main purpose seems to be to let the reader know what she may expect from the book.

Well, first of all, we are not here to be liked. Philosophy is not a seduction technique. And anyway, there is something particularly insidious about a seduction attempted through the identikit 'personal touch' characteristic of the introductory section: this is the traditional venue for the author to show a little—not too much!—of himself as a human being, of his idiosyncrasies and subjective experience; but notice that the 'personal' turns out to be surprisingly *im*personal—most authors emerge as the same quirky, humble, endearingly abstracted Academic and Family Man. The restrained 'personal touch' found in the typical introduction is only the flipside of the *im*personal style of philosophizing that enjoys default predominance everywhere else (why should it be thought 'unphilosophical' to write like a human being?). There are some exceptions, of course, but what this amounts to is mostly just a bit more leeway for eminent old-timers, who are occasionally allowed to spill their guts or their seed over the page in a way that others are not. This is a qualified rule, then: a rule which need not apply to the qualified. Its strictness depends on the status of the author—roughly, the more of a big shot you are, the more the provision of autobiographical detail is appreciated or at least tolerated.[21]

As for the almost universal practice of letting the reader know what is in store for her, the anticipated justification is that this practice is *helpful*, an aid to better understanding and more effective research. Philosophy, it may be said, should not be about entertainment or fun, any more than politics should be, and in both places we should expect transparency to come before mystique. What counts as 'helpful', however, is always going to be relative to *what we are doing* and to *the conditions under which we are doing it*. Judging from the blow-by-blow previews with which philosophers often begin their books, a fair inference is that they envisage their readers (perhaps correctly) as having quite well-specified, though limited, preexisting agendas. In order to succeed in their exams or to compose publishable articles, they require directions to help them navigate through 'the literature', identify the main hazards and stake out an unclaimed patch of the territory.[22] But this end requires the scrupulous elimination of the unexpected. As one philosopher observes, 'To put the last page first is the conventional responsibility of introduction in academic texts . . . [this convention] requires that the author tell the reader precisely whodunit, why, and how.'[23]

There are various different ways to think about the purpose of philosophy and of philosophical texts, and about the relationship between author and reader. The stylistic tics, structure and constitution of the typical introduction seem to me to point towards one particular way, which we might dub the 'commercial model'. It is a relationship between producers, or retailers, and consumers—with the peculiar twist that, in this case, these are basically the same people: academic philosophy is overwhelmingly written *by* academic philosophers *for* academic philosophers. Both author and reader are on a quasi-imperialist hunt for virgin territory to conquer, in cutthroat competition with fellow author-readers. As author, the philosopher displays his wares to their best advantage in the first place the would-be consumer is likely to look; as reader, the philosopher shops around, scanning the shop windows of plausible texts before deciding where best to invest his time and attention. The author imparts certain goods to the reader, goods which are available to view before purchase. But it is also conceivable that there are philosophical and educational ends that cannot adequately be prefigured in this way. [24]

The parallels between this model and the one increasingly applied to higher education in the United Kingdom are clear, and seem unlikely to be coincidental. One of the main foci of criticisms of twenty-first-century 're-forms' to the sector has been the attempt to remodel students as consumers, teachers as providers and education as a 'product'. Against this, voices from across the political spectrum [25] have protested that education *just isn't that kind of thing*, that it is too complex, too variable and unpredictable a force to be described as a 'product' at all, and that it *forms* who we are, rather than being something that can be delivered to a fully formed 'us' in the manner of a take-away pizza.

The configuration of the conventional philosophy text, on the other hand, strongly suggests that what the latter offers is something wholly determinate: describable-in-advance and summarizable-in-conclusion—sealed, at both ends, like a sausage.

NOTES

1. Nietzsche (1993 [1872]; p. 62).
2. It may also be said that this has been pointed out enough times already—some readers will think, for example, of Bonnie Honig's thesis of the 'displacement of politics' (cf. Honig [1993]). It would require too much space to deal satisfactorily here with the relationship between Honig's thesis and mine. Suffice it to say that, while there are some affinities, I see our two projects as very different. I hope that this will become clear, if it is not already, in the

following few pages, as I set out the intent behind the title of this book. In chapter 5, I also clarify my stance with respect to the 'realist' school of political theory, to which Honig's 'agonistic' approach is often assimilated.

3. Cf. Engels (1883) on 'the simple fact, hitherto concealed by an overgrowth of ideology, that mankind must first of all eat, drink, have shelter and clothing, before it can pursue politics, science, art, religion, etc.'

4. See, for example, Hanisch (1970), or more recently, Greer (2000; p. 424): 'The personal is still political. The millennial feminist has to be aware that oppression exerts itself in and through her most intimate relationships, beginning with the most intimate, her relationship with her body.'

5. I'm aware that attacking political philosophy (especially liberal political philosophy) for being too detached from real political concerns is anything but novel. Indeed, this is the starting point of many 'realist' approaches. It should become apparent that although the critique I offer here belongs to this generic category of attack, it is distinctive both in its *approach* (which proceeds in part by analyzing particular debates in political philosophy and demonstrating them to be deficient *by the discipline's own professed standards*), and in its *scope*, which is intended to encompass much more than the (relatively rare) sort of political philosophy that conceives of itself as strictly abstract 'ideal theory'.

6. I offer a fuller treatment of the notion of 'ideal theory' in chapter 5.

7. I'll discuss this at length in chapter 2.

8. I should say at the outset that I'm using the term 'methodology' loosely, to include at least two importantly different things: (i) norms concerning the ways in which philosophy is practiced, in the broadest sense—this includes styles and methods of philosophical writing and argument, characteristic attitudes and presuppositions and espoused intellectual values; and (ii), the activity of theorizing about the things included under (i)—the many conferences about the role and nature of political philosophy are 'methodological' in this sense. I will try to make it clear from context which of these is meant at any given point. But the two are in any case best viewed as continuous—inasmuch as (i) includes intellectual *values*, for instance, it is just a less formal and explicit version of 'methodology' in sense (ii).

9. See Fukuyama (c1992).

10. These words are taken from a recent article by Labour MP Tessa Jowell (2011), but they could equally well have been uttered by a representative of any of the three main British parties.

11. Perhaps equally telling is the breakfast cereal brand Shreddies' use of the phrase 'hunger strikes' (with 'strikes' as a verb). It's hard to see why anyone would think this a felicitous pun, but either someone must have done, or else it must have been regarded as too far-fetched an association to bother about—which seems equally peculiar.

12. For more on the puniness of philosophy, see chapter 6.

13. A similar view is often expressed about the worth of methodological reflection in meta-physics (e.g., Mellor [2008]).

14. Note that this may be put as an extension of my claim about the relationship of interde-pendence between philosophy and its methodology, transposed up one level: a certain *meta*-methodological view (i.e., the view that methodology of political philosophy is a decadent distraction) turns out to presuppose a position—albeit a rather general one—*within* the metho-dology of political philosophy (i.e., the position that the way in which political philosophy is currently practiced is not sufficiently objectionable as to warrant the step backwards to a standpoint of methodological inquiry).

15. 'School?' he said; 'yes, what do you mean by that word? I don't see how it can have anything to do with children. We talk, indeed, of a school of herring, and a school of painting,

and in the former sense we might talk of a school of children—but otherwise,' said he, laughing, 'I must own myself beaten.'

Hang it! thought I, I can't open my mouth without digging up some new complexity; I wouldn't try to set my friend right in his etymology; and I thought I had best say nothing about the boy-farms that I had been used to call schools, as I saw pretty clearly that they had disappeared; and so I said after a little fumbling, 'I was using the word in the sense of a system of education.'

'Education?' said he, meditatively, 'I know enough Latin to know that the word must have come from *educere*, to lead out; and I have heard it used; but I have never met anybody who could give me a clear explanation of what it means' (William Morris, *News from Nowhere* [1970]; p. 23). See also Illich (1970), in particular, his notion of a 'hidden curriculum'.

16. I take up this thought again in the afterword to this book.

17. I develop the thoughts that follow more fully in 'An Introduction to the introduction' (Finlayson forthcoming).

18. Philosophy is what the poet Paul Celan (2003) thought art was: 'a conversation which, we feel, could go on forever if there were no snags'.

19. It might be queried why we should look at introductions, rather than directly at the texts themselves, in order to look for sameness. My answer is that we should try to do that too, but that there is an advantage in taking unexpected angles or indirect routes. Inconstancies are generally more noticeable to us than constancies, and furthermore, philosophers have an interest in pushing their differences onto centre stage. Individually, this makes them seem more interesting. Collectively, it protects the features they share from detection and criticism. It is by looking for omissions, offhand remarks, and subsidiary sections like the introduction, preface, footnotes or acknowledgements—places which the author does not expect or think it reasonable to have scrutinized—that these common features may be most fruitfully sought. The principle is the same as that applied to the detection of art fraud: you recognize forgeries not by looking at the most prominent features of a work, but by seeking out details which were considered unimportant and consequently rendered with less care (that is also, more famously, the approach associated with Sherlock Holmes).

20. If you don't believe me, or if you think that what I'm putting forward is an outdated stereotype of bad old days past, I suggest you try the following experiment: go to a philosophy library or section of a library; look at the introductions and acknowledgements of the first ten books you find published since the year 2000; note down the genders, to the extent that they can be discerned from the names, of the people mentioned in the introductions and acknowledgements. A friend and I tried looking at the fourteen books on the 'new books' shelf of my university's philosophy library (ten of which were by male authors, the remaining four by women), and found that almost 60 percent of academic acknowledgements—that is, acknowledgements for input which would be normally classed as 'academic', such as commenting on the content of manuscripts and discussing ideas—were to male names, approximately 36 percent to female names (in the remaining 4 percent of cases the gender wasn't clear from the name alone). When we isolated those acknowledgements which were presented as non-academic debts—we included both professional (e.g., typing and editing) and non-professional (e.g., emotional support) contributions in this category—the proportions were exactly reversed, with 64 percent female names and 36 percent male. My thanks to Claire Benn for her good-humoured processing of the data.

21. A similar phenomenon exists with respect to the use of swearwords in academic contexts. Some students, knowing that they cannot expect to get away with using a term like 'bullshit', even when the word seems to be right for the context, feel compelled to protect themselves by appealing to authority (despite its irrelevance)—for example, 'But this sugges-

tion is, in Frankfurt's (2005) terminology, "bullshit". . . . .' I am grateful to Ben Colburn for bringing this to my attention.

22. This approach is absolutely antithetical to the 'essay genre', as poet and translator Michael Hamburger (1989; p. 11) observes: 'An essay is a walk, an excursion, not a business trip. [. . .] One walker is interested in wildflowers, another in the view, a third collects insects. Hunting butterflies is permitted—everything except the intentions of surveyors, farmers, speculators.'

23. Honig (1993; p. 1). This partly explains why so many people read only the introductions and conclusions of books.

24. Cf. Geuss (2009).

25. Opponents of the U.K. government's changes to higher education have included not only the traditional left, but also a large contingent of liberals and even conservatives (with both lower- and uppercase letters).

I

Well-Ordered
Political Philosophy

Chapter One

There Is No Alternative

Constructiveness and Political Criticism

[T]here really is no alternative.

—Margaret Thatcher, 1980

Question: how does a book in contemporary Anglo-American political philosophy begin? Answer: it begins by observing the triumph of liberalism, in theory as in practice. Depending on what is meant by 'liberalism' (and 'triumph', and 'theory'), this triumph may be presented as centuries- or merely decades-old. According to one recent introductory text, 'one paradigm has dominated the landscape in many ways, *at least since the seventeenth century* in Europe and continuing to the present day. . . . There are many forms of liberalism and several fundamental components to it, but the domination of this framework for normative political principles in recent decades is notable and is even taken for granted by liberalism's several critics.'[1] The editors of *The Oxford Handbook of Political Theory*, by contrast, comment on the relative newness of liberalism's supremacy—or at least, of a situation where this supremacy is largely unchallenged—observing that while the last couple of decades have been 'a time of energetic and expansive debate, with new topics crowding into a busy field . . . for many in political theory, including many critics of liberal theory, this pluralistic activity obscures a more important point: the dominance that has been achieved by liberalism, at least in the Anglo-American world.'[2] That liberalism is dominant *now*, however, seems to be a commonplace on which all can agree.[3]

Sensing a need to say something by way of explanation of this phenomenon, many authors now make a brief nod in the direction of Marx—or rather,
to the empty place where he once sat. They observe that '[i]n earlier decades,
liberalism had a clear, comprehensive competitor in the form of Marxism,
not just in the form of real-world governments claiming to be Marxist, but
also in political theory.'[4] But this is now over, they announce, in tones
ranging from the sober gravity of the vet about to put a sick dog out of its
misery to the glee of the hunter standing triumphant over the corpse of his
quarry—and usually, in fact, containing elements of both. The influence of
Marxism has 'waned', we are reminded;[5] 'within academia it has lost ground
to the point at which it is not even attacked any more, let alone defended.'[6]

And we know why. As the editors of the *Handbook* observe, '[t]he fortunes of Marxist theory were not helped by the demise of the Soviet bloc in
1989-91, and the determined pursuit of capitalism in China under the leadership of a nominally Marxist regime'[7] (and, of course, as editors of a 'handbook' to political theory, they feel bound to offer something representative of
the current state of that field—whether they like it or not).[8] Liberalism's
main competitors, it is generally agreed, have been refuted by history: '"real
existing socialism" has been abandoned everywhere except North Korea,
which is scarcely an advertisement for it,'[9] remarks one liberal theorist, at the
opening of a three-hundred-page book on equality and 'multiculturalism'; the
events of the twentieth century have shown both socialism and anarchism to
be 'dead ends', remarks another.[10] Concurs the first: '[t]he spectre [of com-
munism] came to life, but it has now been laid to rest, apparently for good.'
Liberalism, in that case, is the last man standing. As one author puts it: '[t]he
Marxist experiment may well have run its course. . . . But the libertarian
philosophy of Mill and his successors deserves a longer probation.'[11]

The scene set, the book can now begin in earnest. All further action will
take place within the framework of liberalism—by which is meant, of course,
liberal capitalism. Within this framework, the proper design of 'just institutions' is debated.[12] It may be asked, for example, when and whether people
should be compensated for bad luck, and whether the liberal state should
allow Sikhs to ride motorcycles without wearing helmets. It is with this sort
of political philosophy—and not with Marxist or anarchist or radical feminist
theory—that I, too, will be concerned in the chapters that follow. My intention is not to participate but to observe from a distance. By doing so, it will
be possible to criticize the framework of liberal political philosophy as a
whole. My approach, however, is not to make a direct argument that the

defining features of this kind of political philosophy are bad ones—for example, to argue that there is something wrong with 'analytic' philosophy per se, or with liberalism, or with capitalism. Instead, I want to look at the ways in which the dominance of this way of doing political philosophy is sustained, and to expose the tricks that seem to underpin its supremacy, warding off or dispatching any significant opposition. I aim to do this through a series of exemplary 'case studies', each focusing in on a contemporary trope or debate in mainstream political philosophy.

In this first chapter, we begin *before* the beginning. I had something to say already, in my own introduction, about the ways in which philosophers write their introductions. And I've now laid out some of the kind of scene-setting specific to *political* philosophy. This scene-setting is typically confined to a few lines in the introduction or first main chapter of a book (although, at least as often, it goes entirely without explicit signalling). In those few lines, however, a complex and crucial communication is made. Janus-faced, it points backwards as well as forwards. It signals a decision, made even before the discussion begins in earnest, as to which political positions are worthwhile objects of that discussion, and which are not. And by that same stroke, liberalism is established as the only game in town. [13] The aim of the rest of this chapter is to shine a spotlight on these crucial few lines—and between them—in order to get a clearer view of what is often thought too obvious to be interesting. In this way, perhaps, we can begin to rattle the throne of a style of political philosophy which, for some time now, has been sitting very comfortably indeed.

I. DEATH CAMPS AND DESIGNER DRESSES [14]

I want now to look more closely at the train of reasoning already described—one which will anyway be extremely familiar: (1) Marxism/socialism has been discredited by history; (2) so THERE IS NO ALTERNATIVE; hence, (3) liberalism. I will not argue directly against the conclusion, or even against the premises—at least in some form, these are plausible ones—but will try instead to disambiguate their various possible meanings and to identify their main presuppositions. Doing so will not show that the conclusion is false [15] or that no form of this basic argument for it is sound. But it will, I believe, reveal a certain shakiness and a certain dodginess to the whole apparatus: shaky, because once a few basic clarifications have been made, the 'argument' seems far less obvious and irresistible; and dodgy, because we can now see the sleight of hand that made it *seem* so commonsensical and must begin to ask what *purpose* the illusion was meant to serve.

What it is feasible to say here about the first step—the claim that socialism is dead, that it has been eliminated from the game of serious politics and political theory—may be said relatively succinctly. The sentiment is a favourite cliché, not only among political philosophers, but among commentators of the liberal intelligentsia more generally—in the media and public discourse as well as in academia. The kinds of empirical events invoked here are also well-known: Stalin's *gulags*, effectively death camps, in which many millions perished; the ultimate collapse of the Soviet Union; the unattractiveness of remaining 'communist' regimes such as North Korea. While being quite willing to concede that such regimes—which one writer quoted above referred to sarcastically as 'real-existing socialism'[16]—are not really 'socialist' or 'communist', in the sense of actually embodying or living up to the relevant ideals, the suggestion by many commentators is that the events associated with the tags 'socialism' and 'Marxism' nevertheless demonstrate the ultimate indefensibility of socialist theory: if its inadequacy were not evident from an examination of its theoretical tenets, it is revealed in the role it has played in real politics.

Now, socialists may feel that this inference—'"real existing socialism" is weak or bad, therefore all forms of socialism are invalidated in theory as well as in practice'—is rather too quick. They may point out, regarding the Bolshevik revolution, that the latter happened in a peasant agricultural society and that there were therefore good *Marxist* reasons for expecting it to be the disaster that it was; that all socialist states so far have lived out their existence encircled by hostile capitalist powers; and that the twentieth century offers endless examples where the United States, in particular, has employed economic and military means to destroy popular and progressive governments in order to replace them with repressive and often murderous regimes (the latter being better suited to U.S. foreign-policy objectives and business interests).[17]

These replies are almost as familiar as the original condemnation but are generally judged to be as feeble as the liberal charge is weighty. Why is that? Perhaps because the historical events in question represent such a catastrophic failure that socialist excuses such as these can't really cut it. As is already apparent, however, the reply to the charge against socialism need not only be a matter of excuses but can also take the form of counter-accusation. The United States that has replaced 'inconvenient' socialist and democratic governments and movements with 'convenient' warlords and dictators is classed as a liberal democracy. 'Real existing liberalism' may not correspond to liberal democratic ideals, of course, but the same was true in the case of socialism—and the point was clearly not regarded as getting the latter off the hook.

It is not difficult to begin to construct an 'empirical' case against liberalism to match the allegedly decisive one against socialism: point to the purges, and I can point to Chile and Guatemala and to the victims of the U.S.-backed state terror in those countries; point to the *gulags*, and I point to the slaughter of as much as a third of the population of East Timor by Indonesia following its 1975 invasion, facilitated by its U.S. ally;[18] point to North Korea, and I point to the U.S.-British invasions of Afghanistan and Iraq—leading directly and indirectly to millions of deaths, and all in the name of the protection and promotion of liberal 'freedom' and 'democracy'. As surely as terrible crimes have been committed by socialist states, the history of liberal nations is the history of systematic acquisitive violence: from the genocide of indigenous populations, to chattel slavery,[19] to contemporary 'regime change' and 'humanitarian intervention'. This much is uncontroversial, even though it may not be thought relevant—or polite, perhaps—to talk about it.

The challenge is now to find a factor which would explain why history must be seen as overturning socialism, *without also overturning liberalism*. Otherwise, we might suspect that the ubiquitous 'socialism is dead—long live liberalism' line rests on a double standard: history and real politics are crucial when we need to discredit socialist theory, but suddenly uninteresting—or 'too complicated'—when it comes to liberalism. What might constitute such a factor? The answer is not at all obvious. There are some clear differences between the kinds of events associated with liberalism and with socialism respectively—for example, the worst of liberal crimes are arguably inflicted on foreign rather than domestic populations,[20] and are often contracted out to 'client states' or paramilitary groups—but it's difficult to see how *these* sorts of differences could be construed as having the required significance.[21] For some, the obvious difference is that the evils historically associated with liberalism—or in any case, those associated with the contemporary 'real existing liberalism' that has emerged from this unsavoury history—are far less bad than those associated with socialism and communism. For others, of course—and in increasing numbers since the spate of economic crises beginning in 2008 and with the growing prospect of ecological catastrophe—this is not obvious at all. But in one sense, this is beside the point. Even if we were to grant liberalism the status of lesser evil, this does not seem to capture very well the spirit of most 'real existing' liberal theorists. Crudely put, they are more *cheerful* than the 'lesser evil' story can tolerate. They typically present themselves as offering visions of a positively 'just' and equitable society, one in which the political order is approximately—though, of course, imperfectly—in tune with liberal ideals as with human interests. In order to make room for that kind of attitude, we would have to put some more distance between liberal theory and the practice of 'real existing liberalism'. But if we do that, we must confront once again the need to identify a relevant difference between the case of liberalism and that of its rivals, one which would prevent the case against those rivals from evaporating along with that against liberalism.

This still leaves one major strand of the 'socialism is dead' line untouched. Alongside the invocation of the historical or contemporary failure of 'real existing socialism', we may also detect an appeal to *testimony* about socialism—or rather, the lack of it—among those deemed worthy of esteem: ' . . . within academia it has lost ground to the point at which it is not even attacked any more, let alone defended.'[22] This appeal to 'negative testimony' or neglect can then be read in two main ways.

First, it may be interpreted as *evidence* that there is some fatal flaw with socialism (which doesn't also afflict liberalism), even if we haven't seen it yet, or else do not have the time and patience to explain it. This falls some way short of a knockdown argument, for reasons conveniently highlighted by the same author whose words I have just quoted. Rebuffing the claim of 'pop academics and their journalistic hangers-on' that the 'Enlightenment project' has become 'outmoded', the liberal political philosopher Brian Barry reminds us that 'ideas are not like designer dresses. There, the latest fashion is the most desirable simply in virtue of being the latest. [. . .] But in the case of ideas we can ask a question that does not make sense in the case of clothes: is the latest fashion right or wrong?'[23] Quite so—and unfashionable anti-capitalists may be among the first to agree. Sometimes, certainly, the unpopularity of an idea may be best explained by its inadequacy; other times, however, there may be an entirely different explanation which in no way tells against the idea in question. The weight we attach to testimony, including the 'negative' testimony of neglect, must depend on a complex series of factors that have to do with the context in which that testimony is found, and must also inevitably be informed by our basic view as to the sort of place the world is.

But this points us towards a deeper problem with any liberal use of the argument from neglect to dismiss socialism. Closely associated with views of the world issuing from a left-of-liberal stance, and with Marxist-influenced traditions in particular, is the notion of 'ideology': the idea that the thoughts and theories we find in a society will not only reflect the kind of society in question, its material conditions and the interests dominant within them, but will shape themselves in such a way as to *reinforce* those conditions and *protect* those interests. From this point of view, it is not at all obvious that a consensus among political philosophers is best interpreted as evidence of truth or validity. If we believe with Marx and Engels, for instance, that the ruling ideas of every epoch are the ideas of the ruling class, [24] then we may attribute a rather different significance to the fact that academics have converged on a liberal-capitalist paradigm. Of course, we are at the beginning and not the end of the book, and so I do not rest what I say now on a prior acceptance of a theory of ideology. I only observe that, if we understand socialism to include a commitment to some theory of ideology, any liberal attempt to exclude it by appeal to academic testimony looks in danger of begging the question at hand: if the theory of ideology is, after all, a defensible theory, then we should at least be receptive to potentially debunking ideological explanations of objects of academic consensus; to make such an uncritical appeal to what academics think, in that case, is already largely to have made up one's mind against something quite central to many forms of socialist theory.

This still leaves a second, seemingly more promising reading of what we might call the 'argument from unpopularity'. There is a distinction between thinking that socialism has been discredited—in the normative sense of having had its deep flaws as a body of theory revealed by the catastrophic failure of attempts to put it into practice—and the weaker claim that, rightly or wrongly, these events have had the consequence that socialism no longer has any prospects of being realized. To put this point in fashionable terminology, rehabilitated liberalism inhabits a closer 'possible world' than rehabilitated socialism (and perhaps even than *un*-rehabilitated socialism). This weaker claim might seem hard to resist—until, that is, we turn the back spotlight on liberalism, just as was done in the case of the empirical argument from 'real existing socialism'. The prospects of *any* attractive ideals being realized in a non-disastrous way are, perhaps, very dim; the claim at hand, however, is that this applies to socialism and not to liberalism. In order to argue that a desirable form of liberalism—which means, *not* the 'real existing liberalism' that is the counterpart of 'real existing socialism', or anything like it—has better prospects of realization than does an attractive socialism, the liberal might point out that liberalism envisages its ideals of freedom, equality, and so on as being realized without such drastic structural and economic change as the socialist requires. But, of course, this possibility is exactly what the socialist is likely to deny. There is a crucial difference between proposing modest means in the pursuit of some goal, on the one hand, and on the other hand proposing a goal that can *actually be achieved* by modest means. If I recommend that you continue to smoke and drink heavily, to overeat and to take no exercise, and also *be healthier*, while someone else suggests an alternative programme involving various tedious and demanding lifestyle changes that you have no intention of making, then in one sense I have given you the more feasible plan. But pretty clearly, I am peddling comforting delusions and should not be listened to. For the socialist and other opponents of liberal 'utopianism',[25] the liberal is a similarly dangerous figure. There is no point banging on about equality and freedom and autonomy, the thought goes, without being willing to criticize the fundamental elements of capitalist society that inevitability destroy those same goods—just as there is no point in simply *recommending* good health while proposing the continuation of arrangements that are incompatible with it. Obviously, the liberal will deny that this is what she is doing, but this is the beginning of the argument and not the end. The liberal's task is to give us some reason to think that she has a vision which is both attractive and more feasible than the socialist's. The task is not discharged merely by being the one recommending the more 'modest' changes.

So far, we have seen absolutely no clear and independent reason to dismiss socialism in favour of a liberal capitalist framework. On the contrary, the more we have looked for a justification of that move, the more the difficulties have accumulated. But we have not yet questioned the underlying assumption that would-be rebels against the liberal framework—or against anything else, for that matter—need to have An Alternative. Like the invocation of 'real existing socialism' already discussed, I'll suggest, this assumption is not nearly so simple and unobjectionable as it might first appear.

II. 'BUT WHAT WOULD YOU PUT IN ITS PLACE?'[26]

If anything, the need to provide an alternative to what we reject, to be 'constructive' in criticism, is regarded as something even more obvious than its habitual sidekick: the thought that socialism has been discredited by recent history. A commitment to it is expressed both within academia and in the mainstream press, not only by liberals,[27] but also by many who continue to identify themselves as anti-capitalists or socialists.[28] It is clear that the absence of 'an alternative' is seen as a big problem, and that this has become a very popular stick with which to beat 'the left' (and with which 'the left' also may, on occasion, beat one another and themselves). This was particularly evident in academic and journalistic responses to the 'Occupy' movement, at its peak between 2011 and 2012. Commentators routinely declared sympathy with the protesters' criticisms of the unfairness and economic inequality they perceived but would immediately follow this up by lamenting their lack of a 'clear focus' or 'positive alternative'—almost as if this were a political party standing for election rather than a large and diverse, loose-knit group of citizens coming together to oppose a system radically out of line with the interests and concerns of 'the 99 percent'.[29] Some sympathetic critics even tried to come to the Occupiers' rescue by offering their own 'constructive' suggestions as to how the movement might become more 'constructive', and we began to hear mutterings that what might be needed to plug the hole is none other than the liberal theory of John Rawls, the most prominent political philosopher of the twentieth century. Writing in the Opinion Pages of the *New York Times*, for example, the philosopher Steven V. Mazie followed a standard first sentence of praise with a friendly warning that 'to move forward and make a difference, Occupy Wall Street needs specific goals backed by a more coherent, more inspiring vision for American democracy'—but fear not, because Rawls's work represents 'a perfect intellectual touchstone', 'a home-grown theory that is ripe for the picking'.[30]

We will deal with Rawls in the next chapter. What I want to address now, however, is this apparently very basic, deeply ingrained and widely shared idea of the need to provide an alternative to what we reject. It may seem obvious why it matters so much: if political philosophy is not to be a completely decadent exercise, it should be willing to make practical prescriptions and not only to analyse or condemn; as some put it, political theory must be 'action-guiding'. Besides, if 'ought' implies 'can', we need to show that things could be better, in order for our criticisms of the political status quo to have any validity. As it turns out, however, the requirement to be 'constructive' is as ambiguous as it is hegemonic. And with a bit of disambiguation, its intuitive power—or rather, the power of certain prevalent versions or instances of it—no longer seems so overwhelming.

The first thing to note is that the demand for 'constructiveness' is not one which is applied to criticism across the board. It is not normally thought impermissible to attack a philosophical theory—for instance, a theory in logic or metaphysics—without being able to propose a better one. I've already mentioned two possible reasons for this asymmetry: the need to guide action and the principle that 'ought' implies 'can', imposed specifically on 'normative' criticism, which suggests that we must show not only that something is bad, but also that it is possible for it to be better. Nor is the demand applied to all criticism within political theory. You are not so likely to be met with the question 'But what would you put in its place?' if all you did was attack a particular theory or claim *within* the general framework of liberalism (without suggesting an alternative). It is only when you start to attack that framework itself that the question becomes almost inevitable. Large-scale criticisms of the status quo—whether that means the general way in which political philosophy is done or the way in which society at large is structured—are those most likely to be challenged and dismissed on the basis of their alleged failure to pass the test of 'constructiveness'. Partly, no doubt, this is because we are more confident of finding replacements for small components than for whole frameworks—the requirement of 'constructiveness' applies, but we are satisfied that it can be fulfilled (even if not here and now or by the particular author of the criticism). Perhaps it is also because we find it harder to see how we can keep going without a general framework for action (including the 'action' of theorizing) than it is to see how we might get along without some particular element within that framework. But let us leave the reasons aside for now. What, more exactly, does it mean to insist that a radical critic of the status quo must offer us 'an alternative'? The options here can be usefully broken up, I want to suggest, with the rather unlikely aid of two conceptual tools borrowed from different areas of philosophy: one from contemporary philosophy of science and another which has already been mentioned, from analytic metaphysics—the notion of a 'possible world'.[31]

Prominent in contemporary analytic metaphysics and epistemology is the diagnosis of a wide range of intellectual phenomena as 'contrastive'. Some philosophers of science, for example, have analyzed *explanation* as a contrastive phenomenon, which may be elucidated through the concepts of 'fact' and 'foil': the 'fact' is what is the case; the 'foil' is something else that *could be the case instead* (but is not); and a contrastive explanation tells us why the fact obtains *rather than* the foil.[32] This structure transfers quite neatly to the

case of criticism: we can criticize the world for being one way (the 'fact')
rather than some other, better way that it could be (the critical 'foil')—and
the contrast (the critical 'foil') that is intended by the critic, or that in any
case is *available* for her to invoke, partly determines the kind of criticism she
can be construed as making.

What kind of 'foil' is being demanded, then, when the political critic is
asked to be 'constructive' or to provide 'an alternative'? Something *less bad*
(in the relevant respect or respects) than the object of criticism, presumably.
Obviously, there will be disagreement as to what counts as 'less bad' than
what—and at least sometimes, this disagreement will be due to what we
would call 'political' differences—but we may put that aside as a very general and unavoidable fact of life. It is clearly not enough, however, just to fix
upon something good or better than what we want to criticize, in order to
pass the test of 'constructiveness': answering 'Beer!' to the question 'But
what would you put in its place?' is unlikely to satisfy (and that is not
because beer is not a good thing). The reason for this, I take it, is that beer is
the wrong *kind* of thing: it is a drink, whereas capitalism is an economic
system; we are not comparing like with like. So it seems that, in order for a
criticism to be 'constructive', the foil must belong to the same category—be
the same 'kind of thing'—as what is being criticized. Of course, part of what
we might want to say, when criticizing something, is that whatever replaces
it (if anything) should *not* be the same kind of thing as *that*. So we will
obviously have to explain the idea of being 'the same kind of thing', and
explain it in such a way that it doesn't undermine what we take to be valid
practices of criticism. If, for instance, you suggest the 'same kind of thing'
should be cashed out in terms of 'fulfilling the same function' (hence being
fit to be put in place of the object of criticism), then—depending, in turn, on
how we interpret 'same function'—this may have the consequence that certain criticisms, namely those which criticize an object precisely *because* it
fulfils the function in question, will be disqualified in advance. Even if we
can all agree that beer is not an appropriate foil for a criticism of capitalism,
it does not follow that there can be agreement, across political outlooks, on
what *is*: does it have to be a system for distributing the wealth of a society? a
system for producing economic growth? for ensuring employment? for keeping the masses down? We might differ as to which of these functions, if any,
is worth preserving—and hence must be plausibly fulfilled by any purported
alternative. We might also want to know what 'system' means. If it means
something that is centrally coordinated by the state, then from certain politi-

cal points of view, the assumption that there must be a 'system' at all is one that should be rejected. But proposals like that, many would say, are ludicrously utopian. And with this, we come to a further crucial specification for the kind of foil a critic needs to have in play in order for her criticism to count as 'constructive'. Not only does the foil have to be 'of a kind' with the object of criticism—and how we see fit to flesh out this requirement will depend on our background assumptions about politics—but it must also offer an alternative that is 'feasible', or 'realistic'.

It is at this point that we may find it convenient to hijack 'possible worlds' talk: to say that something is a '*realistic* possibility' might be expressed by saying that it belongs not only to a possible world, but to a world relatively close to the actual one; to say that something is 'utopian', on the other hand, may be put by saying that it belongs to a world which is 'modally remote'—*far out*. We might even envisage a spectrum stretching from the actual world, off into modal space, with various possibilities strung along it. When the demand for 'constructiveness' or 'an alternative' is made, then, what is being demanded is that the critic be able to provide an appropriate foil which is located somewhere not *too* far along that spectrum. Perhaps we might also envisage successive nested 'bands' of possibility, ranging from the 'softer' kinds at one end—the 'economically' or 'humanly' possible, for example—to 'physical' and finally 'logical' possibility at the other.[33] It is then clear that the usual demand is for a foil that possesses one of the softer, more demanding kinds of possibility: it is not 'constructive' to propose something that is strictly logically possible (that is, non-contradictory), but which requires humans to subsist without food, or grow wings. No, we presumably need to be able to offer something that is at least humanly, psychologically and economically possible. Here is another point at which there are going to be disagreements, and where these disagreements are going to be, once again, partly political. How 'modally remote' is a substantially egalitarian society? Or one in which workers own and control the means of production? Supporters of capitalism are in the habit of declaring that neither complete material equality nor socialism (which they often erroneously regard as one and the same) could work, because of 'human nature'—which, their privileged but unexplained direct epistemic access to the latter tells them, is 'too greedy'. But if their intended targets bought this, of course, they would not hold the positions that they hold. What counts as farflung and 'utopian' depends on what we think the world is like, which is to say that it depends on our politics.

This will apply even to the comparative judgement that one proffered foil is more 'remote' than another, as we saw already in the previous section: is it more fanciful to believe in the possibility of successful socialist revolution, or in the idea that substantial equality and well-being could be achieved under capitalism? These are questions and disagreements of a fundamental and paradigmatically political nature.

But there may yet be further constraints on the sort of foil that a critic must offer, in order to pass the test of 'constructiveness', which we have not yet covered. The question of modal remoteness is not just the question of what 'could be otherwise', someone might say—or, if it is, then this just means that in the context of political criticism we should be concerned about more than just the modal remoteness or proximity of foils. The example of Theodor Adorno's social and political theory may help to clarify the point here. A crucial aspect of Adorno's judgement of the social world after Auschwitz as 'radically evil' is his conviction that the evil is *contingent*: with the available resources, the world *could* have become a paradise for human beings; and it is the contrast between humanly possible paradise and actual catastrophe that underpins his distinctive critical stance.[34] To put this in the terms of my discussion so far, Adorno appears to be able to point to a foil which is 'possible' in an appropriate sense, and which lies close to the actual world—he does not, for example, subscribe to the view that 'human nature' is such as to doom us to an inhumane political order. Yet he is unlikely to be considered a 'constructive' critic, being notoriously sceptical about the existence of any path from the actual world (post-Auschwitz) that might lead us to a system free of the radical evil that pervades this world, let alone a path to the realization of possible paradise.[35] Escape, or whatever might help us effect such an escape, is so radically remote from present reality as to be virtually inconceivable to us even if it is possible (and at least on some readings of Adorno, it is *not* possible).[36]

What this brings out is that the norm of 'constructiveness' requires not only that the critic offer a foil that is modally proximate—a state of affairs that might have been—but one which might actually come to be, *given where we are now*. I might have come within a hair's breadth of having a twin—or of not having been conceived at all, for that matter—but this doesn't make it any more feasible or 'constructive' for me to suggest that my twin should do the washing up as an 'alternative' to my doing it myself.

There is a crucial ambiguity, however, in a phrase like 'given where we are now'. Certainly, I have to make practical suggestions which are compatible with the fact that I don't have a twin, however close the possible world in which I *do* have one. But what does it mean, in the apparently more complex context of political criticism and discussion, to require suggested alternatives to take account of where we are now, rather than where we easily might have been (but are not)?

To propose an alternative that is realizable 'given' some feature F of the status quo could mean one of two completely different things: (i) to propose something compatible with the fact that F obtains now; or (ii) to propose something compatible with F's *continuance*, that is, something which could coexist with F. I've touched already on the fact that there can often be fundamental political disagreement over the question of what is and is not compatible with some feature F. So what would count as 'constructive', in the sense of conforming to (ii), would in any case be a matter of controversy. My further point now is that the demands for (i) and for (ii) are *distinct* demands, and that it is perfectly coherent to accept the first without accepting the second. This is, I hope, fairly obvious: the suggestion that a woman give birth by caesarean section is compatible with its being the case now that she is pregnant, though its implementation is clearly *not* compatible with her continuing to be so. But there is a tendency, I think, for the distinction to be glossed over in the application of certain demands for 'constructiveness', where being 'constructive' is implicitly or explicitly equated with being will- ing to propose an alternative that preserves rather than challenges certain contingent features of the status quo. This need not be the same as the situation already discussed in the last section, and raised again above, in which there is a disagreement over what is compatible with some feature F: all sides may agree that only very modest improvements are possible while the existing framework persists. Nonetheless, we are told, we have to work within the system we have (i.e., in the expectation that this system will continue).

In some cases, this principle might be appropriate, or at least understand- able. If I want to help my student continue with her studies, giving her 'constructive' advice means helping her to write a studentship application which stands the best chance of being successful—even though I may not approve of a system in which students are supported in this inadequate, tokenistic and largely arbitrary way. But it hardly follows from this that we should impose this kind of 'constructiveness' as a blanket demand on the activity of political theory. As political critics, theorists, agents and activists, we do not and should not only think about the immediate, either in time or in terms of the 'space of possibilities'. We might need to criticize things, knowing that they could not ('realistically') be otherwise under the present system, but also believing that the system itself could—and should—be otherwise.

III. CONCLUSION

What has repeatedly emerged in the course of this chapter is that the seemingly obvious and commonsensical status of liberalism as the privileged framework for political-philosophical discussion quickly ceases to be so obvious and commonsensical[37] when subjected to a moderate amount of scrutiny; and that what might initially seem to offer us a reason to be liberals—and even to rule out alternatives to liberalism in advance of the 'main business' of political philosophy—actually turns out to *presuppose* a preference for liberalism over its rivals. The ubiquitous pair of claims examined here—that there is no alternative to liberalism, and that it is incumbent upon liberalism's critics to provide such an alternative—are ultimately no more obvious than the superiority of liberalism is already (and thus cannot unproblematically be used to provide support for the latter). Perhaps it is after all more rather than less charitable to interpret the agenda-setting slogans considered here as just that—slogans—rather than seriously entertaining the possibility that they are arguments. For as *arguments* for liberal supremacy, they appear guilty of serial question-begging.

As I've observed throughout, many opponents of the liberal framework are unlikely to accept the premises on which the superiority of that framework is established—the premise, for example, that socialism has been refuted by history in a way that liberalism has not, or that an end to dire inequality and poverty is possible within a capitalist system. No socialist is going to be floored by these (very familiar) self-justifying statements. So who are they aimed at? At those likely to agree, of course: fellow liberals. A comparison might be drawn here with the traditional justifications adduced for colonial adventures: that the land in question is *terra nullius*, or 'a land with no people'. Who are these pearls aimed at? The people who allegedly don't exist? *They* are hardly likely to accept their own nonexistence as a premise. No, these justifications are surely aimed at like-minded third parties, those who are already on side, but who may feel a reflexive need to *hear* something by way of a rationalization—just as others may feel a reflexive need to *say* something for that purpose. The genuinely uninitiated are offered nothing to lure them in and plenty to repel them. These are nods of mutual approval among friends.

Any not just any friends. The line 'There Is No Alternative' (or TINA, as it is fondly known) is—despite its profession of powerlessness—a line associated with the voice of the *more* powerful party (most often when that party is about to do something unspeakable). It is the *less* powerful party—in this case, the critic of the political status quo—who is expected to carry the burden of providing 'an alternative'. In the end, though, this state of affairs is only as legitimate as whatever it is we are trying to find an alternative *to*. The uninitiated themselves have no reason to accept the burden. And there comes a point when we should be the ones demanding alternatives from the proponents of the status quo, not the other way around.[38]

NOTES

1. Christiano and Christman, eds. (2009; p. 5; my emphasis).
2. Dryzek, Honig and Phillips, eds. (2008; p. 14).
3. Some commentators note, in addition, that a particular *form* of liberalism has recently been dominant and contend that there is currently no acceptable alternative even to *this*. For example, Galston (2010) claims that there is, as yet, no 'coherent affirmative alternative' to what he calls 'high liberalism' (which he designates as a prime target of 'realist' critiques). Similarly, Richard North, introducing the journal issue in which Galston's article appears, opens with the observation that the liberal mainstream as represented by such figures as Rawls and Ronald Dworkin is almost universal and is confronted with no persuasive alternative as yet.
4. Dryzek, Honig and Phillips, eds. (2008; p. 15).
5. Ibid., p. 16.
6. Barry (2001; p. 3).
7. Dryzek, Honig and Phillips, eds. (2008; p. 16).
8. Thus the *Oxford Handbook* is firmly centred on liberalism and its 'critics'—who, as the editors themselves acknowledge, are not always very critical at all. For example, for the section on 'Feminism', they comment that 'many branches of feminism that were once critical of liberalism have made peace with the liberal tradition' (p. 20); 'deliberative democracy', likewise, looked as though it 'would require innovative thinking about alternative institutional arrangements that would take democracies beyond the standard liberal repertoire (Dryzek 1990). By the late 1990s, however, the very institutions that deliberative democrats had once criticized became widely seen as the natural home for deliberation, with an emphasis on courts and legislatures.' (p. 21).
9. Barry (2001; p. 3).
10. Anderson (2008).
11. Almond (2006; p. 192). Of course, the term 'libertarianism' is often used in a way that contrasts sharply with the intended meaning of the different term 'liberalism' (e.g., to indicate the hyper-individualist political philosophy of figures like Robert Nozick). At other times, however, the two terms are used interchangeably, or as indicating two points on a continuum. From Almond's association of the term 'libertarian' with Mill, I infer that she is using the term

to indicate what would usually be classified as a form of liberalism that is broadly Millian in inspiration. But this is not crucial. The point is that liberalism and libertarianism alike are regarded as having escaped 'falsification' by history in a way that socialism and communism have not.

12. Ever since John Rawls's declaration that 'justice is the first virtue of social institutions', discussions within political philosophy—whether of feminism, war or the distribution of re-sources—have been overwhelmingly couched in terms of this value. A number of influential criticisms notwithstanding (Gilligan 1982; Sandel 1998), it is 'justice', rather than rival con-cepts such as 'solidarity', 'care', 'community', 'alienation' or 'oppression', which serves as the main currency of political-philosophical debate. To give one indication, searching the political philosophy section of the online catalogue of Cambridge University Press (accessed 14 April 2014) gave me 103 hits for 'justice' (versus 27 for 'community', 14 for 'care', 9 for 'recogni-tion', 3 for 'solidarity' and 2 for 'oppression').

13. Cf. Lukes's (1975) second dimension of power as 'managing the agenda'.

14. This section draws on and incorporates material from an article I published in *Theoria: A Journal of Social and Political Theory* (no. 126, 2011) under the title 'Death Camps and Designer Dresses: The Liberal Agenda and the Appeal to "Real Existing Socialism"'.

15. In a broad sense of that term, of course—what does it mean, after all, for 'liberalism', or the policy of working within a liberal framework, to be 'false'? It could mean a number of things, but I take it that we can make good sense of the possibility of the 'conclusion', that is, the destination of the train of thought identified here—being an inappropriate or bad one. In that case, 'false' should be understood as equivalent to the German *falsch*, a term much broader than the English one, and one that can be used to indicate any kind of incorrectness, wrongness or inappropriateness.

16. Barry (2001; p. 3).

17. See Chomsky and Herman (1994); Chomsky (2003).

18. See Chomsky and Herman (1994). Still less well known is the mass slaughter, beginning in 1965, of up to a million Indonesians by U.S.-backed military and paramilitary forces, led by General Suharto, after the overthrow of the democratically elected government (as documented in Joshua Oppenheimer's 2013 film, *The Act of Killing*).

19. See Losurdo (2011).

20. Even this point requires that we overlook, for example, the historical and contemporary reality of the treatment of black and indigenous peoples in countries such as the United States.

21. Note that this need not beg questions about the relative status of intended consequences and 'foreseen side effects'. In the case of many of the atrocities backed by liberal states, it appears that civilian death and suffering *have* themselves been aimed at, for example, as a *means* to continued profit or dominance. This feature, which makes the label of 'state terror' applicable where it obtains, is not obviously any less present in the behaviour of liberal states than in 'real existing socialism'. I discuss other candidates for relevant asymmetries in Finlay-son (2011).

22. Barry (2001; p. 3).

23. Barry (2001; p. 9).

24. See Marx and Engels (1987; part I).

25. For example, the 'realists'—see my discussion in chapter 5.

26. A much earlier expression of the arguments in this section is published in *Studies in Social and Political Thought*, under the title 'Constructiveness in Political Criticism' (2009).

27. For instance, Robert Skidelsky (2008) justifies his article's focus on reformist criticisms of the market with the opening line, 'Today, there seems to be no coherent alternative to capitalism'.

28. On the occasion of the 2000 re-launch of the *New Left Review*, for example, the Marxist political theorist Perry Anderson lamented that '[f]or the first time since the Reformation there are no longer any significant oppositions—that is, systematic rival outlooks—within the thought-world of the West: and scarcely any on a world-scale.' Sharing the underlying principle, a journalist for *Times Higher Education* had no trouble in describing Anderson's statement as a 'frank admission of defeat'—although the two writers might well differ as to whether the defeat was moral or 'merely' practical.

29. Cf. George Monbiot's (2000) earlier diagnosis of the failure of 'Reclaim the Streets': 'it might have been able to sustain an attack on global capitalism if it had identified a workable alternative. But without clear proposals for political change, the protests on both June 18 last year and on May Day this year were unmitigated disasters.'

30. Mazie (2011). See also Cohen (2011).

31. Most famously, Lewis (1986). I stress that I am not claiming that this terminology is helpful in general—only that it is in this particular case—and I certainly do not make any Lewisian-Leibnizian commitments to the *reality* of 'possible worlds'.

32. As Peter Lipton puts it: 'A contrastive phenomenon consists of a fact and a foil, and the same fact may have several different foils. We may not explain why the leaves turn yellow in November *simpliciter*, but only for example why they turn yellow in November rather than in January, or why they turn yellow in November rather than turn blue' (2004; p. 33).

33. Another way to look at it would be to think of logical possibility as 'weaker' (admitting more things) than more demanding kinds of possibility. I class the latter as 'softer' only as a play on the conventional distinction between the 'hard' and 'soft' sciences.

34. Adorno (1984; p. 48).

35. See Adorno (1973; §III, esp. p. 367).

36. This point about the conceivability and inconceivability of various political possibilities, from the standpoint of the actual world, is extremely important and is also very relevant to the issue of 'ideal theory' (see my discussion in chapter 5). I only note here that there are principled reasons why some non-liberal theorists, including Marx, have embraced 'anti-utopianism': the view that we do not have the adequate epistemic access to describe a desirable social world in any detail, and that it is inappropriate—after a certain point—to try. Clearly, to the extent that demands for 'constructiveness' ask for exactly what the anti-utopian regards as inappropriate or impossible, these demands presume against anti-utopian approaches in advance.

37. Put another way, what appeared to be common sense turns out actually to be 'conventional wisdom'—a phrase whose pejorative use dates to Galbraith's 1958 book, *The Affluent Society*. Somewhat earlier, the fourteenth-century philosopher Ibn Khaldun makes the interesting argument that unschooled common sense is in fact a much better guide, in thinking about history and politics, than is *taqlid* (i.e., the uncritical deference to traditional authority).

38. 'Recently I saw a house. It was on fire.

The flames licked at the roof. I went up to it and noticed
that there were still people inside.
I went through the door and called to them
that the roof was on fire, and that they should therefore
get outside, quick. But the people
didn't seem in any hurry. One asked me,
with the heat already singeing his eyebrows,
how it was outside, whether it wasn't raining,
whether the wind did not blow, whether there was another house out there,

and so on. Without answering,
I went outside again. These people, I thought,
would have to burn to a cinder before they'd stop asking questions.'

Brecht (1953), from 'The Allegory of the Buddha and the Burning House', translation mine.

Chapter Two

'Beware! Beware! The Forest of Sin!'

Reluctant Reflections on Rawls

... a society may also contain unreasonable and irrational, even mad, comprehensive doctrines. In their case the problem is to contain them so that they do not undermine the unity and justice of society.

—John Rawls[1]

I tried being reasonable. I didn't like it.

—Clint Eastwood

It is a truth universally acknowledged that any work in political philosophy nowadays must have something to say about John Rawls. I have by now said something about the way in which books in philosophy are introduced, and about the way in which political philosophers begin by dispatching the spectre of socialism before getting down to business. No figure looms more largely in what comes next than Rawls, frequently described as the greatest political philosopher of the twentieth century.[2] Since he is so very central to the mode of liberal philosophy currently dominant, he will be the focus of my next two chapters. I did not really want to do this, but in the words of Margaret Thatcher, 'there really is no alternative'—and I'll first explain why.

With uncanny regularity, discussions of Rawls's work kick off with a sentiment along the following lines: 'Love him or hate him, we cannot deny the man's inestimable importance, but must take the trouble to engage strenuously with the Rawlsian canon and to define ourselves in relation to it'.[3] If this just means that Rawls has long been the centre of attention within academic political philosophy—and, to an arguable extent, an influential figure beyond it—then that seems unobjectionable; but I take it that it *doesn't* just mean that. Undeniable things, since they tend not to get denied, don't really need to be endlessly re-asserted; when they are, there is invariably something further going on.

When the 'importance' of Rawls is asserted, this usually comes with a clear implication that the importance in question amounts to something more than column inches, or degree of influence. This something, we may suppose—which is evidenced by the amount of respectful, scholarly attention already lavished on Rawls, and generates an imperative for more of the same—is the presence of some deep philosophical value which can be acknowledged by followers and opponents alike: theoretical elegance or sophistication,[4] impressiveness of argument or ambitiousness of vision, sensitivity to questions of central human importance, embodiment of some particularly fruitful or appropriate methodology, contribution to understanding or progress,[5] and so on and so forth.

The presence of any or all of these virtues in Rawls's political philosophy ought at the very least to be *deniable*, however—above all in a subject such as philosophy which prides itself on keeping nothing off-limits—and it seems legitimate to ask why Rawls's philosophical virtue should be any more obvious a matter than the correctness of his specific claims or the ultimate defensibility of his theory. For one thing, we can hardly expect to find a sharp separation between 'correctness' and 'value'. The claim that Rawls pursues a worthless (or worse-than-worthless) approach to political philosophy might equally be put by saying that he is *wrong* in a particularly drastic way.

Nevertheless, the etiquette of discussion in political philosophy seems to be that while some disagreement with Rawls's claims and arguments is approved, even compulsory[6]—so that the atmosphere is frequently perceived by his sympathizers as one of all-pervasive Rawls-bashing—dissent that denies the serious *value* of his work is less tolerable.[7] I have in mind, here, objections which (a) represent relatively more fundamental or radical disagreements with Rawls, (b) tend to find fault with his approach or 'methodology' rather than with the explicit content of his theory,[8] and (c) question the positive valuation usually placed on Rawls's contribution—that is, they cast doubt on the idea that political philosophy is or has been better off thanks to the presence and prominence of Rawls.[9]

Clearly, it is neither a problem in itself, nor evidence of any injustice, if some philosophical positions are more popular than others, some taken seriously and others derided. But I'll briefly criticize prevalent attitudes to what we may call 'sanctioned' and 'unsanctioned'[10] dissent. The problem is twofold. First, the extent, occurrence or even the *possibility* of the kind of dissent characterized by (a) to (c)—call it 'deep dissent'—is often denied or played down. One example of this is the already-noted ubiquity of statements to the effect that no one can deny Rawls's value, even though they may disagree with him: to the extent that this is an exaggeration, it helps to conceal the instances, however few, where the value of Rawls's work *is* denied. Another manifestation is the tendency to mis-render deep dissent as shallower, more manageable disagreement. This is what I will argue is going on in the case discussed in the next chapter, on philosophical 'charity': deep dissent is denied or interpreted out of existence.

The second aspect of the problem is that, in addition to being concealed in the ways just described, both deep dissent and deep *agreement* are 'depoliticized'. The statements asserting that 'we' can all acknowledge Rawls's great worth are, it seems to me, not presented as *political* judgements at all, but as springing from a kind of political philosophers' 'common sense'—the same 'common sense' that tells us that socialism is dead, and that there is no alternative to the liberal framework. The idea, it seems, is that anyone who knows 'the trade' knows a decent political philosopher when they see one and has to allow that Rawls cuts it. The more prominently displayed sentiment here is the (correct) one that an acceptance of Rawls's worth (this is the 'deep agreement') is independent of an acceptance of various of his specific claims ('shallow agreement').

What is easily overlooked, however, is that deep agreement (or disagreement) is *not* therefore independent of one's political-philosophical position *tout court*. If, for example, one has a view of the social world which accords a big enough role to ideological illusion, the use Rawls makes of 'intuitions' in his central devices of the 'original position' and 'reflective equilibrium' may appear sufficient to render the whole of his system fatuous; and that would be an archetypically *political* (and *philosophical*) reason for denying Rawls's worth as a philosopher. Deep agreement, by the same token, must be premised on the rejection of such a view of the social world. The suggestion of obviousness, universal acceptability and the apparent lack of felt need for justification or elaboration (other than to emphasize the extent of Rawls's influence), which come with the insistence on Rawls's philosophical worth, contribute to the impression that the assertion of this worth somehow has an apolitical basis. And by way of flip side, such deep dissent as is recognized at all takes on an equally apolitical sheen and thus appears inexplicable, save as a philosophically uninteresting defect of personality (which, as we will see in the next chapter, is a popular diagnosis of certain criticisms of Rawls).

To be absolutely clear, then, my complaint here is *not* 'I think that Rawls's political philosophy is not only incorrect but also of little merit; everyone else thinks this is a ridiculous position; I feel stifled; in conclusion, a dominant Rawlsian paradigm must be conspiring against me in unfair ways.' The complaint, which does not actually presuppose any particular estimation of Rawls's philosophical value, is that discussion tends to proceed in such a way as to *conceal* or *depoliticize* the kinds of opposition to Rawls which the consensus position of 'deep agreement' finds disreputable, to the systematic and unwarranted benefit of this dominant outlook. Thus we have a climate which, without being so transparently dogmatic as to present the 'correctness' of Rawls's ideas as beyond doubt, instead presents their 'importance' or 'value' as indisputable and thereby preserves those ideas as the centre around which political-philosophical discourse must turn, entrenching a dominant paradigm that is Rawlsian in this broad sense (though not in the narrow sense of demanding acceptance of the particular tenets of Rawls's major works).[11]

The 'deep dissenter' is therefore in a difficult position. Her criticisms will predictably be ignored or mischaracterized either as (plausible or implausible) 'shallow' disagreements or as inexplicable petulance. The problem is intensified by the fact that there is virtually nothing one can say about Rawls without being jumped on from all sides by those who want to point out that what you have said touches upon a matter of 'deep controversy', about which there already exists 'voluminous' literature with which one must 'engage' in order to be taken seriously enough to have the chance of contributing to the already vast pile—which will, in its turn, confront the next would-be critic. The result is that the sphere of 'sanctioned' discourse on Rawls is rather like the forest of Roald Dahl's *The Minpins*, into which the unsuspecting are lured by the Devil's whispered promises of wild strawberries: 'Beware! Beware! The Forest of Sin! None come out, but many go in!'[12]

Another option—quite attractive, given the alternative—is to adopt a boycott policy, and more or less refuse to talk about Rawls.[13] Entering deep into the Rawlsian Forest can, I believe, be neither necessary nor sufficient for getting Rawls right—or if it is, then this just goes to show that trying to 'get Rawls right' is not worth the cost, when we have no prior assurance that this path will lead us to political-philosophical wild strawberries—a very real possibility is that the path is a dead end, camouflaged by the failure of the greatest political philosopher of the twentieth century to write properly.[14] I am, however, going to talk about Rawls all the same—as opposed to the *talking about talking about* Rawls that I've been doing so far—although I've found it almost impossible, for the noted reasons, to do so in a way that seems to me (or to others)[15] anywhere near adequate. My reason for choosing this over the boycott course is that I explicitly conceive of my task here as one of meta-reflection on the state of political philosophy—although I see this sort of endeavour as continuous with the 'first-order' practice of that discipline—and in that context it would seem negligent to omit sustained comment on such a central character. What follows should therefore be seen as subordinate to the broader project of *talking about talking about* Rawls— and, in particular, about the notion of 'reasonableness', in his work and in political philosophy more generally. I've tried both to resist being sucked into the forest of interminable Rawls discourse and, at the same time, to appease those likely to raise interpretative concerns, by using the strategy of crude-brevity-plus-generous-notes.[16] I realize that this strategy will not please everybody—perhaps it will not please anybody—but it is the best I can think of.

I. THE RHYTHM OF THE REASONABLE

There is a good deal of controversy as to the extent to which the transition from Rawls's first major book, *A Theory of Justice*, to the later *Political Liberalism*[17] marks a decisive break in his thought, as opposed to a harmonious development or shift of emphasis. I cannot stress enough how little I care about this question. What is important here is that the move to 'political liberalism', whether it is best seen as an addition to or a repudiation of what came before, is to be understood as an attempt to produce a political theory that makes the correct kind of contact with what Rawls sees as the realities of the contemporary political world: in particular, to produce a response to what he calls the 'fact of reasonable pluralism'.[18] Rawls seeks an answer to the question of what principles of justice might be legitimately enforceable given this fact. For Rawls, this means advocating a 'political' conception of justice, understood as one which is acceptable to all 'reasonable' persons, with their divergent 'reasonable comprehensive doctrines'.[19]

The language of 'reasonableness' is therefore extremely prominent in the post-shift Rawls—as Leif Wenar puts it, Rawls's conception of justice ('justice as fairness') 'proceeds through *Political Liberalism* to the soft rhythm of the reasonable'[20]—and there has unsurprisingly been a large volume of secondary literature on Rawlsian reasonableness.[21] Much of this attempts to reform the notion so as to repair various defects;[22] but some critics have maintained that no such reform can succeed, and that political liberalism's reliance on the notion of reasonableness is such that the former must be abandoned.[23]

I'll suggest that a version of the second view is correct. In particular, I'll argue that, given a certain simple fact—one concealed, like Marx and Engels's own 'simple fact' (that man must eat, drink and have shelter before he can do anything else) 'beneath an overgrowth of ideology'[24]—the notion of reasonableness cannot support the possibility of the peculiar transcendence which a 'political conception of justice' is meant to possess. A consequence of this is that Rawls's 'political liberalism' fails in its entirety, but I'm well aware that similar arguments have been made before (most notably by 'comprehensive' or 'perfectionist' liberals). The main interest of what I have to say, however, lies elsewhere—although it does depend on my sort of objection to political liberalism being found persuasive—and is articulated towards the end of this chapter, where I describe the way in which the idea of 'reasonableness' functions so as to conceal political liberalism's fraudulence and to constrain the discourse of political philosophy more generally.

Rawls's 'political liberalism' turns on the idea that a conception of justice should be 'political', in a peculiarly Rawlsian sense of that term: a 'political conception of justice' is 'freestanding',[25] in that it is 'neither presented as, nor as derived from' any particular 'comprehensive doctrine'—a term which Rawls employs extremely vaguely to refer to a set of attitudes an individual may have as regards what is valuable, but also concerning various controversial metaphysical matters (such as whether there is a god or an afterlife).[26]

On the kinds of issues with which comprehensive doctrines are concerned, Rawls says—and here comes the 'real politics'—there is ineradicable and, crucially, *reasonable* disagreement. But Rawls thinks that principles of justice should only be imposed on reasonable persons on condition that those persons can be given reason to accept those principles from their own points of view (this is his 'Liberal Principle of Legitimacy').[27] Therefore, given the noted 'reasonable pluralism', it follows that principles of justice should be acceptable from the points of view of the holders of various and divergent 'reasonable comprehensive doctrines'. This is possible, according to Rawls, when a set of principles legislates only for the 'basic structure of society'—another vague Rawlsian term, which refers to the state and other major social institutions.

So in sum, political liberalism says that a conception of justice fit for the social world that confronts us must be 'political', in that it restricts itself to the 'basic structure' and presupposes no particular comprehensive doctrine; its being 'political' makes it possible for the holders of reasonable comprehensive doctrines to view it as 'derived from, or congruent with, or at least not in conflict with, their other values',[28] so that it may form the centre of an 'overlapping consensus' between these doctrines, making its coercive implementation legitimate.[29]

What conception of justice, Rawls then asks, might achieve this? His suggestion: 'justice as fairness', that is, the ordered combination of the Principle of Equal Basic Liberties, the Principle of Equality of Opportunity and the redistributive Difference Principle advocated by Rawls twenty years earlier as the content of his 'ideal' theory. Passing over the audacity of that twist for the moment,[30] what I want to show now is that reasonableness does not just figure importantly in Rawls's *motivations* for espousing 'political liberalism'; it plays a crucial supportive role, such that without the appeal to the notion of reasonableness, the theory would be transparently ludicrous.

This argument begins from the basic observation that people care and disagree about politics—or to put it in Rawlsian terminology, they value incompatible sets of arrangements for the basic structure: Rawlsians may value the application of the principles of 'justice as fairness'; Marxists may value the successful overthrow of capitalist relations; and so on. The human activities of thinking and valuing, of forming evaluative and descriptive judgements about the world, are not confined to matters of personal conscience or interior decoration, but continually spill over onto questions of social organization and trends, exploitation and injustice, relations of power, and so on.

Now, it is not as if Rawls doesn't know this—or perhaps, it precisely is *as if* he doesn't. Without denying that people care and disagree about basic-structural questions, he construes 'comprehensive doctrines' in a way that gives prominence to other matters: comprehensive doctrines cover such things as 'what is of value in human life', 'ideals of personal character, [. . .]

of friendship and of familial and associational relationships'.[31] If we think of comprehensive doctrines in this way, it makes it easy to imagine a set of principles for the basic structure (and only for the basic structure) sitting at the centre of an overlapping consensus: you believe in the immortal soul; she values loyalty most of all in a friend; I like cheese; we all like justice as fairness.[32] But, of course, it is not so easy as that. As noted, Rawls's motivation for advocating a 'political conception of justice' in the first place is a concern for *legitimacy* in the enforcement of liberal principles of justice under conditions of 'reasonable pluralism'; and what that means for him is that all 'reasonable persons', or holders of 'reasonable comprehensive doctrines' (Rawls is unclear on the details, but it doesn't matter here), must be able to recognize adequate reasons for accepting the conception of justice in accordance with which they are required to live. How can that be achieved, when people vehemently disagree with one another about how the 'basic structure of society' should be organized—the very question on which a 'political conception of justice' takes a stance? The fact that 'justice as fairness' presupposes nothing about the soul's immortality, the value of loyalty or of cheese will not make it any more acceptable to (for example) a cheese-loving Marxist.

At this point the political liberal must make one of two moves. One possibility is to say that there is a least one conception of justice (perhaps 'justice as fairness') such that no one *reasonably* disagrees with its prescriptions for the basic structure. So one might say that it is unreasonable of the Marxist, for example, to advocate the common ownership of the means of production. The claim might be that she is not a 'reasonable person', or, more kindly, it might be said that she is merely unreasonable *in respect of her views about the basic structure*. Either way, for the purposes of evaluating the imposition of a liberal conception of justice on her, she is to be regarded as unreasonable, and so the question of legitimacy in Rawls's sense does not arise. She is to be considered as someone (globally or locally) insane: we cannot, of course, simply do what we like to her,[33] but we do not have to offer reasons which she, in her insanity, can recognize as adequate.

The second option, which seems to be the one Rawls favours, is to allow that there is reasonable disagreement on the proper organization of the 'basic structure', such that there can be no conception of justice with which nobody can reasonably disagree, but to hold that it is possible to have a 'political' conception which is somehow acceptable in the required sense even to such dissenters.

I suspect that someone confronted with these options for the first time would likely judge the first one unattractive and the second impossible—and I'll suggest that this is pretty much right. But the point to take now is that the Rawlsian needs to make one of the two moves, if the suggestion that there can be a set of principles of justice which everyone can find acceptable is not simply to shatter against what we might call the 'fact of political disagreement'.[34] And the 'reasonableness clause'[35] in 'political liberalism' is what seems to preserve the possibility of its possibility. For Rawls doesn't talk about *everyone* finding the same 'political conception of justice' acceptable, or about people finding it *simply and straightforwardly* acceptable. He talks about 'reasonable' persons, or the holders of 'reasonable' comprehensive doctrines, finding it acceptable; or about people finding it acceptable '*as* reasonable persons'[36] or finding it acceptable 'in the light of their common human reason'.

So the salvation of 'political liberalism' depends on an account of reasonableness being given which can allow Rawls to tell a story of this kind. In the next section, I'll outline two constraints that a Rawlsian account of reasonableness must satisfy and argue that, for a very simple reason, they cannot both be satisfied at once.

II. CAN'T WE ALL JUST GET ALONG?

Rawls, I noted, wants a conception of justice to be acceptable not *in every way* and *to every person*, but *to certain people* and *in a certain way*. We may think of this as implying two basic constraints on an account of 'reasonableness'.

The first, the 'constraint on reasons', concerns the sense in which a conception of justice must be 'acceptable' (to those people to whom it must be acceptable): a Rawlsian account of reasonableness must be able to support the claim that the relevant set of people has *reasons of the right kind* for accepting the conception of justice on which they converge. The point can be put with the aid of a distinction made by Bernard Williams, between 'internal' and 'external' reasons:[37] a reason is 'internal', for Williams, if it is 'magnetic', that is, capable of motivating us by creating in us *desires* to act in certain ways; and internality, on this understanding, is a matter of degree—a reason can be more or less capable of motivating us, and capable of motivating us under more or less remote possible circumstances.

What seems clear is that Rawls needs the reasons which citizens have for accepting a political conception to be relatively *internal*. In the first place, a political conception would once again lose its alleged advantage of stability if the reasons underpinning it were only recognized by citizens in remote counterfactual scenarios. The fact that I *would* accept some regime, if only I had some wildly different set of beliefs and values, is hardly going to deter me-as-I-am from rioting. A second and related point is that political liberalism will lose what it presents as its distinctive feature, once citizens' reasons for accepting a conception of justice are allowed to reach a certain degree of externality. Inasmuch as *any* political theory will present its favoured basic-structural arrangements as being *desirable*, it will posit the existence of reasons for citizens to accept those arrangements. Rawls, of course, is trying for something more than this. He demands that people have reasons *from their own points of view* to accept the conception of justice that is imposed on them. And it seems natural to interpret this as meaning that they should be able to recognize and find motivation in the reasons in question. That, after all, is why it is important for Rawls that a 'political conception' should not presuppose any particular comprehensive doctrine—if it did, it would preclude reasonable doctrine holders from having sufficiently internal reasons to accept that conception, since their finding it acceptable would require them to give up important aspects of their worldviews.

To move now to the second constraint: one of the few certainties in all this is that Rawls intends a conception of justice fit for legitimate implementation to be acceptable not to some clique, nor even to half the population, but to typical, normally functioning, mature inhabitants of a liberal democratic society *in general*. This does not mean everyone, but it must not be too far from it. If even a significant minority were to have no adequate reason to accept the conception of justice, branding this minority as 'unreasonable' might be a way to preserve the possibility of 'legitimate' enforcement, but the connection Rawls makes between this legitimacy and *stability* would be broken: if although a conception of justice can be said to be 'legitimately' enforced, a sizeable part of the population nevertheless can find no reason to accept it, then the 'legitimacy' in question cannot be expected to bring stability, since the 'unreasonable' may revolt en masse.[38] It is therefore essential that the Rawlsian's account of reasonableness be faithful to the everyday usage of the term to refer to a *fairly minimal, widely satisfied condition*. Call this the 'constraint on scope'.

To summarize these two constraints: what the political liberal needs is an account of reasonableness that identifies a feature or features of people *in general*, which gives them relatively 'internal' reasons for accepting one and the same conception of justice.

Now, I said that the political liberal, with the aid of an account of reasonableness, must make one of two moves: deny that there is reasonable disagreement about the 'basic structure of society', or allow such reasonable disagreement but deny that this precludes the possibility of a conception of justice being acceptable to the right people in the right way—which, we can now say, means *people in general having relatively internal reasons.*

Assuming the fact of political disagreement, the first move seems to violate the constraint on scope. If we agree that for any conception of justice, there will be at least a significant minority that rejects that conception's basic-structural prescriptions, then dismissing this dissent as 'unreasonable' cannot be satisfactory. Rawls, in any case, does not take this path. [39]

Rawls appears instead to attempt the second move: there *is* reasonable disagreement on political matters, including the matter of the proper organization of the basic structure; yet a political conception of justice can be supported by 'reasonable persons' who diverge from one another not only in their views on religion, morality and the good life, but also in their views on such things as political structures. If this line is to be upheld, it must somehow be shown that even basic-structural dissenters 'may reasonably be expected to endorse [the essentials of the conception of justice from which they dissent] in the light of principles and ideals acceptable to their common human reason.' [40]

It is not easy to see how this is supposed to work. It would be one thing if political beliefs were fairly peripheral and unimportant to the people who held them. But I take it that often enough they are as deeply rooted and integral to a person's identity as are religious and moral attitudes. And that suggests that a good political liberal cannot require that such beliefs be given up in order for their holders to accept the conception of justice. But in that case, it looks as though what is expected of reasonable basic-structural dissenters is dissent and assent at the same time. No surprise, then, that political liberalism has been criticized on the grounds that it requires citizens to be 'schizophrenic'. [41] Rawls's 'ideal of public reason' purports to offer a way of making sense of this: reasonable persons will see only some considerations as being fit to bring into the realm of political discussion and decision making. But although it might make sense to talk of keeping aspects of one's 'comprehensive doctrine'—for example, certain forms of Catholicism, or love of cheese—out of politics, how is a Marxist supposed to do the same with her commitment to the communal ownership of the means of production? Asking people not to bring their politics into politics makes no more sense than asking them to keep their Catholicism out of religion, their utilitarianism out of ethics.

This talk of paradoxical injunctions against 'bringing one's politics into politics' requires further comment. The Rawlsian may say that if there is a paradox involved here, it is not a vicious one, and perhaps that there is a parallel with the so-called 'paradox of democracy'. We can quite easily believe in the desirability of some policy while also believing in the desirability or even sanctity of some procedure for determining policy—for example, by lot, by first-past-the-post representative democracy, or single-transferable, or through referenda. Similarly, it is possible to believe (e.g.) that the means of production should be owned in common, where 'should' has a force which is compatible with also believing that *given the assumption that common ownership of the means of production is not (under our contemporary contingent-but-permanent conditions of reasonable pluralism) acceptable to all reasonable persons*, the means of production should not be owned in common but rather in accordance with the particular form of regulated market capitalism prescribed by a given liberal conception of justice. [42]

What is needed, then, is a conception of reasonableness, weak enough to satisfy the constraint on scope, which gives people a set of principles to which they can appeal in order to arbitrate between their clashing basic-structural views and arrive at a consensus, without having entirely to renounce those clashing views—just as the members of a group might espouse different immigration or taxation schemes, while all accepting whatever is the outcome of a first-past-the-post procedure in which they all enter their preferences. Rawls, in fact, seems to want reasonable persons to find the political conception of justice acceptable in a much stronger sense than the sense in which the first-past-the-post democrats accept policies they voted against and which they may find totally repugnant (hence his talk of reasonable persons' finding the conception of justice 'congruent' with their other values). The vision is perhaps more like a scaled-up version of a compromise over what to have for dinner: we all have our tastes and dietary requirements, but we all also (a) accept an arbitrating principle to the effect that what we end up eating should be sufficiently in line with everyone's tastes and requirements, and (b) are sufficiently similar in our tastes and needs for this to be a realistic goal—none of us are dung beetles or carrion-eating birds; so I may want anchovies most of all, and Seb may want olives, but we both know that I hate olives and that Seb is a vegetarian, but that garlic bread is acceptable to both of us; so we put our anchovy and olive preferences to one side— although these are undeniably *culinary* preferences—and eat the garlic bread without either of us feeling too oppressed by the outcome.

The formidable task of an account of reasonableness is to show how something like this can happen at a national level, on complex and large-scale questions of political organization. But at the very moment where he needs to perform a miracle, Rawls proffers what is perhaps the most magnificent dud of his theoretical arsenal. 'Reasonableness', we are told in the manner of a primary-school code of behaviour, is a matter of recognizing the 'burdens of judgment' (i.e., recognizing that moral, religious and philosophical questions are difficult and hence objects of reasonable disagreement)[43] and being 'ready to propose principles and standards as fair terms of cooperation and to abide by them willingly, given the assurance that others will likewise do so' ('reciprocity'),[44] where 'fair terms of cooperation' means terms which others can 'reasonably' be expected to accept 'as free and equal'.[45] As it stands, this is in danger of circularity: 'reasonable persons' are *those who are prepared to propose things that are acceptable to others insofar as those others are prepared to propose things that are acceptable to others insofar* [. . .]. If reasonableness is to be a pot from which we can draw reasons sufficient to enable us to accept the same conception of justice, there will have to be more in this pot than the bare commitment to proposing and accepting some conception of justice that 'we can all accept'. Otherwise it will be as if Seb and I had said to each other only 'I'll have something that is acceptable to both of us', over and over again, until we both starved. On top of this commitment, we had to draw on the overlap in our gustatory tastes and physical (and perhaps ethical) requirements. It is the same kind of common basis of agreement that the Rawlsian needs to identify in the political case.

At this point, all that Rawls has left to offer is an extremely vague commitment to the idea that people should be treated as 'free and equal', and an implication that when they disagree on the many difficult matters that confront them, their divergent views should be respected, and that we should be 'ready to discuss them'.[46] The problem is, of course, that this could mean pretty much anything.[47] Even if this 'public political culture' is widely enough shared (as Rawls thinks it is) to form a broad base of reasonableness, people are liable to disagree on what such things as 'equal respect' or 'treating others as free and equal' amount to, so that the acceptance of such values massively underdetermines acceptance of any particular set of political arrangements: plenty of socialists see the justification of their views in terms of something like 'equal respect' or the value of 'freedom'; and if people habitually (and we will have to say, on pain of violating the constraint on scope, *reasonably*) disagree on this, then their common attachment to the bare *words* 'equal' and 'free' will not bring them to converge on a conception of justice. If reasonableness consists in allegiance to this vaguely defined set of values, the constraint on reasons is clearly violated: 'reasonable' people will not find in these values internal-enough reasons for accepting the same conception of justice.[48] If, on the other hand, we specify more precisely what is meant by (e.g.) 'treating others as free and equal', we can no longer expect (if, indeed, we could have expected it before) that a sufficiently broad cross-section of citizens will subscribe to the resultant ideal: that is to say, the constraint on scope is violated.

A common defence of political liberalism, and one which may be prompted by my use of examples of dissenting Marxists, is that Rawls is only concerned to address himself to fellow liberals, not to justify either his principles or the fundamental liberal values on which they are based to those who stand outside liberalism.[49] Therefore, the reply goes, it is no objection to Rawls's project if a political conception of justice cannot be justified to a Marxist. This may well be how Rawls conceives of his project, but it will not get him anywhere. Either 'liberal' in this context means something like 'sharing in a view of people as free and equal', in which case it includes many who are not 'liberal' in any usual sense of the term, and who would not conceive of themselves as liberal but (e.g.) as Marxists. Or it is used more narrowly—for example, to indicate those who work within the broad framework of capitalist liberal democracy. In the first case, arguably there are enough 'liberals' around to satisfy a constraint on scope, but many 'liberal' Marxists will not find a Rawlsian conception of justice acceptable—and this violates the constraint on reasons. In the second case, there will be a significant 'non-liberal' minority who must be deemed 'unreasonable'—thus violating the constraint on scope. What is more, even within 'liberalism' as understood in the narrower, more everyday sense of the term, I take it that there will be significant differences of opinion both on what constitutes a satisfactory way to organize the basic structure, and on the interpretation of terms like 'free' and 'equal' and 'respect'; and we have seen no reason to expect there to exist among even this subgroup—in any case too narrow a group to ensure for political liberalism 'stability for the right reasons'—a basis of agreement sufficient to provide all its members with internal-enough reasons for accepting the same conception of justice.

This more or less exhausts my patience with the subject, but there is one further important point still to be made. What I have said so far may give the impression that this is a so-called 'Goldilocks issue':[50] it is a question of avoiding accounts that are either 'too strong' or 'too weak', and the Rawlsian may yet hit upon a notion of reasonableness which is 'just right' for the task, satisfying both of the constraints I have described.[51] This impression would be mistaken. What I want to emphasize now is that, in contrast to the ever-increasing convolution of any attempt (or of my attempt, at any rate) to assess the central claims of political liberalism, the reason why it cannot work is embarrassingly simple.

The constraints on scope and on reasons must both be satisfied, I said, if an appeal to an account of reasonableness is to support political liberalism. But the constraints cannot be jointly satisfied. And the reason why they cannot is the simple fact of political disagreement. If reasonableness is characterized in such a way that the bulk of the population counts most of the time as 'reasonable', then the constraint on scope is satisfied. But in that case, since persons who are 'reasonable' in this sense will disagree fundamentally with one another about how the 'basic structure' should be organized, and since they will predictably also disagree on the proper procedure or values that should determine how these disagreements are to be reconciled (or on the proper interpretation of the supposedly shared values that might arbitrate in this conflict), they cannot all be 'reasonably expected' to endorse the same conception of justice.

This is, in fact, the same basic and fatal problem that afflicts social contract theories in general—and perhaps one of the things obscuring the fact that political liberalism is beset by it is that the latter theory is not generally thought of in social contract terms (the social contract element of Rawls's political philosophy being generally associated instead with his idea of an 'original position', introduced in *A Theory of Justice*). Since all citizens have not and will not actually sign a contract, agreement must be hypothetical. This immediately raises the question 'Who would agree to what, and under what imagined circumstances?' Either—and this rests again on the observation of the fact of political disagreement—we're talking about what people would agree to in conditions not-too-remote-from-actual-ones (e.g., conditions in which they retain their basic identities, the essentials of their comprehensive conceptions of the good, and their beliefs about the basic structure of society, etc.), in which case there can be no contract; or, on the other hand, we will have to refer to conditions that are more remote (e.g., if they were all to 'see the light'), in which case the contract is so hypothetical that it is entirely unclear why it should have any bearing either on anyone's motivations or on when and whether people may legitimately be coerced by the state. It is the observation that there exists significant political disagreement, it seems to me, which assures us that there will be no contract that is 'just hypothetical enough'. [52] And the same observation tells us that no account of reasonableness will be 'just right' for the political liberal's purposes. The correct response to 'political liberalism' is therefore an analogue of Johnson's response to Berkeley: kick a large Marxist and say, 'I refute it *thus*.' [53]

To argue as I have argued here should not be confused with the kind of 'tough luck realism' which holds that, since we're never going to agree, we must accept the coercive imposition of some regime or other, even on those who can find no reason to submit to it. [54] I did not even say that we are *never* going to agree, and I left it an open question what lesson might be the best one to draw from the current reality of political disagreement. One response, certainly, would be to abandon altogether the idea that citizens ought to be able to find reasons, from their own points of view, to accept what is coercively imposed by the political scheme under which they live. Those liberals who reject the philosophy of the later Rawls typically lean in this direction: the important thing is whether a given scheme is just or not; if it is, people may or may not recognize it—efforts should be made to explain it to them, and it should only be imposed on them in the context of the right kind of democratic process (most will say), but that does not remove the awkward fact that it will need to be imposed on some significant minority who unfortunately can see no reason to accept it. People should be given reasons which apply 'from their own points of view', in the sense that a just political order should respect all citizens and seek to represent their interests, but that is not to embrace Rawls's political-liberal project. In fact, any palatable political proposal will make a claim of this sort. A different response would be to focus not on the content of what is to be imposed on people—the 'conception of justice', the set of policies, the distributive scheme or however we prefer to think of it—but on the *process* by which that content is determined: for instance, we may shift focus onto models of 'democracy', or 'revolution', for that matter—still with the assumption that some kind of centralized coercive agency would impose something or other on citizens at the end of this process (something which they may not all find reason to accept, especially if they have not found reason to accept the process in question). A different kind of response again would be to get rid of the assumption that there must be a central body that wields coercive force—those who favour this response may see the very 'problem of legitimacy' as a product of this unwarranted assumption.

I'll touch again on these issues shortly, in the concluding section of this chapter. Whatever we think about the relative merits of the alternative responses mentioned above, I want to note now, they all have something in common: the powerful advantage of *not doing what Rawls's political liberalism does*. They do not attempt to deal with the reality of political disagreement by pretending that it isn't there—and then presenting this denial as unique sensitivity. It is this double deceit which accounts for political liberalism's deadly attraction, just as it encapsulates its fatal flaw.

III. CONCLUSION

The point of all this, as I indicated much earlier, is not primarily to overturn political liberalism (though, clearly, I do regard the factors discussed above as overturning it). Those with the greatest motivation to engage in an assessment of political liberalism are those who are attracted to liberalism in general, and wish either to vindicate political liberalism over comprehensive liberalism, or to derive support for comprehensive liberalism from the defeat of the political liberal challenge. From a point of view marked by a general *wariness* of liberalism, the specific faults or relative merits of the later Rawls's theory do not have the same import. That political liberalism cannot work is not necessarily the greatest of its defects. Even if the fact of political disagreement were altered, and there really did exist a consensus broad and deep enough to make possible a political conception of justice 'reasonably acceptable' to citizens in the sense Rawls intends, there are further questions to ask. What, for instance, is the source and nature of this agreement? Whose interests does it tend to further, and might it admit of an ideological explanation of the kind to render it problematic to us? What are the practical effects, so far as we know, when the kind of conception that is the object of this remarkable convergence actually gets implemented? Does it lead to poverty, inequalities of wealth and power, a deficit of meaningful control over our lives and a spate of worsening economic and environmental crises?

Figure 2.1. *Beware! Beware!* Artwork © Patrick Benson. Reproduced by arrangement with The Random House Group Ltd.

So if anything makes the pain and nausea of thinking about Rawls on reasonableness worthwhile, it is not the prospect of refuting political liberalism—and I suggested that no purported refutation is likely to be accepted in any case. The real interest is in the deceptive mechanics of the notion of reasonableness at work within political liberalism and elsewhere. Given that reasonableness cannot perform the function Rawls wants it to, it makes sense to ask what sort of function it *does* perform.

The first thing to note is that the phenomenon of reasonableness follows the same pattern I identified in the first chapter, in my discussion of 'constructiveness': what is presented as politically neutral 'common sense' turns out to be politically controversial, and the illusion to the contrary serves to reinforce the philosophical and political status quo. Rawls himself does not conceive of reasonableness as apolitical, of course: he ties it closely to the idea of a liberal public political culture. But if what I've said here is correct, he does portray it as having a measure of independence from political questions—and a capacity to arbitrate in political disagreements—which it cannot have. Quite apart from the rhetorical effect of using the term 'reasonable' as a byword for 'liberal' . . . (he might as well have talked about 'sensible' persons, or about justifiability to 'decent chaps'). The appeal to 'reasonableness' may not work, in one sense of the word 'work', but the danger is that it nevertheless succeeds in lending an unearned glow to liberalism in general, and to Rawls's position in particular.

Rawls may be seen instead as effecting a split, not primarily between political philosophy and its 'methodology', but between 'first-order politics' and the 'methodology *of politics*': there is the matter of how the basic structure is regulated, the principles applied to it; then there is the *procedure* by which this is determined, the conditions of a given set of principles being 'legitimate' and the bedrock of liberal values which is supposed to underlie both. This split is highly artificial. Questions as to *who has, and should have, the power to decide what* are both continuous with other political-philosophical questions—any useable set of principles for regulating the 'basic structure' is in reality going to involve specifications as to what persons or institutions get to decide or enforce this or that—and also archetypically *political* (cf. Lenin's conception of political philosophy as concerned with the question 'who whom?'—who gets to do what to whom, and why, and to what end?). Rawls creates an artificial division and then uses the lower, methodological stratum to lend artificial support to a higher level of 'policy'. This division, at least, is not at all atypical of the practice of political philosophers. Commonly enough, they do not even pretend to address the most definitively political side of this contrived split (the 'who whom?' aspect). Instead, they treat their task as an exercise in megalomaniac fantasy, like the project some-times given to schoolchildren, 'If I were King (or Queen) . . . ' The political philosopher stands to people at large in the same relation as a stranger who, entirely unsolicited, drew up detailed blueprints for a suggested improvement to your home. However shyly the blueprints were offered, their status as 'mere suggestion' emphasized, your thoughts might still turn to a restraining order.

Rawls's treatment of the 'methodology of politics', of the questions of legitimacy theorized in *Political Liberalism*, in fact preserves and develops this megalomaniac aspect. It is not really a treatment of the question of who gets to decide what and how. The assumption is still that 'I, Rawls', or 'we, the political philosophers', are deciding that. It is not actually up to 'us', of course (except insofar as 'we' are identified with the broader 'political class' to which 'we' belong). But 'we' can think about what 'we' would like to happen, and set that out in creepy detail, and publish it for the students of PPE at Oxford to read and to bear in mind when they are in the Cabinet. This is still Rawls's basic mode when he asks what reasons 'we' can offer the citizens to accept what 'we' propose to inflict on them. Political philosophers in this mode are like home-designing creeps who are pathologically unable to recognize what is creepy about their activity. Their response to a shout of 'It's not up to you!' is to draw up another proposal, this time a proposal as to the decision-making procedures and distribution of authority that should ob-tain among the members of your family when it comes to matters of home improvement. You would say, 'You really don't get it, do you? *It's not up to you!*'

A different way to do political philosophy would be to think about it in terms of the conditions under which 'we' *the citizens* should submit to this or that—a mere difference in phrasing, but an important one; I suspect that the suggestions of *Political Liberalism* will take on a very different air when we switch viewpoints in this way. Or we might even do political philosophy by *really* thinking about the question of who has and who lacks this or that kind of power, about who might and can and should take power, rather than who should be graciously 'allowed' various powers by our envisaged regime. But that would be to allow political matters into political philosophy—something which Rawls, in line with currently dominant attitudes in his discipline, strenuously avoids.

Even the opponents of political liberalism too easily fall into the trap of seeing it as benign—too *nice*, if anything: an inevitably unsuccessful but honourable attempt to give more respect to 'reasonable' people, to accommodate their disagreement, to 'tolerate' more and 'impose' less than any liberal has done before; unfortunately, says the opponent, you can't accommodate as much as the political liberal says you can, and we have to reconcile ourselves to the idea that liberalism must be imposed like anything else (but that's ok, because as things to impose go, it's pretty decent); the political liberal, in being squeamish about this, is too soft. No doubt many of its adherents are well-meaning in precisely this way, but the kind of opposing attitude just described nevertheless misses the respects in which political liberalism—and in particular the use it makes of 'the reasonable'—is genuinely sinister.

Political liberalism is sinister, first, in what it does to the opposition it faces from other political theories. Rawls creates the false impression that certain sets of liberal principles can—and that his own proposed set plausibly *does*—have the extraordinary advantage of being acceptable even to their opponents. The stance the political liberal takes towards persons as citizens and towards persons as fellow philosophers is in this respect similar: 'Even though you disagree with me on one level, that's fine; I can accommodate your disagreement, and that's what gives me the edge.' Leif Wenar, in his address to a seminar on Rawls in 2006, emphasized this aspect with evangelical zeal. I remember him saying to me, 'So it doesn't resonate with you? *That's fine too.*' Probably the reason why this was so effective in reducing me to a small ball of rage was that it seemed to undermine the possibility of my even *objecting* to political liberalism, and to do so under the guise of the utmost respect for my 'reasonableness'. Incoherent as it is, this hyper-liberal move is extremely powerful, for it appears to deal with all opponents in a radical way—not by justifying itself in the ordinary ways that those opponents attempt to justify themselves, but rather by changing the rules of combat and appearing to defeat them all in the new game thus conjured, precisely by *yielding* to them in a way that they are apparently dogmatically unwilling to yield to others.

The role of reasonableness in political liberalism, in fact, has an authoritarian potential that would not go unnoticed for five minutes in a theory further to the left. This comes out most clearly in the stance taken towards the dissenter *as citizen* (rather than the dissenter as rival political philosopher). One possibility is that you are 'reasonable', in which case you are told that you do have reasons from your own point of view—though you don't know it—to accept the conception of justice. If Berlin has a point about 'positive liberty', when he identifies the potential for excusing coercion on the grounds that people must be 'forced to be free',[55] then something similar may be said about the potential for imposing political schemes on the unwilling under cover of the rhetoric of 'what they have reason to accept qua reasonable persons'. This is what comes of the political liberal's attempt to *avoid* 'forcing people to be free' in a different way—namely, through imposing on them a Western liberal autonomy-minded vision of the good life with which not everyone can identify.[56]

On the other hand, your dissent may be 'unreasonable'. In that case, you are excluded from the group of potential subjects to whom questions of legitimate or illegitimate enforcement even apply. Here Rawls is uncharacteristically and chillingly concise: 'Of course, a society may also contain unreasonable and irrational, even mad, comprehensive doctrines. In their case the problem is contain them so that they do not undermine the unity and justice of society.'[57] You are a problem for the police, in other words. Kettle the unreasonable! This tactic of preserving noble principle by excluding certain 'problematic' people from the relevant category has a long pedigree, of course. All men are created equal—but women are not men. All humans must be treated with dignity—but those natives are not fully human. Prisoners of war have certain rights—but these people are terrorists.

The effect of Rawls's use of the notion of reasonableness is to conceal and deny the extent and depth of political disagreement—a disagreement for which opponents of the political status quo must be thankful, while perhaps regretting that its extent and depth is not greater. It is ironic, then, that Rawls's work is so often seen as having 'resuscitated'[58] political philosophy at a time when it seemed as though there was nothing interesting left to disagree about. In any case, it seems to me that if there really were the degree of liberal agreement that Rawls's theory requires, we would not need Rawls's theory—or any political philosophy—to point it out. Rawls seems to be committed to the view that although everyone really agrees (or everyone who matters, at least), we haven't noticed yet, so we just need to sit down and talk things through—a view which seems to betray a low view of human intelligence, even for a political philosopher.

NOTES

1. Rawls (1993; pp. xvi–xvii).

2. This is not, of course, to deny or belittle the existence of other influential figures and traditions. While the prominence of Rawls is hard to miss in most U.K., U.S. and many European philosophy departments, there are notable exceptions (such as, in the United King-

dom, certain programmes at the universities of Essex and Sussex), and many departments of political science or political theory (particularly in the United States) pay more attention to the work of thinkers such as Foucault and Arendt than they do to Rawls.

3. See, for example, Nozick (1974), who strongly opposes a Rawlsian stance: 'Political philosophers now must either work within Rawls's theory or explain why not' (p. 183); see also Mulhall and Swift (1996; p. 1), who emphasize 'the extent to which [Rawls's] theory established the terrain upon which subsequent political-theoretical battles were to be fought', noting that 'in many ways Rawls simply *did* define the agenda and continues to do so'. Alvineri and de-Shalit (1992) observe that Rawls's 1971 book, *A Theory of Justice*, is 'often regarded as the most important text of political thought in the post-war Western world' (p. 1).

4. Nozick has some particularly nauseating words of praise: '*A Theory of Justice* is a powerful, deep, subtle, wide-ranging, systematic work in political and moral philosophy which has not seen its like since the writings of John Stuart Mill, if then. It is a fountain of illuminating ideas, integrated together into a lovely whole.' See also R. P. Wolff (1977), who (albeit from a different angle) in general opposes Rawls at least as much as Nozick does: Wolff (p. 16) describes Rawls's idea of the 'original position' as 'one of the loveliest ideas in the history of social and political theory'.

5. For example, Scheffler (1994; p. 5): 'John Rawls's book *Political Liberalism* constitutes a major contribution to this project of liberal self-understanding.'

6. Developing one's own distinctive pattern of agreement with and departure from Rawls is sometimes simply *identified*, implicitly or explicitly, with the task of being a modern political philosopher.

7. It might be objected that it is unsurprising if people who write about Rawls affirm his value, since they are a self-selected sample of people who at least consider him worth writing about. But first, that need not be the case, since there are important senses in which you can deny Rawls's value and still think it worth writing about him—for example, if you think that he is influential, pernicious and overrated. Secondly, granted that those who write on Rawls are unrepresentatively keen on him, my impression is that they constitute a large enough slice of the population of political philosophers as to be nevertheless quite a good indicator of that field's characteristic attitude towards Rawls.

8. (a) to (c) are intended as a loose bundle: the claim is about criticism of Rawls that combines these sorts of features; it is not that *all* criticisms with *any*—or *any* criticisms with *all*—of (a) to (c) will be frowned upon. Most notably, there are some acclaimed criticisms that might be classed as 'methodological' (e.g., Michael Sandel's [1998] communitarian critique; or, though more accepting of Rawls's general approach, Susan Moller Okin's [1989] critique of his treatment of gender in *A Theory of Justice*).

9. Note that this last strand is independent of finding any fault with Rawls's methodology or competence: Rawls could be going about things completely ineptly or otherwise badly and yet have a good and stimulating effect, or he could be a methodologically virtuous philosopher whose influence, for whatever reason, has damaged political philosophy.

10. I should stress that I'm making no claim of any organized conspiracy against the 'unsanctioned' dissenters, just the usual case of informal social and academic pressures; nor am I suggesting that there is anything wrong, per se, with such pressures existing and shaping people's thought (as it is in any case unavoidable).

11. Cf. Lukács (1971; p. 1): 'Let us assume for the sake of argument that recent research had disproved once and for all every one of Marx's individual theses. Even if this were to be proved, every serious 'orthodox' Marxist would still be able to accept all such modern findings without reservation and hence dismiss all of Marx's theses in toto—without having to renounce

his orthodoxy for a single moment.' Something analogous might be said about the 'orthodox' Rawlsian (who need not necessarily realize that she is one).

12. Dahl (2008; p. 7).

13. Better still would be a 'no platform' policy, although I have found this to be an unpopular suggestion.

14. *Justice as Fairness*, in particular, reads like an instruction manual for a household appliance. Even the staunchest Rawlsians, in my experience, admit that the gospel is badly written. I do not mention this out of irritation or mean-spiritedness alone. The bewildering effect of the appalling prose of Rawls's major works might form part of an 'error theory' (if we were minded to demand one), explaining why—if his theory is, as I would maintain, not only representative of a fundamentally wrongheaded approach to political philosophy but also poorly crafted—people have taken them so seriously.

15. Versions of the midsection of this text were rejected from journals on at least five occasions, the main stated reason being failure to 'engage' closely enough with the literature (some of which had not yet been published at the time of submission).

16. Noel Coward apparently said that reading a footnote was like being called downstairs to answer the door in the middle of making love. I suppose marginalia would be more like having the cat walk in. In any case, I don't think he would have said this if he'd had the typical prose of political philosophy in mind. Perhaps his remark could be adapted in the light of Marx and Engels's famous statement, in *The German Ideology*, that '[p]hilosophy and the study of the actual world have the same relation to one another as onanism and sexual love.'

17. The ideas of *Political Liberalism*, it's worth mentioning, do not actually appear for the first time in that text but in Rawls's 1985 article, 'Liberalism: Political Not Metaphysical'.

18. Rawls (1993; pp. 36, 54, 303–4); Rawls takes the term 'reasonable pluralism' from Joshua Cohen (1993; p. 282).

19. Rawls (1993).

20. Wenar (1995; p. 34).

21. See, for example, Kelly and McPherson (2001; esp. pp. 38–55); Wenar (1995; esp. p. 36); Cohen (1993); Larmore (1996).

22. Wenar, for example, proposes a modification of Rawlsian reasonableness in the context of what he describes as an 'internal critique' of political liberalism. By 'internal critique' Wenar appears to mean a sympathetic critique of Rawlsianism—a critique whose premises and conclusions alike remain within a broadly Rawlsian framework: in criticizing Rawls's view of the reasonable, Wenar is making a relatively minor modification to political liberalism by making a relatively minor modification to something central to it.

23. See, for example, Caney (1995), Gaus (1996).

24. Engels (1883).

25. Larmore (1990) puts this in terms of a 'principle of political neutrality'. I've chosen to avoid the term 'neutrality' here, since it tends to invite misunderstanding (as Larmore himself acknowledges [1990; p. 341]).

26. Rawls (1993; p. 12).

27. Rawls (1993; p. 137) gives the full statement of his 'Liberal Principle of Legitimacy' as follows: '[O]ur exercise of political power is fully proper only when it is exercised in accordance with a constitution the essentials of which all citizens as free and equal may reasonably be expected to endorse in the light of principles and ideals acceptable to their common human reason.'

28. Rawls (1993; p. 11).

29. Ibid., p. 10.

30. Perhaps this is a bit cheap of me. As Scheffler (1994; p. 8) points out, Rawls's earlier device of the 'original position' is itself meant to model 'weak and widely shared assumptions'. If the theory of 'political liberalism' is thus seen as a development and accentuation of this feature, then it makes some sense that the principles of justice it vindicates should be the same as or similar to those put forward in *A Theory of Justice*—this just shows that Rawls hasn't changed his mind about what the 'widely shared assumptions and values' are. It is remarkable, all the same, that Rawls should first arrive at specific principles of justice while consciously *sidelining* the question of how to ensure legitimacy of enforcement (since there is no need for enforcement at all under the assumption of full compliance), only to come back to the very same principles after consciously considering (at great length) how such legitimacy can be preserved given real-world conditions. Either the earlier Rawls had an almost supernatural implicit grasp of what would be acceptable in the light of the theory he was later to articulate, or the elaborate architecture of that later theory is an ad hoc attempt to vindicate the liberal and 'realist' credentials of the earlier one—a long-winded and grandiose version of the unsurprising claim to offer principles which are an articulation of 'widely shared assumptions and values' (a claim made by most political theories). Or it really is a hell of a coincidence. Cf. Farrelly (2007; p. 848), who appears to share my reaction here.

31. Rawls (2005; p. 13). It is worth emphasizing at this point that I am not making the following, probably familiar objection to his position: that is, neutrality is bogus if it obtains only between 'individualistic' conceptions of the good, while privileging these over 'communalistic' conceptions. As Waldron (1989; p. 80) points out, there is no logical inconsistency in being neutral between some things but not between others, and one might recommend neutrality between individualistic conceptions and *non*-neutrality between these and communalistic conceptions for the same fundamental liberal reasons—reasons which are not themselves held to be neutral.

32. Of course, we *could* all like the common ownership of the means of production. The kind of neutrality being described here is one possessed in good measure by *any* political scheme which leaves a fair amount of room for individuals to live as they see fit. Liberals do not have a monopoly on this (cf. most obviously Marx and Engels's famous passage in *The German Ideology*: 'in communist society, where nobody has one exclusive sphere of activity but each can become accomplished in any branch he wishes, society regulates the general production and thus makes it possible for me to do one thing today and another tomorrow, to hunt in the morning, fish in the afternoon, rear cattle in the evening, criticize after dinner, just as I have a mind, without ever becoming hunter, fisherman, herdsman or critic.').

33. Quong (2011), who defends his own version of political liberalism, assures us that the 'unreasonable' would have the same full package of rights and benefits as other citizens—despite having quoted Burton Dreben approvingly in his introduction as saying, 'When I go around speaking for Rawls, sometimes I am asked, What do you say to an Adolf Hitler? The answer is, Nothing, you shoot him.' It is telling, I think, the stock examples of 'unreasonable' persons are lunatics, racists, fascists and religious fundamentalists. But assuming that the right not to be shot is among the package of the rights and benefits of citizens, Quong is not seriously recommending that Dreben's suggested treatment of 'an Adolf Hitler' should be generalized to all of the 'unreasonable'. We are to be reassured that, although the dissent of the 'unreasonable' has the same status as the dissent of a Nazi or madman, 'unreasonable persons' will be treated well—like in Bedlam, or Guantanamo Bay.

34. I am using the word 'political' here in the normal sense, not the Rawlsian one.

35. My made-up term, not another piece of Rawlsian jargon.

36. Emphasis mine.

37. Williams (1981). Williams's concern is to argue that there are no 'external' reasons, understood as reasons that can have no effect whatsoever on our motivations. I make no judgement on this claim. Confusion on this point can be avoided by noting that when I speak of 'external' reasons as both possible and actual, I will be using the term to refer to '*relatively* external' reasons and *not* the *absolutely* external reasons that Williams denies.

38. It is also possible, of course, that they would *not* revolt. Rawls doesn't think that legitimacy is necessary for stability, or else he would have to judge all existing stable societies, past and present, to be legitimate. (It's interesting to note, as an aside, that Rawls's claims in *Political Liberalism* appear to commit him to the view that *no* existing society is one in which the authority of the state is legitimate. This is a plus, as far as I'm concerned, but I don't think Rawls would see it that way.) Stability can also be ensured through tyranny. But Rawls is explicitly concerned with what he calls 'stability for the right reasons'—as Raz observes (1990; p. 14), his main ambition is to show how 'social unity and stability' are possible 'without excessive resort to force'.

39. Not only would this break the link between legitimacy and stability by violating the constraint on scope, but it would also sit badly with Rawls's characterization of reasonableness in terms of, for example, respect for the 'burdens of judgment' (see my discussion later in this section).

40. Rawls (1993; p. 137).

41. See, for example, Mulhall and Swift (1996; p. 197 and p. 223 onwards) for a discussion of this objection.

42. A different way of putting it might be that a person can espouse a communist 'ideal' theory and a liberal 'non-ideal' theory. I discuss the distinction between these two types of theory in chapter 5.

43. Rawls (1993; pp. 58–59).

44. Ibid., p. 49.

45. This is a crude summary of what may be gleaned, I believe, from the sum of Rawls's statements about 'reasonable persons' and about the 'idea (and 'ideal') of public reason'. As far as I can see, there is no difference between 'reasonableness' and adherence to an idea of 'public reason' that is important for my purposes.

46. Rawls (1993; p. 49).

47. Cf. Trotsky (1973; p. 22): 'The so called "generally recognised" moral precepts in essence preserve an algebraic, that is, an indeterminate character. They merely express the fact that people in their individual conduct are bound by certain common norms that flow from their being members of society . . . The vacuity in the norms obligatory upon all arises from the fact that in all decisive questions people feel their class membership considerably more profoundly and more directly than their membership in "society." . . . The moral norm becomes the more categoric the less it is "obligatory upon all."'

48. We can, of course, say, 'But Rawls is *right* about what equal respect, and so on, consist in.' But that does nothing to solve the problem that the reasons people have are not internal enough to yield for political liberalism the advantage it claims in terms of 'stability for the right reasons'.

49. Quong (2011) understands political liberalism in this way (see the section entitled 'The Modesty of Political Liberalism'). See also Scheffler (1994). It is worth noting that Quong defends his brand of political liberalism against essentially the same objection as the one I make here: 'If reasonable people disagree just as much about justice as they do about the good life, then why are perfectionist reasons, but not reasons of justice, deemed illegitimate grounds for state action? I call this the *asymmetry objection* to political liberalism.' (pp. 192–93). However, Quong's project appears to be sufficiently different from Rawls's and other political

liberals' that his defence—which involves distinguishing between 'foundational' and 'justifica-tory' disagreement on matters of justice—is irrelevant here. Quong construes political liberal-ism as 'a theory that explains how the public justification of political power is possible among an *idealized* constituency of persons who are committed to certain fundamental, but fairly abstract, liberal values.' (p. 5; emphasis in the original). Now, my view is that so long as the shared values were 'fairly abstract', convergence driven by internal-enough reasons would not occur—unless Quong also 'idealizes' the way in which people reason from and interpret their core values. In other words, I am saying that his idealization would have to be more radical than he seems to acknowledge: it would have to involve people in general *becoming political liberals of a particular kind*. But in any case, I have said that for Rawls, political liberalism is above all an attempt to produce a theory that is applicable to (something close to) real political conditions. It is *this* that I argue cannot be upheld. I include a brief remark in the final section on what we should think about the hypothetical situation in which there *is* enough political agreement to get political liberalism going.

50. Arneson (2008; p. 5).

51. Kelly and McPherson (2001), for example, seem to be arguing for a construal of Rawl-sian reasonableness that makes 'political reasonableness' weak enough to include the 'philo-sophically unreasonable', while being strong enough to do the work Rawls needs it to do.

52. There is, of course, wide variety within the social contract theory tradition, and I should allow that some hypothetical contracts might be capable of playing the role the theory in question requires them to play. If, for example, the contract device is just a convenient way of expressing the claim that the political authority that is exercised is rooted in reason, or respon-sive to human interests, then the problem doesn't arise—although it is unclear how much point there would be in referring to a contract at all. Suffice it to say that insofar as social contract theorists resemble Rawls in claiming a special advantage of acceptability or stability, they face the same problem as he does.

53. See Boswell (1986; p. 122).

54. I discuss the relationship between varieties of 'realism', pessimism and conservatism at greater length in chapter 5.

55. See Berlin (1970).

56. This is the worry about 'comprehensive' liberalism which exercises political liberals and other critics. Larmore (1990; p. 345), for example, takes the view that comprehensive liberal theories such as those he associates with Kant and Mill cannot adequately respond to the problem of reasonable disagreement about the nature of the good life, but are 'simply another part of the problem.'

57. Rawls (1993; pp. xvi–xvii).

58. Being resuscitated by Rawls's philosophy must be a bit like being given mouth-to-mouth by a dead fish. Nevertheless, the idea is quite widespread. Mulhall and Swift (1996; p. 1), for example, refer to the 'commonplace observation that the publication of Rawls's *A Theory of Justice* was the single most important stimulus to the renaissance of political theory during the 1970s and 1980s'. Those who were around before that time tell me that there was, in fact, quite a lot going on.

Chapter Three

Foul Play

The Norm of
Philosophical Charity

[The principle of charity] constrains the interpreter to maximize the truth or
rationality in the subject's sayings.

—*The Oxford Dictionary of Philosophy*[1]

The referee's a wanker!

—Popular British football chant

I promised two chapters on Rawls. Strictly speaking, that was a lie, because
this chapter is going to focus on the philosophical virtue of 'charity'. But one
issue leads naturally to the other. The verdict I advanced in the previous
chapter on the work of the later Rawls was a pretty harsh one, and I would be
very surprised indeed if a common reaction to it were not that I have been
'uncharitable'—although I made every effort to provide textual support for
my claims and to anticipate possible responses on behalf of the Rawlsian.
What I argued there must stand on its own. The purpose of this present
chapter is not to repeat the attack on Rawls, or to extend it—for instance, by
turning my attention to the earlier *A Theory of Justice*[2]—but to have a closer
look at a value which plays a crucial role in regulating criticism and debate in
political philosophy, and discussions of Rawls in particular. As I observed at
the start of the previous chapter, some kinds of dissent against Rawlsian
political philosophy are tolerated and even encouraged, while others—partic-

ularly cases of what I called 'deep dissent'—are found to be beyond the pale. In such cases, the notion of 'charity' plays a crucial justificatory role: these forms of criticism, it is often judged, are unacceptable because they are based on 'uncharitable' readings of Rawls. One of the more dramatic examples is a paper by Raymond Geuss, in which he notoriously accuses Rawls of being 'generically the same kind of thing' as George W. Bush and Condoleezza Rice.[3] Now this, it is generally accepted, is uncharitable *if anything is*. This verdict goes even for those who consider themselves fairly sympathetic to Geuss's general approach to political philosophy, an approach which views Rawls as the archenemy. Such sympathizers, unlike most Rawlsians, may regard the comment as amusing—perhaps even 'onto something'—but nonetheless ultimately impossible to take seriously as a criticism. Why? Because it is so obviously 'uncharitable' to Rawls: whatever you think of him, he is no Condoleezza Rice.

Once again, however, I will argue that things are not so simple. Philosophers continually stress the importance of 'charity' and castigate each other for falling short of the ideal. But since these judgements are generally made in the course of talking about something else—or perhaps just because the matter is thought to be obvious or uninteresting—there has been little attention given to the question of what the value of philosophical charity actually *is*, why we should prize it, and how we might detect its presence, absence or violation. Thus far, the case of 'charity' resembles that of 'constructiveness', discussed in chapter 1. And the basic line I want to take on these two informal methodological values is the same: like 'constructiveness', I'll argue, 'charity' is deeply ambiguous (or rather, incomplete), so that the way in which we construe and apply it must ultimately be informed by our politics; and as with 'constructiveness', the tendency to overlook this results in the disproportionate penalization of dissent against the political-philosophical status quo.

But the norm of 'charity' has its own peculiarities. For a start, it seems both stricter and more universal. As I observed, not every kind of criticism is required to be 'constructive'. But in the analytic tradition, at least, to describe something as 'uncharitable' is to refuse it recognition as a serious philosophical criticism (while perhaps continuing to appreciate it for its comic or aesthetic value): it is to say that the criticism ultimately does not 'work'—and this is so whatever the subject matter or object of criticism. On the face of it, this sits oddly with the overtone of supererogation (the ethicists' term for 'going beyond the call of duty') that is carried by the term 'charity', both in the methodological sense dealt with here and in the more everyday sense of charity-as-philanthropy.[4] Pre-theoretically, to be 'charitable' is voluntarily to do *more* than is required of us, to give what we could legitimately opt to keep for ourselves. To make this compulsory therefore looks rather paradoxical: we are required to do more than is required of us.[5] This is perhaps the first sign of the thick fog of confusion that surrounds the informal norm of philosophical charity. It is important to dispel this fog, I'll argue, not just so as to correct any illusion that this norm is a neutral referee, regulating political-philosophical debate according to a methodological principle acceptable to all—an illusion which tends to work to exclude certain kinds of dissent against the status quo from the circle of sanctioned disagreement. It is important also because the notion of charity nevertheless does seem to have an important role to play in philosophical discussion. It is not clear that we can do without it: even if norms of charity are shown to be laden with political content, we will still want to say, from our various political points of view, that certain interpretations and criticisms are 'uncharitable'. As I'll indicate towards the end of this chapter, there are occasions when this seems to be what the accused should say, in response to an accusation of violating the norm: it is the accusation itself, and not the accused, that is uncharitable. We need to be able to make sense of these claims, and of the basis on which we might favour one over the other.

A worry may arise at this point, a worry which was already lurking in the background during my discussion of 'constructiveness'. I have made no suggestion that there could ever be a truly politically neutral incarnation of an informal methodological value like 'constructiveness', even in principle—although I haven't exactly ruled it out. If these things are *always* political—which is the direction I seem to be heading in—then aren't all manoeuvres in philosophical argument open to the kind of 'critique' I've been waging? Do not all (tacit or explicit) appeals to (informal or formal) methodological norms and values 'beg the question' against those at whom they are directed? How, in that case, can we ever choose between different political positions (since, by hypothesis, there is nothing we can reach for which doesn't already presuppose some political positions over others)?

This worry touches upon some very deep and general questions in epistemology and the philosophy of science, and I will try to say something about them—albeit necessarily schematic—in the conclusion to this book. But the short answer is, unsurprisingly, that I *don't* regard the more radical option which I favour, which holds that 'everything is political', as committing us to an 'everything goes' relativism. In the first place, I do not criticize my targets on the basis that they turn out to presuppose political content per se, but on grounds of a tendency for this to be somehow denied or disguised. Ok, in criticizing *that*, I must appeal to some principle of 'anti-duplicity', which says that philosophers should be up-front about the political presuppositions of their methodological moves. Isn't this going to turn out to be a politically loaded principle, too? Some, of course, may simply answer 'no': there are some philosophical standards which *are* politically (perhaps also ethically) neutral. My preferred policy is to allow that all such standards will be 'political', at least in *some* sense (sometimes a very remote one).[6] And this raises a further crucial point: nothing may be neutral, but some things are more non-neutral than others. Towards the end of this chapter, I'll make a distinction between 'relative' and 'absolute' independence. The latter, I suggest, is impossible. But the former may be enough to allow us to distinguish between more or less neutral usages of a value like 'charity'. This distinction can be used to lend support to a surprising conclusion: whether or not it is uncharitable to say that Rawls is like Condoleezza Rice, it can be uncharitable to call someone 'uncharitable' for saying it.

I. REASONS TO BE CHARITABLE

Before going any further, it is helpful to give a preliminary description of philosophical charity, understood as a norm governing interpretation and criticism. This norm seems to amount to the demand that when we criticize others, we do so on the basis of an interpretation of those others which makes their positions *as defensible as possible*. There are obvious similarities between this informal norm and the more formal 'principle of charity', which, having been first formulated by Neil L. Wilson in the late 1950s and made familiar in particular by the work of Donald Davidson, has received sustained attention from philosophers of language in a way that the informal norm that concerns me has not.[7] The 'principle of charity' tells us to interpret speakers (for Wilson, especially speakers of other languages) *in such a way as to make their statements come out mostly true*. There is, of course, plenty of room for doubt and disagreement as to how to make sense of this, and of Davidson's accompanying claim that adherence to the principle of charity is a prerequisite for regarding the other's language as one in which meaningful utterance is possible at all. That need not concern us, however. All I want to do here is briefly to set out the ways in which the informal norm of philosophical charity resembles and differs from the Davidsonian principle.

There is a similarity between the two notions inasmuch as both involve 'giving the benefit of the doubt', where this means interpreting others in such a way as to ascribe to them more truth (or something of comparable import—I'll come back to this shortly) than would be ascribed by alternative interpretations. But the kind of charity considered here also differs in important respects from Davidson's. In the first place, the norm of charity is not only applied at the level of a language or other body of discourse as a whole but is also applicable to the criticism of individual theories, schools of thought, statements, and so on. Thus, it might make sense to complain, 'You interpreted what I said on that occasion uncharitably.' Relatedly, with the informal norm of charity, there is no obvious analogue for the Davidsonian rationale about securing the possibility of meaningful utterance. The norm of charity, unlike the principle, is specifically a rule for the conduct of *criticism*, and accordingly comes with its own distinctive rationale, which I'll now try to describe.

The reason why it should be important to interpret philosophical opponents in a way that maximizes their defensibility, I take it, is not merely that it is good etiquette or an act of kindness. Interestingly—and also slightly jarringly, considering the use of the same term for altruistic material generosity—an important part of the rationale for 'charity' in the present sense is a strong *prudential* value for the critic, in the form of a kind of argumentative security. The idea is that we are actually better off tackling positions in their most formidable guises, because if we direct our attacks at the more feeble versions, we buy temporary or limited argumentative success at the cost of leaving better versions of those views unaddressed, and this is self-defeating. It is tempting, but incorrect, to explain this thought as follows: If we want to overturn view *V*, then we should attack version A rather than version B (where version A is better), because since A is better than B, then if our attack works against A, it must work against B as well. A moment's reflection finds that this rests on a false picture of the workings of criticisms. Criticisms and objects of criticism are not like weightlifters and weights respectively, where if I can lift 70kg then I can be confident that I will also be able to lift 50kg. Criticisms play on particular weaknesses of their targets, weaknesses that will not necessarily be shared by overall weaker possible versions of those targets. It might be judged that I am a more formidable creature, *overall*, than my elderly cat (in the ways that are deemed relevant in the given context), but I nevertheless have weaknesses that she does not have: you might systematically undermine my self-confidence with your barbed comments and withering looks; the cat, however, is entirely immune to such things. In the same way, a criticism of a philosophical view might perfectly well take advantage of a weakness that is specific to the *strongest* version of that view, and in such a case the criticism would have no force against less defensible versions. So this first thought cannot be quite right. A better explanation of the rationale for charity might suggest that the best version of a given view will be acceptable 'if any version is', and that therefore, if we are interested in showing that the view is unacceptable, it makes sense for us to attack *that* version. To take a stupidly oversimplified example, we might judge that if liberalism is true, then liberalism's best version A is true. In that case, if we can argue that version A is not true, it follows that liberalism *tout court* is probably not true; whereas if we merely argue that inferior version B is not true, the general conclusion about liberalism does *not* follow.

Let us suppose, then, that this accounts for the prudential value of abiding with a norm of charity. In addition, I take it, the value of charity is also a *social* one, in the following sense. It is not merely that my criticisms are more likely to be successful if they are charitable, and that yours are too—so that, therefore, if we both argue charitably, there will be better philosophy around than there would otherwise be. What that statement of it doesn't adequately capture is the idea that charity is meant to promote some goal of philosophical 'meritocracy': if we all argue charitably, the thought goes, this contributes to the attainment of a state of affairs in which thinkers, positions and theories that are good, valid and interesting (or 'meritorious' in whatever way we deem relevant) are recognized as such, while untenable positions are more decisively and thoroughly refuted. Two unfortunate scenarios may issue from a failure to criticize charitably, and both scenarios threaten to undermine rather than promote a condition in which the worth of competing philosophical positions is correctly appreciated. First, there is a danger of inefficiency: if I criticize a 'straw man', or an otherwise weak version of my intended object, I leave it an open question whether a better version might be defensible; an opponent might come back at me with this better version, and if I want to succeed against my object, I will then have to confront this version too—but in that case, it would have been better to have done this in the first place, rather than waste time and energy on a dress rehearsal. But the more serious danger, I take it, is that I might get away with it: I might successfully create the illusion that I have overturned *V*, when at best all I have done is overturn an inadequate shadow of *V*. In that case, it seems we would want to say that there is some kind of miscarriage of intellectual justice.

A good example here is a comment by Simon Blackburn (incidentally, the author of *The Oxford Dictionary of Philosophy*, from which I took the definition of 'charity' cited at the start of this chapter). In the early pages—always a danger zone—of his very popular introduction to philosophy, *Think*, Blackburn briefly considers the eleventh and best known of Marx's 'Theses on Feuerbach': 'The philosophers have only interpreted the world, in various ways. The point, however, is to change it.' This, Blackburn reflects, is

> One of the silliest famous remarks of all time (and absolutely belied by his own intellectual practice). He would have done better to add that without understanding the world, you will know little about how to change it, at least for the better. [8]

This may seem unobjectionable—as long as we forget to do what the title tells us, *think*. Once we do that, the very obviousness of Blackburn's point should ring alarm bells. Are we really expected to believe that Marx was enough of a moron to think that we ought to make our efforts to change the world *without* knowing anything about it? This, as Blackburn himself points out, sits badly with the fact that Marx spent his life attempting to understand the world. Or are we supposed to think that he was not so much an idiot as just spectacularly stubborn or hypocritical? Some people *are*, of course, stupid, stubborn, lazy, hypocritical and many other things besides, but a concern for 'charity' would seem to dictate that we do not diagnose such conditions when more generous alternatives are available. In the present case, it is hardly much of a challenge to come up with such an alternative. Marx's point is that the historical function of philosophy has been to describe, mirror and even to help preserve the world as it is, and not to change it—or not to change it *enough*, anyway. Marx believes that the world is now due for revolutionary change. So if we're going to do philosophy at all, we must radically overhaul the way in which we perceive and practice it, so that it can play the right kind of role in that revolutionary change. Blackburn's objection seems to have no force at all against *this* Marx, who has an underlying view which both makes sense of the eleventh Thesis and clears him of any commitment to the stupid-or-stubborn claim that we should try to change the world blindly. By failing to heed this, Blackburn attacks a 'straw Marx'—an exercise made *more* rather than less harmful, I suggest, by the fact that it takes place not in an up-front political polemic but as a passing comment in a best-selling introductory text for newcomers to philosophy. This makes Blackburn much more likely to get away with it—and to do so in front of a large audience—with all the damage that this entails.

II. THE CHARITABLE IS POLITICAL

It should be obvious, even from this preliminary sketch of philosophical charity and its rationale, that this norm will have to be elaborated on at crucial points if it is to give us any useable guidance as to how to criticize or evaluate the criticisms of others. Charity is a matter of interpreting others so as to maximize the defensibility of their positions, I said. But what constitutes the 'defensibility' of an object of philosophical criticism? The value of charity itself does not pretend to provide an answer to that. So what counts as 'charitable' cannot be divined by an examination of the value of charity alone but will require input from elsewhere.

This gap in the notion of charity widens once we note that the 'What is defensibility?' question lies downstream of another. We will not only have to specify the *content* of 'defensibility'. We also have to decide upon the *standards* relative to which defensibility is to be interpretatively maximized. I could interpret you so that your position emerges as being as defensible as possible (i) by *my* standards, which may or may not be ones that I take to be (ii) *objectively correct*; or, on the other hand, I might interpret you as being maximally defensible (iii) according to *your* standards. Within the tradition of 'internal criticism', for instance, the value of 'charity' might be construed as demanding that I interpret you so as to maximize the merit of your position *by your own lights*, before arguing that even on this charitable interpretation, you are internally inconsistent. Depending on which set of standards we deem relevant, an adherence to a norm of charity can prescribe drastically divergent courses. And, of course, the question of whether and how we should make our criticisms 'internal'—and thus of what standards are the relevant ones—is no more straightforward a question than that of the correct characterization of philosophical defensibility.

Another place in which the notion of charity displays a gap is in the constraints on what qualifies as a permissible *interpretation* (as opposed to an invention, say). If you say that *p*, and I consider that a stupid and false thing to say, I may decide to 'interpret' you as making the more plausible claim that not-p. But although I may well see myself as having taken on a more noble task in so doing, this is pretty clearly not what is, under normal circumstances, demanded by charity. Plausibly, I have been neither charitable nor uncharitable towards you, but rather have destroyed the required preconditions for being either of these things, by refusing to respond to *your* view at all. So we should see the distinctive constraint that charity places on interpretation—the constraint to interpret so as to maximize defensibility—as subordinate to a prior constraint, which we may call the 'constraint of conservation': a requirement that we interpret in such a way as to conserve the *identity* of the object of criticism—that is, that we really do criticize what we claim to criticize. Operating with these two principles combined, charity requires us to select and attack the most defensible target from the range of the interpretations which satisfy the constraint of conservation. But what determines the range of interpretations which satisfy this constraint?[9] If the object is a statement written by a particular philosopher, is the range of permissible interpretations limited by what she (consciously?) meant, or perhaps by what it is plausible for us to *suppose* that she (consciously) meant? Or is it sometimes permissible to attribute to people statements that they did not (consciously) intend to make? Again, answering these questions is neither straightforward nor something which can be guided by the ideal of charity itself.

In sum, the norm of charity seems to be a thing with holes in it bigger than the thing itself. And even at a glance, it seems clear that the way in which we choose to fill those holes, so as to end up with an ideal of charity substantive enough to apply to criticisms within political philosophy, is going to be in part a *political* decision. What we will count as 'defensibility' or 'merit' in a political-philosophical position obviously depends on the political-philosophical commitments we have. If I think, for example, that ideological illusion is an extremely important feature of the social world, I will judge that an appropriate sensitivity to this will be one of the characteristics of a defensible or meritorious political-philosophical theory. Likewise with the question of whose standards should be the ones relative to which we seek in our interpretation to maximize the defensibility of what we criticize. The tradition of internal criticism is, to a significant extent, bound up with a certain sort of *political* position, and some of its advocates go as far as to connect 'external' criticism with 'imperialist' attitudes.[10] To use the example of ideology again: if you have a political outlook which takes this phenomenon seriously, you may be drawn towards a form of criticism which seeks to unearth internal contradictions in opponents' views, rather than judging them wanting in the light of ideals which you have satisfied yourself are correct— through, for example, consulting your 'intuitions'—since you may reject the idea that such intuitions can afford us access to undistorted Truth. And turn- ing, finally, to what I've called the 'constraint of conservation': what it means to be 'true to' or 'mindful of' the nature and significance of the object of one's criticism, and how important a consideration this is, are also matters that are not easily detachable from background commitments and attitudes. If, for example, one takes a view of political philosophy whereby the latter is simply a matter of arriving at abstract truths, then it may not be all that important whether the view one attacks is recognizable as belonging to a given philosopher: I may interpret V, which I associate with you, and attack it; and it doesn't really matter, except perhaps for social or practical reasons, whether V-as-I-interpret-it can sensibly be said to be *your* view (much as it might be annoying for you to be misrepresented); the point is to get at the truth, and in principle one could renounce arguing *with other people* alto- gether and simply engage with *positions*. In that case, it may even be of little interest where one 'position' (such as the position we call 'liberalism') be- gins and ends—I might have an interpretation of 'liberalism', L1, and a criticism of it, and have no particular interest in whether what I have criti- cized is still apt to be called 'liberalism' or not, my only concern being whether my argument *works* (i.e., whether it works against L1, however one chooses to classify that object). If, on the other hand, I have an approach to political philosophy which places greater emphasis on real politics, I will have a far greater interest in the question of what certain political figures stand for and in the actual significance of political affiliations or labels such as 'liberal', and I may therefore insist on a much stricter conservation con- straint when applying or testing for charity.[11]

This already shows that the interpretation of the value of charity must be informed by *methodological* commitments (i.e., views about what political philosophy is, what it is for and how it should be done)—and it is a central hypothesis of this book that the methodological cannot be neatly separated from the political. But to put that aside, assuming that our methodological approach does tolerate our being concerned to get the meaning and signifi- cance of our real-world targets right, the way in which the constraint of conservation is interpreted will be a more clearly and directly *political* mat- ter: what we think some view really means or 'stands for' will depend on our background political beliefs and values, and these will also inform the degree of similarity or difference we perceive between two or more parties or positions: it often seems correct to place on some party or political intervention the interpretation that it is 'racist', although, more often than not, the racism will not be fully explicit—and to do so is to make a political judgement, one which is controversial at least in the sense that those supportive of that party or intervention (otherwise known as the racists) will deny that this is the correct interpretation; equally, to say that Labour, the Conservatives and the Liberal Democrats are all the same—that they stand for the same basic set of interests—may be to make a legitimate point, but the similarity will likely not be so salient to a Conservative, to whom the differences are very important (whereas 'the Left', of course, *are* 'all the same').

From some political points of view, then, to say that Rawls is like George W. Bush or Condoleezza Rice is no less perverse than interpreting *p* as not-*p*. As the legions of infuriated Rawlsians can point out, there are seemingly huge differences between Rawls's views and those of the neoconservatives. For example, in the *Law of Peoples*, Rawls advocates as a part of his conception of international justice a 'principle of non-aggression'. At the level of domestic policy, too, the difference from neoconservative policy is stark. Although it is a matter of endless controversy exactly how much redistribution would, could and should be sanctioned by Rawls's 'Difference Principle', the ideal of maximizing the welfare of the least well-off hardly *sounds* like a Reaganite slogan.

So why would anyone claim something so peculiar as that Rawls and the neo-cons are 'the same kind of thing'? As with the earlier example of Marx and Blackburn, we may construct two theories: the 'stupid-or-stubborn' reading and the 'underlying background view' reading. As in the case of Blackburn and Marx, it is not hard to imagine what such a background view might look like. It would have two important features, for a start. First, what I referred to in the previous chapter as 'deep dissent': fundamental opposition to Rawls's whole way of going about political philosophy, not just a quibble with the content of his theory or even a wholesale rejection of his specific prescriptions. Second, and equally important, a view to the effect that political theories should be evaluated in the light of their political 'resonance', their apparent relation to real politics, both in terms of the politics they seem to reflect and in terms of the role (if any) they might be seen to play in the real world—the sort of view which we saw, in chapter 1, being rather selectively held and applied (to socialism but not to liberalism).[12] If this background is held in mind, when considering the comparison between Rawls and the neoconservatives, that comparison suddenly makes a lot more sense: of course, there are obvious differences between the outlooks of Rawls and George W. Bush, but (the thought goes) there are also some under-acknowledged *connections* between them, connections which can more easily be seen once we look at Rawls's theory in its political context; and the acknowledged respects in which the content of Rawls's philosophy is superficially opposed to neoconservatism do not tell against a criticism focused on those deeper connections.

Now, of course, this background position might not ultimately be the right one. Maybe the reading of Rawls's political resonance is wrong—many defenders of Rawls would certainly say so.[13] Or maybe it is wrong in the first place to reject abstract approaches to political philosophy and to place so much emphasis on the actual historical role and origins of a political theory. Either way, it may also be legitimate to say that the comparison between Rawls and the neo-cons is a breach of what I've called the 'constraint of conservation'. But if the diagnosis of a violation of charity is made only on the grounds that there are numerous divergences between Rawls's explicit commitments and those of the neoconservatives, differences which the comparison in question (almost inexplicably) ignores, then it seems appropriate to say that what is *really* uncharitable here is the diagnosis itself: instead of acknowledging and criticizing the view that forms the background of the comparison, the accusation acts as if this deeper opposition did not exist— deep dissent is mis-rendered as shallow dissent, because no other kind of dissent is thinkable—which leaves us with the conclusion that anyone who makes a critical comparison of this sort is simply being stupid or perverse. And that, as they say, is not very charitable.

III. POLITICAL 'ALL THE WAY DOWN'

I've tried to show how the way we view even the most apparently obvious example of an uncharitable criticism might be turned on its head, so that we see the failure of charity as lying instead with the initial assumption that the first criticism is uncharitable. And the strange thing is that we can say this even if that criticism *is* uncharitable, since then it is being correctly diagnosed but for the wrong reasons, that is, on the basis of an interpretation which violates the requirement for charity.

But it is clear that this cannot be the last word on the matter. The above applies, I noted, only if we interpret the objection against the Rawls-Rice comparison in a particular way—if, that is, our reading of it is that the claim that this is 'uncharitable' is just an unthinking reflexive response, which acts as if the person making the comparison somehow hadn't noticed (or was pretending not to have noticed) the various obvious features which distinguish Rawls's political philosophy from that of neoconservatism. That, of course, is one among many possible interpretations, and may itself be criticized. It may be countered that those who object to Geuss's original claim about Rawls know perfectly well that the claim is made against a certain background: when they say that the claim is uncharitable, part of what they are saying is that the background view in question is wrong, and in particular, is wrong because it depicts Rawls's political resonance—the relationship between Rawlsian theory and real politics—in such a way as to fail to make it as defensible as possible (i.e., it is uncharitable). In that case, my own suggestion above was itself uncharitable against those who make the objection that likening Rawls to the neo-cons was uncharitable.

In this way, things can get very messy very quickly. I am not mainly interested in defending the interpretation which says that those who cry 'Uncharitable!' on Rawls's behalf have reduced deep dissent to shallow dissent in order to dismiss it as merely foolish—although I do think that this is often at least part of what is going on. Obviously enough, such an interpretation will be more or less appropriate in some cases than in others, and it is quite plausible that, at least sometimes, those outraged by claims like Geuss's about Rawls are outraged precisely because they *do* recognize the background view (and find it outrageous).[14] For example, as I noted earlier, many of Rawls's defenders vehemently contest the claim that Rawls stands in the kind of relation to neoconservative politics that Geuss insinuates: in particular, they point out, Rawls can hardly be held responsible for Reaganite politics; rather, they claim, his effect on actual politics has been either negligible or benign.[15] My impression is that this version of the reaction is not usually couched as an accusation of violation of 'charity': the objection is not that Rawls's role in real politics has been interpreted in a way that fails to maximize its defensibility prior to criticism, but, more straightforwardly, that the depiction of Rawls's real-political significance is simply *false*. But let us leave that aside. The point I want to develop here is a general one about the structure of 'charity' as a methodological norm. We can already see, from the imaginary back-and-forth I've begun to construct above, that the progression of accusations and counter-accusations could go on forever: to complain that a criticism is 'uncharitable' is itself to make a criticism, based on a particular interpretation; as such, the second criticism is also open to a further (third) criticism to the effect that it interprets the first criticism 'uncharitably'; and this third criticism, and the interpretation *it* rests on, can also be criticized—and so on ad infinitum.

An attempt could even be made to rescue Blackburn's breezy critique of Marx, by turning the value of charity against the critique of that critique: '*of course* Blackburn knows that Marx has a background view of the kind you describe,' someone might say, 'so when he says that the eleventh Thesis represents one of the silliest famous remarks of all time, this must be understood as extremely pithy shorthand: he means that this background view is false, and that, after this view has been ruled out, the only other thing left that one could plausibly mean, by saying what Marx says, is something very silly indeed.' To give an analogy, suppose you tell me that you are going to the shops, and I (very wittily) say, 'Oh? Have you built a time machine?' Because I happen to know that all the shops are shut, you see. So although you clearly have a background view less ridiculous than the delusion that you are able to travel back to before closing time, that view is false; and given this fact, the only remaining possibility is that you intend to head for your time machine. To mock you for allegedly suffering from this delusion is my charming way of letting you know that it is a bank holiday. In the same way, perhaps, Blackburn is engaged in a kind of low-energy *reductio* of Marx's theory of history.

Well, maybe. There is a general question to be asked here as to how we are supposed to choose between rival stories as to who is violating 'charity' (and how). The most fundamental answer must be that it depends on *who has the best politics*. But that is not very helpful: apart from being an unfathomably big question, we still face the problem of how to evaluate and compare different political views in order to decide which are 'better' or 'best'. This is not a problem peculiar to anything I've said here, to be sure. Still, the accounts I offer of notions like 'charity' will be of limited value, at best, if they answer all methodological questions—questions like 'Is charity important?', 'Is this a charitable argument?' and so on—with the same reply: 'It all depends on your politics.' How are we ever supposed to get anywhere with trying to understand politics, or with arguing for one view over another, without any of the usual tools (i.e., methodological norms and values like those of constructiveness and charity in criticism)? Ok, I haven't said that we should stop using those notions, only that we should acknowledge their essentially political nature in order to avoid illusions of neutrality. But how are we actually supposed to *use* them, if we need to know what politics to endorse before we can say what a value like 'charity' should mean, or when it is being correctly instantiated and when it is lacking?

As I warned at the outset, these are very deep and general questions about the structure and grounding of our knowledge and practices, questions which I cannot hope to take on here. I suspect that any adequate solution must involve ridding ourselves of the habit of making 'foundationalist' assumptions (i.e., of assuming that our claims must rest on a basis that is somehow established in a way that is fully independent of those claims, and that, otherwise, any claim will be as good as any other). A more immediate way to allay some of these worries, however, is to acknowledge what I think is an important distinction between different types or levels of 'neutrality' that a statement might possess. As already noted, my suggestion has not been that we stop talking about 'philosophical charity' altogether, only that we correctly apprehend its structure. And one of the things we observe when we examine that structure is that criticisms which allege a violation of charity get their leverage through adopting a kind of *local* neutrality: to say that A is being 'uncharitable' to B is not necessarily to assume that B is right or wrong; it is to say that, regardless of how *that* question is best resolved, A is criticizing B through an improper procedure (and that this impropriety damages the criticism's ability to contribute to a resolution of the question it aims to address, i.e., that of the merit of B's view). This independence, though, is possible only *relative to* the (inevitably political) background view with which the critic operates, and in line with which she construes and applies the ideal of 'charity'.

This distinction is important, I'll suggest finally, not only because it helps us to capture the point of the norm of philosophical charity. It might also be of use in evaluating and comparing rival diagnoses of criticisms as 'charitable' and 'uncharitable'. I've shown how easy it is to generate alternative diagnoses of the same conflict, and that each diagnosis may itself be diagnosed, in principle, as 'uncharitable', and that this process might continue indefinitely. But that does not mean that each diagnosis is as good as any other—for instance, I considered an alternative reading of Blackburn which perhaps stretched the bounds of credulity somewhat. What I want to suggest now—although the matter looks rather tricky—is that the relative neutrality of a criticism invoking the value of charity, and the leverage which this relative neutrality affords, might yield one important reason to favour some diagnoses of 'uncharitableness' over others.

Take, once again, the example of the comment likening Rawls to the neo-cons. This comment is then met with the response 'That is uncharitable'. If this response is to have the leverage that is supposed to be a central advantage of claiming that one's target is 'uncharitable'—as opposed to simply saying that the target is *wrong*—this must come from its possession of the kind of relative or local neutrality I identified above. And the second critic may well lay claim to an independence of this kind: she may well say, '*Whatever you think of Rawls*, he's no neo-con!' Her judgement, in other words, is presented as neutral between views of Rawls. Not *all* views of Rawls, of course—the view that he's a neo-con is obviously excluded—but a wide range of views, nonetheless. That might seem like enough to give the criticism purchase, since it can easily be established that Rawls doesn't endorse anything recognizable as neoconservatism. But what was the original conflict about? The answer, it seems: precisely the relationship between Rawlsian theory and neoconservative politics. While it may be easy to establish that Rawls doesn't explicitly support Reagan, or say the same sorts of things as Reagan does,[16] I pointed to a more complex view, according to which Rawlsian theory—despite its explicit pronouncements—reflects and reinforces a neoliberal, neocolonialist status quo, which the so-called 'neo-conservatives' have been instrumental in creating. Suppose or imagine, just for the sake of argument, that this view is right. Now does it seem 'uncharitable' to compare Rawls to Condoleezza Rice? No, it seems blunt, pithy or polemical, perhaps, but that—and this is a point which it will be worth coming back to—is not the same thing.

What this shows, I think, is that the diagnosis of uncharitableness actually presupposes something which is very central to the initial conflict about which that diagnosis is made: on my interpretation, at least, the allegedly uncharitable comment about Rawls and the neo-cons is an expression of exactly the sort of view which this application of the norm of 'charity' rules out. In that case, it isn't really any different from the pantomime shout 'Oh no he's not!' in response to the initial provocation of the claim that Rawls is like the neo-cons. Of course, sometimes 'Oh no he's not!' is a true and appropriate thing to say. But it is an unnecessary and misleading aggrandizement to dress this up as an appeal to the cherished philosophical virtue of 'charity', *especially* if this is done as if this virtue is not already something political—and I would submit that it very often *is* done with this air (although this is not a claim which admits of any easy proof).

So what is the advantage of the local neutrality that I acknowledged this diagnosis to possess? Much as I suggested in the case of 'constructiveness' at the end of chapter 1, it seems to work only if addressed to a third party—or rather, in this case, a fourth party, since the one making the diagnosis of uncharitableness is already cast as the third party on my presentation. The diagnosis is made to an audience, who may be assured that the diagnosis can hold regardless of what—within a circumscribed range—you think of Rawls: certainly, you don't have to be a Rawlsian, in the usual sense of that word, to think that it is uncharitable to liken Rawls to Condoleezza Rice. Well, that is something, but I would have thought it was something that had been obvious all along (who ever said that you had to *agree* with Rawls in order to avoid classing him with the neo-cons?). That is the kind of binary thinking ('Either you are with us, or you are with the terrorists') which we might very well associate with the likes of Bush.

Now consider the verdict I suggested: that the diagnosis of uncharitableness is itself uncharitable. Again, this verdict lays claim to a limited neutrality: I presented it as independent of the question of whether Geuss's comment about Rawls is right or wrong, and even as compatible with the view that the comment is indeed uncharitable. The initial conflict, in this case, is between a comment about Rawls and a comment about that comment: that is, it is a conflict over what it is and is not legitimate to say about Rawls, and over the status of a particular comment made. What does my verdict presuppose on this matter—or to ask the same question another way, what does it rule out? The answer, as far as I can see, is that it doesn't rule out much at all. What it does assume is that seeing the significance of (at least part of)[17] Rawlsian theory as basically reflective and supportive of neoconservative politics is *less obviously indefensible* than the attribution of simple misunderstanding, ignorance or wilful blindness—and thus that being charitable means prefering the first interpretation over the second.

But nor is the independence of my verdict absolute. It depends on my decision as to what interpretation is permissible for the purposes of my criticism, and also on the way in which I furnish the norm of charity with answers as to what counts as 'defensible'—and so on. The 'neutrality' here is thus of a local and limited kind but can be useful nonetheless. It should be seen as one species of the more general (and indispensable) form of argument: 'Whether p or not-p, q'—that is, the argumentative strategy of making it the case and announcing it to be the case that some primary claim is independent of various others (while of course being dependent on *further* others, others which can be expected to have *some* bearing on our assessment of the claims between which the primary claim is independent). At least, it is more than just another 'Oh no he's not!'

IV. CONCLUSION: THE RIGHT TO RUDENESS

While this chapter has certainly not been 'about' Rawls, I hope to have shed some light on an informal norm which is instrumental in policing the division between what I've called the spheres of 'sanctioned' and 'unsanctioned' dissent against Rawlsian political theory. As with the norm of 'constructiveness', a central purpose of this discussion has been to lay bare the inevitably political character of this under-examined but universally prized methodological virtue. And what often happens when something is covertly rather than overtly political, of course, is that the illusion works to the advantage of the status quo.[18] I've tried to show how we might use the same notion of charity as a weapon with which to resist this tendency, and why my own attempt to do so enjoys an advantage of relative neutrality over the more dominant verdict which it aims to invert. At the very least, I hope to have demonstrated that we have a reason to be on guard when we encounter appeals to 'charity'—especially where such appeals function so as to deflect criticism of dominant figures and strands within political philosophy—and to ask, in each case, what the political presuppositions of a given appeal are, and in what relation they stand to the main issue of dispute.

Charity in criticism is perhaps best seen as a piece of philosophical safety equipment: it makes the critic's attack *safe from* uncertainties of interpretation; it aims to leave the object of criticism nowhere to run, by sealing off the possible escape route of turning out to be (or morphing into) a more defensible object than the critic had reckoned on. As such, charity has its place. But I want to end with some considerations as to why the place of judgements of charity—even self-conscious, openly political judgements of charity—should be a limited one.[19] The thing about pieces of safety equipment is that they are not costless—they are not even costless in terms of safety: they make you safer from some kinds of dangers in particular situations, but expose you to other dangers (not to mention inconveniences). It is certainly a good idea to wear a visor when welding, so that you don't get arc eye. But welding visors are a bit heavy and uncomfortable and hot—and also very dark, so if you were to wear one around the house, this might not make you safer, all things considered, because you would probably fall down the stairs.

Safety equipment protects us from specific dangers, but also inevitably limits what we are able to do, how much we are able to do, and in what manner and state we are able to do it. In the case of philosophical argument, the cost is clear: making an argument or criticism independent of various considerations rids it of a certain kind of vulnerability, but it also sets limits on the kinds of claims we are able to make. In particular, we can anticipate that the less an argument depends on, the less ambitious or interesting it will be able to be. Sometimes there can be good reasons for taking what are in some sense 'risks' with our criticisms, making them depend on more. The right way to interpret Enoch Powell's 'Rivers of Blood' speech is as expressing various racist sentiments. Given his relatively careful use of language, you *could* interpret him 'charitably', as making only the descriptive claim that immigrants are likely to face problems in the process of integrating into British society. You could then say, '*Even if* that's all he means, he's still wrong for X reasons.' But even if correct, this criticism would obviously miss the point.

We might try to get around this by saying that the problem in this case is an inadequate construal of 'charity', because the 'constraint of conservation' in play is too loose—it is certainly not very plausible that the banal descriptive claim is all that Powell intended. But *why* would we demand that the constraint of conservation be tightened? Because, it seems to me, what we (rightly) judge to be important in this case is correctly identifying the political and social significance of Powell's speech. The pursuit of this objective can be squared with the demands of 'charity' only if we tighten the conservation constraint implicit in our conception enough that the norm ceases to be a relevantly applicable or useful one. Beyond a certain point, it becomes appropriate to describe the critic's activity straightforwardly as trying to interpret the object of her criticism *correctly*. We might describe such a case as one of 'critical interpretation'—the point being that the artificial separation between criticism and interpretation that the norm of charity involves is not appropriately made here, as the two occur as a unity: Powell's interpreter criticizes by interpreting his speech *as racist*. This sort of thing—which not only may sanction a coldly 'realist' interpretative policy on occasion, but may also accord a place to the almost archetypically 'uncharitable' strategy of *caricature*—seems to me a legitimate and crucial form of political criticism. Allowing the norm of charity to maintain a stranglehold on philosophical disagreement and criticism may therefore distract from and even undermine the attempt to identify and de-mask the actual significance of particular interventions—a project which, I would have thought, ought to be seen as one of the most important tasks of political philosophy.

This brings me to my final point. It is clear that, sometimes, the proper role of political philosophy is to engage not only in criticism, but in *harsh* and *wholesale* criticism, not to pussyfoot around or to tinker with the details of a view which deserves to be thrown out of the window. Such criticism is only in tension with the value of charity to the extent that we choose to construe that value in such a way as to discourage radical criticism—a choice which stands in need of justification, and which is not in any way dictated by the concept of charity per se, as analyzed here. And it should be even clearer that charity, on this analysis, has nothing to do with politeness—a quality with which it is often confused. As I've described it, philosophical charity is a value with a particular *structure*, which promises to lend certain advantages to the practice of criticism—and how that structure is fleshed out is then an inevitably political matter. Politeness, on the other hand, is a *style of presentation*. Without wishing to draw a sharp separation between style and content, it seems safe to point out that the same basic proposition may be communicated in various different ways: some milder and more polite, others blunt or even rude. Whatever the merits of politeness, it seems clear that it is a quality which may be present or absent quite independently of whether the proposition in question is 'charitable' or 'uncharitable' towards its target. And it is equally clear that the prudential advantages of efficiency in criticism, which may issue from the characteristic structure of charity and from the relative neutrality this structure imports, are *not* attendant on politeness (although other prudential advantages might be). Besides, there perhaps ought to be a place in philosophy, especially political philosophy, for bile and bad manners—if only to keep us all awake. If Marx had felt compelled to conform to the norms of our contemporary philosophical prose, he probably wouldn't have called Bentham 'that insipid, pedantic, leather-tongued oracle of the ordinary bourgeois intelligence of the 19th century',[20] but it seems to me that this would have been a loss rather than a gain to philosophy. To allow such losses to pile up, under the banner of 'charity', is to allow a tyranny of the tedious to be established on the basis of a confusion.

NOTES

1. Blackburn (1994; p. 62).
2. This is not because I think the early Rawls is any more defensible than the later. If anything, I find the idea of the Original Position—the device introduced in *A Theory of Justice*,

in which rational choosers determine principles of justice from behind a 'veil of ignorance'—more transparently ludicrous than the argument of *Political Liberalism*, which at least is able to fox us for a time with its sheer convolutedness. But I think that anything that I would want to say about the Rawls of *A Theory of Justice* is likely to have been said many times before, and so I will let it be.

3. Geuss (2005; p. 34).

4. A similar uncomfortable ambiguity is arguably also present in the 'political liberal' notion of 'reasonableness' (see my discussion above, chapter 2). See Benn (2014) for a discussion of the problem of obligations to perform supererogatory actions.

5. This sense of going beyond what is required presumably harks back to the root of the English word 'charity' (via French *charité*) in the Latin *caritas* (meaning 'esteem', 'costliness', 'dearness'), which at a certain point came to be used to refer to the Christian ideal of non-sexual love or benevolence towards others, and it is striking that the appearance of paradox is already present in this ideal: Christianity seems to *require* love and benevolence of us, not merely to recommend them; and access to certain benefits, such as admission to heaven, may even be conditional upon them. It is perhaps worth noting the linguistic specificity of the fusion of this ideal with the notion of *generosity* (there is, for instance, no obvious equivalent for the word 'charity' in Arabic).

6. I have in mind, here, the same sort of sense in which, for Quine, all statements are open to empirical refutation: this applies even to tautological statements such as 'All bachelors are unmarried men', which a pre-Quinean consensus placed on the 'analytic' side of a rigid 'analytic'/'synthetic' distinction. Quine's view is that all statements are part of the same 'web of belief', and are all open *in principle* to being empirically overturned; but this is not to say that they are equally open, nor that statements traditionally viewed as 'analytic' are empirically overturn-able in any very close or obvious sense.

7. See Wilson (1959); Davidson (1984; p. 27, and 2001; p. 211); also Gauker (1986), Saka (2007).

8. Blackburn (1999; p. 12).

9. My view is that there can be no fixed, complete or simple answer to this, and that the best we can say is that there will be a loose cluster of features, varying according to context and according to the interpreter's purposes, on the basis of which we can say that an interpretation is permissible or impermissible—for example, ordinary or 'correct' use of the English language, internal coherence, *fit* with a text, with the author's body of work, biography or school of thought, and so on.

10. For example, Walzer (1993; p. 38): 'We might compare [the critic, on the 'conventional' view] to an imperial judge in a backward colony.'

11. In fact, it's worth noting that at either extreme, charity threatens to slip out of the picture altogether: if I don't care about the belongingness of views to particular persons, nor about the limits of recognized positions like 'liberalism', then it's hard to see how I can be interested in charity at all, since I am not interested in interpretation or in the line between this and invention—only in formulating and criticizing abstract positions, which may or may not be held by actual persons; if, on the other hand, I am very strongly interested in uncovering the real allegiances of certain characters or the significance of actually espoused positions, it is not clear what role 'charity'—which abstracts away from this question—can have. I come back to this point at the end of this chapter.

12. Note that Geuss, who makes the comment about Rawls and the neo-cons, explicitly takes the view that the way to evaluate a political theory is by studying the 'systematic, long-term effects of applying it' (2005; p. 36).

13. See the comments left at leiterreports.typepad.com/blog/2007/10/geusss-skeptici.html.

14. This seems to be what is going on in many of the responses on the Leiter blog, cited above. See, again: leiterreports.typepad.com/blog/2007/10/geusss-skeptici.html.

15. Note that such responses tend to leave out the equally important issue of where a view like Rawls's *comes from*, that is, what sort of political context it reflects. In fact, the issues are closely connected, because if our analysis of a certain political philosophy is that it reflects and affirms U.S.-style capitalist constitutional democracy (for example), that might form a significant part of our *grounds* for saying that its real-political effect is to support that kind of political order—something which may not admit of independent proof. That is, we may, to some extent, infer something's effect from its nature and origin. If this thought has any value, then it may give some substance to the worry that Rawls's 'Difference Principle' plays into the kind of politics represented by the so-called 'trickle-down theory' of wealth—a staple of political theory and practice whose ascent maps quite neatly onto the rise of Rawlsian political theory. Something similar may be said of the eerie correspondence between Rawls's (1999) and Reagan's (1985) use of the term 'outlaw state' (with 'rogue state' as an alternative term heavily used by officials of the Reagan administration).

16. Depending on what you mean by 'same sorts of things', that is. Rawls's use of the term 'outlaw state' might spring to mind again here.

17. The comment under scrutiny here, after all, is one made in the specific context of a discussion of Rawls's *Law of Peoples*.

18. *Think* has sold however many thousands of copies, and to my knowledge, nobody has complained in print about Blackburn's uncharitableness towards Marx. Imagine if he had taken aim at Rawls instead.

19. Christina Cameron suggested to me another reason for thinking that the role of charity must be a limited one. If, as I have suggested, conformity to a norm of charity is often thought of as a binding obligation, then this will severely limit the scope for judging criticisms to be 'uncharitable' (since this is to interpret them as indefensible, an interpretation admissible only in the absence of any alternative). Charity is thus self-undermining in a peculiar way: if we subscribe to a universally binding norm of charity, this will constrain our ability to point out violations of this norm without violating it ourselves in the process.

20. *Capital*, vol. I, chapter 24, section 5.

II

With Radicals Like These . . .

Chapter Four

How to Screw Things with Words

Feminism Unrealized

In general, and increasingly in recent years, scholars have laboured to place the facts of abuse uncovered and analysis of dynamics developed on its own ground into one academic straightjacket after another, attempting to prise apart and recategorize and cabin and control and ratiocinate their meanings and implications, abstracting the work into tiny fractionated bits to be confined and domesticated and thus, seemingly, made newly credible and acceptable, even important. The process could be a subject of study in itself. Why are ideas seen as valuable, exciting, worth thinking about, only if cast backwards into already familiar words and pre-existing frameworks, only when reconfigured within the principles of some big man's prior thought?

—Catharine A. MacKinnon [1]

By now, I've looked at the way books in the dominant mode of political philosophy begin, and at the way in which the notions of 'constructiveness', 'reasonableness' and 'charity' function so as to chasten dissent against that dominant mode. It may be felt, by this point, that I am attacking a 'straw mainstream'. I haven't defined the mode of political philosophy I claim is dominant, except to observe that it is liberal and analytic (themselves admittedly vague terms). This is as it must be: a more detailed picture is being built up, in the course of these chapters, through the critical analysis of examples of philosophy in this mode; but any attempt to give a detailed, abstract definition of it would end up being false and reductive, much as would be the case if our object of study were a person or group, such as punks in 1980s Britain—in fact, our object of study really *is* a group of humans and their activity, after all, although these humans are not much like 1980s punks (more like the WI, perhaps).[2] But that, someone might say, is exactly the problem: my coverage is falsely reductive. Not only is there deep dissent against Rawls, it may be claimed, but there is also a good deal of dissent against the broadly liberal framework that I describe. What about the powerful challenges to liberal theory posed by communitarians, feminists and others? Why think that the sort of critiques I've developed so far apply to them? By reducing the mainstream to one strand within it, this thought goes, I overlook the diversity that exists within the contemporary discipline of political philosophy.

On the face of it, this seems right: there is a lot of diversity in political philosophy—and not just in the form of the consciously 'alternative' or 'radical' work, for example in the socialist and anarchist traditions, which is generally confined to the margins. Within the mainstream itself, there is debate and division: besides the well-established communitarian challenge to traditional liberal theory,[3] feminist philosophy has made a place for itself in almost all philosophy departments and courses; and accompanying the growth in interest in the 'methodology of political philosophy', another prominent challenge has emerged, in the form of the 'realist' critique of what is perceived as a dominant tendency towards abstraction and 'ideal theory'. But then again, there are feuds and factions in the WI too.

The remaining chapters of this book will focus on the two areas just mentioned: in the present chapter, I'll examine a popular debate in feminist philosophy; then, in the last two chapters of the book, I'll turn to consider some of the main topics within explicitly 'methodological' discussions of political philosophy. The feminist issue I want to consider now is that of pornography,[4] an area where the tensions between feminism and liberalism have been most apparent. By way of introduction, I'll now very briefly tell the story of this conflict.

Once upon a time there was an argument over pornography. Liberals held that expression should not be restricted unless it could be shown to be in clear violation of Mill's 'harm principle'. Some feminists took the view that pornography *did* harm, degrade and brutalize women. Liberals replied that the issue was complicated, and that they had not seen enough evidence to justify taking such a drastic step as censorship. Freedom of speech was paramount. The debate seemed to have reached an impasse. And then, suddenly, a new argument was discovered, which had the potential to meet liberals on their own most sacred ground. This argument—which has come to be known as the 'silencing argument'—held that one of the harms of pornography is that it *silences* women. In that case, there might be an argument for censoring pornography *precisely because* freedom of speech is so important. But does it work? The jury—it seems to be agreed on both sides—is still out.[5]

At least, that is how the story is often told. In fact, the silencing argument did not appear so suddenly. The idea that pornography robbed women of a voice had always been a part of the radical feminist critiques of porn which began to appear in the late 1970s and 1980s—most notably by Andrea Dworkin and Catharine A. MacKinnon[6]—at a moment when pornography had unmistakably ceased to be a niche or specialist good and was instead becoming one of world's biggest industries and a staple of mainstream culture.[7] MacKinnon's version of the argument was then translated into terms more readily digested by analytic philosophers by Rae Langton in a 1993 article, 'Speech Acts and Unspeakable Acts',[8] sparking a lively debate and research programme which has been running ever since.[9]

My intention here is not to join in the existing debate on the silencing argument but to observe it from the sidelines, in order to get a better sense of its shape, structure and function. I should emphasize that in what follows, neither MacKinnon nor Dworkin nor their liberal feminist interpreters, defenders and critics are meant to 'stand for' feminism. I choose the example of the debate over pornography and the silencing argument as a case study, which illustrates the general point that what may look at first glance like a powerful challenge to dominant ways of doing political philosophy often turns out, on closer inspection, not to be so. Insofar as the silencing argument contains genuinely challenging and subversive elements, I'll argue, these elements are decisively tamed, obscured or cancelled out in the course of the current debate.

I. THE 'SILENCING ARGUMENT' AGAINST PORNOGRAPHY

In a reaction against the liberal debate over the alleged harms caused by pornography, Catharine MacKinnon argues that pornography does not just cause harm: it *is* harm. Rather than regarding pornography primarily as an act of speech or expression (which may then go on to have various effects), we should recognize pornography for what it is: the very act of subordination. [10] More particularly, pornography subordinates women partly by *silencing* them: 'The free speech of men silences the free speech of women.' [11]

Many philosophers have struggled to make sense of this. As MacKinnon herself observes: 'to say that pornography is an act against women is seen as metaphorical or magical, rhetorical or unreal, a literary hyperbole or propaganda device.' [12] One commentator notes that while philosophers may appreciate the idea that pornography *depicts* or *perpetuates* subordination, they cannot see how it could literally *constitute* subordination. [13] MacKinnon's claim is duly dismissed as a particularly strident expression of a claim accepted even by prominent opponents of restrictions on pornography: depictions of subordination tend to perpetuate subordination. [14] We remain firmly stuck in tedious empirical disputes over cause and effect, and it seems that MacKinnon has added nothing of interest.

Enter Rae Langton. Langton's project is to show, in terms acceptable to analytic philosophers, that MacKinnon *is* making a distinctive claim after all—not just adding a rhetorical flourish—and, moreover, that the claim is both coherent and plausible. Langton does this by developing a connection which MacKinnon also makes—albeit only in passing [15]—between the phenomenon of silencing and the work of J. L. Austin on 'speech acts', as set out in his 1962 book *How to Do Things with Words*. Austin makes a threefold distinction between 'locutionary', 'illocutionary' and 'perlocutionary' speech acts: a locutionary act is the act of speaking certain words (e.g., 'I do'); an illocutionary act is an act performed *in speaking those words* (e.g., the act of marrying); and a perlocutionary act is something which happens *as a consequence* of speaking certain words and thereby performing an illocutionary act such as marrying (e.g., irritating the bride's family). [16]

Langton suggests, with MacKinnon, that we interpret the silencing claim as the claim that pornography performs a certain *illocutionary act*. Pornography does not just depict things, and does not merely *say* something about women: it *does* something to them. Just as the speech act of saying (or writing) the words 'Blacks are not permitted to vote' can discriminate against black people, so pornography can be seen as an act of relegating women to an inferior, subordinated status as sex objects. In particular, it is claimed that pornography constitutes an illocutionary act of *silencing* women, and that it does so through the projection of a certain image of what women are and how they behave. As MacKinnon and others have observed, much pornography propagates a 'rape myth': the idea that all women, at all times, whether they admit it or not, 'really' want sex, and that their refusals of sex are not sincere or authentic; women say 'no' but mean 'yes'. If this myth is accepted and internalized, this can result in a situation where women suffer 'illocutionary disablement': they are free to speak words of refusal—e.g., to perform the locutionary act of saying 'no'—but are debarred from performing the illocutionary act of refusing. The silencing performed by pornography is 'illocutionary' in a double sense: it is an *illocutionary act* of silencing, and it silences women *at the illocutionary level*, by preventing them from doing things with their words.

Langton makes further use of Austin in order to explain exactly how this is possible. Austin is interested not just in how we do things with words, but also in how we can *fail* to do things. Successful performance of illocutionary acts depends on the fulfilment of what Austin terms 'felicity conditions'. For instance, the words 'I do' can only function as an illocutionary act of marrying if they are said in the presence of a priest (or equivalent), and if neither the bride nor the groom is already married. And according to Austin—although this is disputed—certain illocutionary acts have as one of their felicity conditions the 'uptake' of the words and their intended meaning by the hearer. Borrowing an example from Donald Davidson, in which an actor shouts 'Fire!' but is assumed by hearers to be merely performing the script of a play, Langton concludes that the speaker in the case fails to warn at all. [17]

Langton then transfers this to the case of refusal. MacKinnon's claim is that pornography projects an image of women that prevents their refusals from *counting as* refusal. Langton translates this into the claim that pornography's perpetuation of the rape myth removes a 'felicity condition' of successful refusal. A woman can speak the words that would otherwise constitute the act of refusing sex, but if the man has internalized the rape myth, he may not interpret her as refusing at all: she may fail to secure the 'uptake' required in order to perform the act of refusal. If this is what pornography does to women, argues Langton, then it silences them. The value of freedom of speech can therefore be turned against the liberal opponent of censorship: the restriction of the pornographer's freedom of speech is arguably justified by the need to protect the freedom of speech of women. At least, the question is no longer about the correct balance between freedom of speech and some other good such as equality—a balance which usually swings in favour of freedom of speech. Rather, it's a question of balancing freedom of speech *against freedom of speech*. 'Freedom of speech' can no longer be played as a trump card against the feminist critic of pornography. The question becomes: *whose* freedom?

The silencing argument as laid out here is commonly perceived—by its proponents and opponents alike—as having important advantages over the standard, harm-based arguments against pornography: first, it is seen as offering to bypass empirical questions of cause and effect (porn just *is* the harm of subordination and silencing); second, its exclusive focus on the value of freedom of speech is thought to carry with it both a certain elegance and also the possibility of an 'internal critique' of the liberal opponent of censorship which exposes her position as self-contradictory ('if you really think freedom of speech is the most important thing of all, then you have a reason to restrict pornography'). Nevertheless, the argument remains highly controversial. In the next section, I examine some of the reasons why.

II. RED HERRINGS AND DEAD WHITE MEN

After an initial murmur of appreciation, the silencing argument is typically met with a barrage of objections. It's helpful to sort these into two main categories. The first strategy is to accept, if only for the sake of argument, the essentials of Langton's story about what pornography does to women, but to deny that this constitutes 'silencing'—or at least, that it's the sort of silencing that threatens freedom of speech. The second strategy is to deny Langton's story outright: rather than 'That's not silencing!', this response says 'That's just not what happens!' I'll look at each of these strategies in turn.

i. 'That's Not Silencing!'

The first strategy usually takes one of three paths. The best-known traveller of the first is Ronald Dworkin (in an early direct response to MacKinnon).[18] Making use of Isaiah Berlin's famous distinction, Dworkin argues that if pornography only prevents women from being able to *do* certain things with their words (like refuse sex)—as opposed to preventing them from uttering those words at all—then it restricts their 'positive' freedom (a freedom *to* do something); but if the state intervenes to censor pornography, this removes a 'negative' freedom (a freedom *from* artificially imposed constraints).[19] According to Dworkin, negative freedoms 'trump' positive ones—in this context at least—and so the freedom of the pornographer to produce and distribute pornography must be upheld.

There is no shortage of possible replies to this one. We might doubt that the distinction between 'positive' and 'negative' liberty can be as clearly drawn as Dworkin needs it to be.[20] Even accepting the distinction, we might reject the premise that negative liberty should always take priority over positive liberty—the legal enforcement of speed limits is a restriction of negative liberty, and most people think that this is justified by the protection of our positive freedom to travel in safety and comfort. But in any case, Langton's claim is that pornography compromises women's *negative* freedom: it's not just that women are unable to make themselves understood—as might be the situation of someone with a severe speech impediment. The claim is that they are *prevented* (by pornography) from making themselves understood.[21] To borrow an analogy used by Caroline West, it is as if the government were to install a chip in the brains of citizens, enabling it to switch off those citizens' ability to understand English whenever a member of a particular group speaks. This, it seems clear, would be to restrict the freedom of speech of members of that group, by actively preventing their comprehension by others.[22]

Whichever of these replies we favour, one thing is clear, and that is that there are two separate distinctions here which must not be run together. On the one hand, there is a distinction between merely being *unable* and being actively *disabled by some external agency*. This, such as it is, is the distinction relevant to the contrast between 'positive' and 'negative' liberty. Then there is the different distinction between ways of conceptualizing speech: for example, as the uttering of words (Ronald Dworkin's understanding) or as the performance of successful communicative (and other) acts (Langton's understanding). These distinctions really do not have much to do with one another, and so if we think of freedom of speech as a matter of the freedom to perform certain 'illocutionary' rather than 'locutionary' acts, this leaves it an open question—at least on the face of it—whether we are concerned here with a 'negative' or a 'positive' freedom.[23]

Rather than dwell on this objection any further, I'll now briefly mention two further versions of the first strategy. Like Dworkin's, both of these objections make use of a famous distinction by a dead white man. This time, however, the dead white man is not Berlin, but Austin himself—although the distinction, I'll suggest later, is just as dubious. Seeking to turn the Austinian machinery back against Langton, proponents of these two objections target one or other aspect of the double sense—identified in section I—in which pornography's silencing of women is held to be 'illocutionary'. The first

version denies that pornographic expression is an *illocutionary* act of subordination or silencing: at most, it has these as 'perlocutionary effects'.[24] We
must therefore examine the evidence; and the evidence, many believe, is
inconclusive. Proponents of the second version of this strategy hold—with
apparently straight faces—that what women allegedly suffer from as a result
of porn is not 'illocutionary disablement', but merely a case of 'perlocutionary frustration':[25] they perform acts such as refusal, all right; they just can't
rely on their refusals being respected.[26]

If these distinctions don't seem very satisfying, they shouldn't. What
difference does it make whether we say that women are silenced, or 'caused
to be silent'? Does it really matter whether women are 'illocutionarily disabled' or 'perlocutionarily frustrated'? Do these states feel any different from
the inside? I'll return to these matters in the next section, but it's worth
making one point now. This is that the distinction between 'illocutionary'
and 'perlocutionary' has as little to do with the contrast between 'negative'
and 'positive' freedom as the distinction between 'illocutionary' and '*locutionary*' did. Although proponents of the two sub-strategies just mentioned
often run together their appeals to the 'illocutionary'/'perlocutionary' distinction with the Ronaldian[27] argument that freedom of speech isn't a matter
of being able to do whatever you want with your words—thrill an audience,
convince them that the world is flat, and so on—that move is as clearly
invalid as it was in the previous case. To revisit West's analogy: the government installs the brain chips; every time I try[28] to say something, my audience's ability to understand me is switched off. It seems natural—to the
extent that applying the 'negative'/'positive' distinction is *ever* natural—to
say that my negative freedom is infringed. Does this change, depending on
whether we think of the event of my being understood as a 'perlocutionary'
effect, rather than as a condition of my performance of an illocutionary act?
No. Suppose we change the example, to make it more Cassandra-like: I am
understood, but the government flicks a switch which prevents anyone from
believing me. Or the government erases people's memories five minutes
later, so that I never achieve my objectives in speaking to others. Does that
mean that we can no longer say that my *negative* liberty is infringed, in the
standard sense, that is, that I am prevented by another agent from doing
things? I see no reason why it should. Although 'frustrated' would be a pretty
good description of my state in this scenario, we shouldn't forget that this is a
word with not only an adjectival form but also a transitive verbal one: '*x*
frustrates *y*'; 'the government frustrates *me*'.

ii. 'That's Just Not What Happens!'

I turn now to the second main strategy mentioned earlier: the line which denies that Langton's account of what pornography does to women's speech corresponds to reality. This objection is rarely developed very far in the literature, but it seems to be in the background—and used as back*up*—in almost all discussions of the silencing argument.

As we have seen, Langton's influential presentation of the silencing argument gives a central place to a rather abstract, deliberately simplified rape scenario: a woman says 'no' to a man who is making sexual advances on her; she fails to secure the 'uptake' which is required—on Langton's extrapolation from Austin's philosophy of language—in order for her utterance to constitute the illocutionary act of *refusal*—that is, because the man does not understand her 'no' as a refusal (having been exposed to the 'rape myth' via the powerful medium of pornography), she doesn't (and cannot) really refuse; hence, she is silenced (*qua* illocutionarily disabled). She is also raped.

One thing that should be immediately clear about this is that it does not work well as a realistic description of rape, for any number of reasons: in real life, many other words than 'no' may be uttered; sometimes 'no' will *not* be uttered; sometimes there will be physical resistance (although sometimes not); and the rapist's attitude towards and interpretation of the woman and her behaviour is likely to be complex, partially ambiguous or even indeterminate, and imperfectly represented at the level of conscious thought or belief. The scenario envisaged is instead a *model* or *device*, employed to make a point—a point about the way in which social context, itself a partial product of speech acts, can make a difference to the sorts of speech acts that are and are not possible for us. Whether the model is a helpful or appropriate one is arguable.[29] But a model is certainly what it is.

That, however, is not always how it is treated. Leslie Green, for example, notes that this is 'almost certainly the least likely form of date rape'—with the distinct air of someone who thinks he is saying something relevant.[30] Daniel Jacobson, meanwhile, obligingly goes through the motions of supposing 'that exposure to pornography has, as Langton imagines, brought some man sincerely to think that a woman's saying "no" to sex is just another way of consenting', in order to consider how we should judge such a case, but 'confesses' to finding it 'unlikely'.[31] The gentle, headmasterly condescension of Green and Jacobson is almost ulcer-inducing, and Langton herself is sometimes guilty of encouraging their mistake. She concedes that she 'does not know' how common the scenario described actually is,[32] in a way which seems to affirm that this is the empirical question on which our attitude to porn and its regulation should hinge: *her* project as a philosopher is to establish the conditional, 'If scenario *S* obtains, then that counts as silencing', and the contribution of empirical social science must be to establish whether or not the antecedent is satisfied (if it is, then 'it may be wrong for a government to allow pornographers to speak').[33]

The problem is that it does indeed seem extremely implausible to suggest that a common way in which rapes happen is by the rapist simply, sincerely and consciously believing that the woman (equally simply, sincerely and consciously) means 'yes' when she says 'no'. Rape is not some kind of hilarious sitcom-style case of crossed wires. The closest that can be found to a documented real-life instance of rape-by-misunderstanding—a case which is duly seized on by those attracted to the silencing argument—is the 1975 case of *DPP v. Morgan*, where a husband invited his friends home with him to have sex with his 'kinky' wife, who, he promised them, would put on an entirely insincere show of resistance.[34] Even in this case, however, the jury's verdict was that the men had in fact been aware that Mrs. Morgan's refusal was genuine.

The literal-minded interpretation of Langton's scenario is surely uncharitable, rendering her point implausible to the point of offensiveness: rape does not happen through simple misunderstanding. It may be perfectly legitimate, however, to use an artificially simplified example to make a general point about how speech can (and does) affect the way in which people are and can be understood, which means affecting the speech acts they are able to perform, which means—it's not crazy to suggest—affecting their freedom of speech. In this sense, Langton's device should be understood primarily as a *pedagogical* one, and to worry that it might not accurately reflect the reality of rape is like worrying that the plastic models used to teach medical students how the human body works are defective because the human body is not made of plastic. And if we want to know what, more exactly, this pedagogical device can teach us, I think the answer is that it can illuminate something about how the politics of sex and agency under patriarchy work. That something may be too complex to be reduced to a simple formula, or to be neatly proved or disproved; but the lesson is not that men simply misunderstand women when they say 'no', because they've watched porn and so they think that women say 'no' to sex when they mean 'yes'. It is something more like: the particular system of unequal power between men and women, to which porn contributes (or of which it forms a part), is one in which women's agency and worth is denied in such a way that their protest or refusal—not just to sex or to sexual advance, but especially to these—is effectively *defused* or *nullified* in ways that are not always easy to detect, let alone to articulate or to combat, but which have to do with the social status and identity that are accorded to women and, relatedly, with the way in which their attempts at protest and refusal are interpreted. And *that*, I would suggest, *is* what happens—happens *so much* that all but the most disruptive, traumatic or inconvenient instances of it are virtually invisible.

This is one point at which reflection on the parallels with Austin's work *could* act as a useful corrective. When Austin considers a scenario in which the vicar conducting a marriage ceremony turns out to be a monkey in disguise—so that the unfortunate couple's words 'misfire' and they fail to marry—nobody gently explains to Austin that, while this would be deeply unsettling were it to come to pass, this sort of thing rarely, if ever, actually happens. It is taken for what it is: a device which is meant to illustrate something about the practical functioning of speech and language. Not how it *might* function, but how it *does*.

III. MACKINNON UNMODIFIED

> The work we did has provided, among other things, fodder for caricature and pornography and libel, ideas to be appropriated without reference or attributed to others, concepts to be twisted or made superficial as their clear original articulation is elided, intellectual background to be taken for granted, and grist for numerous academic mills, as various schools of thought contend to dismiss it from or subordinate it to pre-existing methodologies. Sometimes the attempts have been tortured, sometimes illuminating, if frankly modestly so. Frequently our work is treated as a trampoline on which others perform showy tricks or described as a distant land seen from an overflying jet or a war zone visited by tourists.[35]

In the last section, I sketched the shape of the debate over the silencing argument and also tried to give a sense that there is something unsatisfactory about it. From the passage quoted above, it seems clear that the dissatisfaction is one which MacKinnon herself shares—although it's striking that this is rarely, if ever, acknowledged even by those who take themselves to be her defenders and allies.

What I want to do in this last main section is to try to get a clearer overview of what it is that has gone wrong, and of what a better shape might be for the debate to take. To a very large extent, I'll argue, this can be done simply by reminding ourselves of what MacKinnon herself has known and said all along.

As we saw in section II.i, a common strategy against the silencing argument focuses on the Austinian distinction between 'illocutionary' and 'perlocutionary'. What one side calls 'illocutionary' the other calls 'perlocutionary'.[36] But all seemed to be satisfied that this is a dispute which is both meaningful and important. Against this, I expressed a suspicion that the distinction is both collapse-prone and beside the point. And MacKinnon seems to agree, noting with characteristic brusqueness: 'Although [Judith] Butler does not seem to understand it, both illocution and perlocution are causal theories, the former more immediately and with fewer intervening contingencies than the latter.'[37] In other words, these are two alternative ways of describing cases where we bring about some change or other in the world, with one term tending to be used to describe cases where the effect is more immediate, direct or inevitable—but neither description would be strictly incorrect.

MacKinnon's impatience with the fetishization of the 'illocution'/'perlocution' distinction reflects her more general impatience with the tendency to fetishize Austin, whom she clearly views with respect rather than deference: 'Austin is less an authority for my particular development of "doing things with words" and more a foundational exploration of the view in language theory that some speech can be action.'[38] Elsewhere, she objects to the tendency for commentators to view her and Andrea Dworkin's work on pornography through the lens of Austin's work on speech acts, 'as if our work, now unnamed, is really, although we did not know it, a subprovince of Austin to be confined and tilled as such, also implying we cannot be doing something he did not do.'[39]

Of course, one reaction to this might be to say that MacKinnon is cutting off her nose to spite her face. If we dispense with the Austinian apparatus exploited by Langton, are we not back in the same situation which Langton aimed to remedy? That is to say, we are back with a set of claims which sound hyperbolic and obscure: that porn 'is' subordination and that it 'silences' women (when we know very well that women can open their mouths and talk just like anybody else). For MacKinnon, however, the appearance of mystery is merely a function of the sort of approach she rejects.[40] That appearance can be dispelled fairly easily without the aid of heavy Austinian machinery. We don't have to set the whole of that machinery in motion in order to hold on to the insight that speech *does things*—and that one of the things it can do is affect (for better or for worse) the sorts of things people are able to do with their speech. That much seems clear. And what MacKinnon thinks porn does is subordinate and silence women. The claim may be found plausible or not, but it's only *baffling* if we make the mistake of assuming that this is being presented as a strictly non-causal claim (recall MacKinnon's explicit acknowledgement that 'both illocution and perlocution are *causal* theories').[41]

Does this mean that MacKinnon's claim is empty rhetoric, after all, adding nothing to existing causal claims about harm? Not really, because what is to be rejected is the *reification* of distinctions, not distinctions per se. The distinction between 'illocutionary' and 'perlocutionary' may only be a distinction between two modes of description—'She broke the glass', versus 'She caused the glass to break'—but in any given context, some modes of description will be more appropriate than others. In the light of MacKinnon's own explanation of the relationship between 'illocutionary' and 'perlocutionary', it seems clear enough that by *identifying* porn with subordination (rather than following the more usual practice of identifying it as a cause), MacKinnon is making a claim about the intimacy, immediacy and systematicity of the relationship she sees between pornography, on the one hand, and violence and discrimination against women, on the other. That is not empty, nor is it mysterious. In fact, MacKinnon emphasizes how mundane her claim is, drawing constant comparisons with cases where we would be inclined to find a 'perlocutionary' description of a speech act highly perverse: it would be odd to insist that the putting up of a 'Whites Only' sign was not an act of discrimination, but merely 'caused' discrimination to occur further down the line. But that, thinks MacKinnon, just shows that we have understood something about racial hate speech that we have not yet understood about pornography.

To claim that pornography subordinates and also silences women is to suggest that views of what women *are*—what they are *for* and what they are *worth*—can become so profoundly distorted that there is a sense in which women become what they are seen to be, and say only what they are heard as saying. This is what gives us the sense in which the woman who says 'no' to sex does not count as *refusing* at all—in this sense she is silenced. But there is *also*, of course, a clear enough sense in which she does refuse—in this sense, she is raped (or 'perlocutionarily frustrated', as some prefer to put it). Evidently enough, some ways of putting things are better than others.

Analytic philosophers, notoriously, often have great difficulty with claims of the form '*p* and not-*p*', even where the contradiction can easily be shown to be of a superficial and benign kind (logically, if not politically). MacKinnon has no such trouble. This comes out especially clearly in her approach to the question of whether porn is or is not speech—another hotly contested issue in the debate over silencing.[42] On the one hand, she refers to the 'lie' that pornography is speech,[43] and remarks: 'To take the claim seriously enough even to rebut it that this practice of sexual violation and inequality, this medium of slave traffic, is an opinion or a discussion is to collaborate, to some degree, in the legal and intellectual fraudulence of its position.'[44] And on the other hand, a little later: 'I am not saying that pornography is conduct and therefore not speech, or that it does things and therefore says nothing and is without meaning, or that all its harms are noncontent harms. In society, nothing is without meaning. Nothing has no content. . . . '[45] Demonstrating beyond doubt that this is not the result of a simple amnesia but is instead a self-conscious and deliberate stance, MacKinnon continues:

> Society is made of words, whose meanings the powerful control, or try to. At a certain point, when those who are hurt by them become real, some words are recognized as the acts that they are. Converging with this point from the action side, nothing that happens in society lacks ideas or says nothing, including rape and torture and sexual murder. . . . It is not new to observe that while the doctrinal distinction between speech and action is on one level obvious, on another level it makes little sense. In social inequality, it makes almost none. Discrimination does not divide into acts on one side and speech on the other. *Speech acts. Acts speak.*[46]

None of this, of course, shows that MacKinnon's specific claims about what porn does are correct. What it shows is that MacKinnon does not need Austin. Her claims can be shown to be coherent and contentful without him. And no amount of staring at the pages of *How to Do Things with Words* will get us anywhere with the question of whether they are *true*—that is a question about concrete political reality.

Perhaps the most striking thing about this whole debate, in fact, is just how *abstract* it is, for the most part. Even Austin, as an 'ordinary language philosopher', was interested in the way in which words are actually used in real life—even though he was never able to fit that reality into the neat categories he had designed for it. One of the perceived advantages of the silencing argument, by contrast, was the promise of a kind of 'flight from reality': a promise to airlift us out of difficult empirical questions of harm. That promise has in one sense been confirmed to be unkeepable: illocution and perlocution alike are contingent, causal phenomena, and we still obviously have to ask, of alleged instances of such phenomena, whether they *happen* or not. In another sense, recent incarnations of the silencing argument have kept the promise all too well, fixating not only on inflated Austinian distinctions but also on hypothetical rather than actual scenarios. We saw this most clearly in the treatment of a highly artificial 'rape myth' situation, discussed in section II.ii. True, I argued that this was to be understood as a pedagogical model—and there need be nothing wrong with that. But a model has to be a model *of* something. In this case, the actual world, of which Langton's scenario might serve as a model, tends to slip out of view, with the result that the model is confused with a naturalistic representation of the real thing—as which it is quite rightly rejected.

MacKinnon, for her part, treats this flight from reality with evident contempt:

> One cannot help wondering why some schools of philosophy have become a place where what something actually does is not considered pertinent to the exploration of what it could or might do. Life is not a game of logic, an argument's plausibility is not unaffected by the social reality to which it refers, and power's denial of abuse is not a function of not having read a philosophical proof that such abuse is possible.[47]

IV. CONCLUSION

I've argued that, while there is something laudable in the attempt to render the silencing argument in terms acceptable to analytic philosophers, much is 'lost in translation' (as MacKinnon puts it).[48] Too often, it appears, what is lost is nothing less than reality itself—while a lot of unnecessary baggage is picked up along the way. I've argued that the debate over the silencing argument is continually derailed by a widespread fetish for J. L. Austin (and that MacKinnon understands this very well). Those involved in that debate do not, of course, regard themselves as effecting derailments, or as performing 'showy tricks'. Many see their project as one in the service of greater clarity and rigour, thereby potentially increasing the accessibility and persuasiveness of the silencing argument to an analytic audience. They should have given MacKinnon a bit more credit—and, perhaps, analytic audiences a bit less.

Of course, it's not only porn that affects the way in which women are seen—and hence what they can say, and how freely—in a way which renders them subordinate and *un*free. Anyway, if we understand 'pornography' not as a class of material, but as an element which runs through the life and speech of patriarchal societies—their literature, their films, their music— then pornography, understood as the eroticization of hierarchy and oppression, really is everywhere.

This is often raised as an objection to the argument that porn silences women: 'if it applies to all that, then surely the argument proves too much!' Since it is assumed that this is a debate about what the liberal state may and may not censor,[49] and since nobody wants too much censorship, anything which threatens to reveal the full scope of the silencing argument's central insight is taken as a refutation. This phrase—'proves too much'—is deeply telling. You can't 'prove' that pornography should (or should not) be censored. That is a practical question, sensitive to a whole range of historical, social, political and strategic variables. It is also not the only question we might be interested in. What is too much to censor does not have to be too much to criticize or to fight. What is 'too much' to prove, or to say, always depends on what is true and what needs to be said. If the silencing argument really applies to 'all that', then we have to change all that. The crucial insight shared by Austin, MacKinnon and her interpreters is that speech does things, and moreover, that the speech of one person may affect what another is able to do with *her* speech—through shaping the way in which she is viewed, the identities that are constructed for her, and as a consequence, the way in which she is understood when she speaks. There can be no sharp disconnect between (i) *what is said about us*, (ii) *who we are*, and (iii) *what we are able to say*. This very simple point is already enough to show what is wrong with the tendency to equate freedom of speech with the absence of censorship. Freedom of speech is a matter of having some control over our own voices, which means having a say in who we are and how we are seen, and not having these things fixed for us by those in positions of superior power. Contrary to appearances, then, the silencing argument is not just—or even primarily—an argument about censorship or other legal measures.[50] It is not just about porn. And it's not even 'just' about women. It's about the relationship between speech, identity and freedom. It would be hard to think of anything more central to politics.

I've chosen to look at the debate over the silencing argument because it is currently such a popular one, and because I think it is particularly instructive as to the character of the mainstream in contemporary political philosophy. Feminism now belongs to that mainstream—a recent achievement, and one not to be relinquished—and this debate has found a place at the heart of mainstream feminist philosophy. At the heart of this debate, in turn, is a potentially extremely subversive idea: the insight that speech is not just about what words we can say, but about what we can do with our words; and that what we can do with our words is profoundly affected by what others do with theirs. Why is that idea so subversive? For a start, because it highlights the inadequacy of an approach which only asks what the liberal state should and should not allow, pushing us to ask instead the much broader question of *what sort of society we want to live in.* Of course, it is still possible to insist on addressing the issues raised by the silencing argument from within the framework of *what the state should do*: for example, we could suggest, as many liberals do, that the state promote better education about pornography in schools. For some critics, MacKinnon, too, is unduly constrained by a legalistic framework narrowly, although it must be borne in mind that these remedies are not proposed in the spirit of 'designing just institutions' for a liberal state (a project from which MacKinnon explicitly distances herself), but rather as measures which MacKinnon, rightly or wrongly, regards as the most effective available tools with which the current situation of women might be improved—a process which could only be completed by a more drastic overhaul of the status quo. However we interpret MacKinnon's approach, though, it seems valid to be sceptical of the extent to which action by the liberal state alone can remedy the sort of problems exposed by the silencing argument's central insight. Wherever there are relations of domination, oppression or significant inequalities of power, it will be the case that those in subordinate positions will be less free to do things with words. Freedom of speech is not a default situation, one which obtains in the absence of interference, but something which cannot be understood separately from the question of the relations of power which exist in society. In order to get a situation where people in general (including women) have control over their own voices, then, we would need to reorganize social life so as to combat oppressive relations of power and domination in all their forms.

Whether this can be achieved within the framework of the liberal capitalist state is at least questionable. While it is obvious enough that this framework is compatible with various policies on the regulation of pornography, it is *not* so obvious that it is compatible with the eradication of the relations of power which can render women—along with other disenfranchised groups, such as immigrant and traveller communities, the working class, the so-called 'precariat', the long-term unemployed and children—effectively voiceless. *This*, it seems to me, is the sort of fundamental question that political philosophers should be addressing: what are these problematic relations of power, how are they constituted, and what are the preconditions of their eradication? But that, as we have seen, is not what happens. Instead, another 'forest of sin'—an Austinian one this time—draws all comers into its depths, never to emerge.

The idea of silencing, it seems to me, has resonance here, too. It is not only pornographers and the mass media that can silence, and not only the sexually subordinated or socioeconomically underprivileged that can *be* silenced. The phenomenon that concerns MacKinnon, Langton and others has its counterpart in the sheltered sphere of academia. I don't just mean that some academics are women—and that the relative privilege they enjoy does not shield them from misogynistic discrimination and abuse. One of the main emerging themes of this book is that there is a kind of silencing which occurs in the sphere of political philosophy, in particular (while surely reflecting similar phenomena outside of that sphere, e.g., in other academic disciplines and in the media): the silencing of dissent against a dominant framework in which political-philosophical discussion is expected to take place. Women are silenced by patriarchal constructions about their desires and identities, constructions which many feminists trace to pornography, in such a way that their ability to refuse unwanted sexual contact is hampered—that is a form of silencing which pervades the sphere of everyday life. But the upshot of my discussions over the course of the last few chapters suggests that a more rarefied version of this phenomenon pervades the sphere of academic political philosophy: dissent against a dominant framework is systematically silenced, this time through the medium of a series of methodological norms and principles that operate so as to keep the peace—the dissenter is condemned as insufficiently 'constructive', castigated as 'unreasonable', interpreted uncharitably or as 'uncharitable' (or both). In these ways and more, deep disagreement is denied out of existence, mis-rendered as something more manageable and dismissed.

In each case, I've suggested that this phenomenon may be usefully understood as a process of depoliticization. Frequently, the form this takes is that an argument, empirical claim or methodological category is presented as if it were politically neutral in a way that it is not, thus allowing its actual political content—invariably one favourable to the political-philosophical status quo—to pass under the radar. But perhaps this is just one important manifestation of a more general tendency within recent political philosophy, one which is often remarked upon but which is far from transparent: the tendency for political philosophy to become divorced from politics. The course taken by the existing debate over the 'silencing argument', I've argued, provides one example of this tendency. But on the face of it, at least, it would be wildly misleading to suggest that the flight from politics has gone without comment and criticism, even in the political-philosophical mainstream. On the contrary, the last few years have seen a marked upsurge of interest in the debate between 'ideal' and 'non-ideal' theory, and in the 'realist' critique of traditional liberal political theory. These related themes will form the focus of my next chapter.

NOTES

This chapter is adapted from a paper of the same title, which appeared in *Hypatia: A journal of feminist philosophy*, vol. 29, no. 4 (2014): 774–89.

1. MacKinnon (2012; p. vii).

2. WI = the Women's Institute, best known for making jam and singing 'Jerusalem'.

3. I won't deal in depth with communitarians—I have never met one, and the signs are that the communitarian 'challenge' may have been a brief ripple largely confined to the 1980s. Besides, to the extent that I understand what 'communitarianism' means, it seems to me that it is often a warmed-over form of liberalism, one which calls for a greater emphasis on bonds of community and culture—a call echoed by many mainstream liberals.

4. It should be emphasized that what I offer here is a discussion of certain philosophical treatments of pornography, rather than a direct comment on the issue of pornography itself. I discuss pornography more fully in a forthcoming introduction to feminism (Finlayson 2015).

5. For example, Langton (2009) only claims that the argument is 'coherent' and 'plausible', not that it is ultimately sound.

6. See, for example, Dworkin (1979), MacKinnon (1987), Dworkin and MacKinnon (1998).

7. Since then, the porn industry has continued to flourish and evolve, and in 2003 is estimated to have grossed $34bn globally (and more than $8bn in the United States alone).

8. Reprinted in Langton (2009).

9. Proponents of versions of the argument include MacKinnon (1987; 1994); Maitra (2009); McGowan (2009); West (2003; 2012).

10. MacKinnon (1987; p. 176).

11. MacKinnon (1987; p. 156).

12. MacKinnon (1994; p. 8).

13. Saul (2006; p. 229).

14. In ruling Dworkin and MacKinnon's 'Indianapolis Ordinance' unconstitutional, Judge Easterbrook agreed: 'We accept the premises of this legislation. Depictions of subordination tend to perpetuate subordination. The subordinate status of women in turn leads to affront and

lower pay at work, insult and injury at home, battery and rape on the streets . . . but . . . this simply demonstrates the power of pornography as speech' (771 F.2nd 329 [7th Cir. 1985]).

15. MacKinnon (1994; pp. 86–87, fn. 31).

16. The distinction between 'illocutionary' and 'perlocutionary' is not unproblematic, as we'll see later, but this must be temporarily set aside in order to describe the contemporary formulation of the silencing argument and the debate that ensues.

17. Langton (1993; pp. 316–17).

18. Dworkin (1993).

19. Berlin (1970).

20. See MacCallum (1967) for an influential criticism of the 'positive'/'negative' framework.

21. Langton (1999; 2009). We might also take issue with Dworkin's choice of analogy. Dworkin (1993; pp. 38, 40) compares the situation of a woman attempting to refuse unwanted sex with that of a 'flat-earther' who cannot find an audience that will take his views seriously. Aside from its offensiveness, the analogy is also badly designed, since—as Langton (1999; p. 129) points out—Dworkin does not suggest that the flat-earther's words fail to secure *uptake* (i.e., minimally correct comprehension) in their hearers.

22. West (2003).

23. Green (1998) also confuses the two distinctions. Green distinguishes between silencing in a 'broad' and 'narrow' sense: we are silenced in a broad sense, he concedes, if rendered unable to perform certain illocutions, whereas we are silenced in the narrow sense only if we are gagged or otherwise prevented from performing *locutions*—and we are not justified in silencing in the narrow sense in order to prevent silencing in the broad sense. He connects this with an interpretation of the silencing argument as holding that one is silenced 'whenever one's words fail to be taken with the force one intends' (p. 302), which is an independent claim, and in any case obviously incorrect as an interpretation of Langton. Similarly, he reads Hornsby as equating silencing with 'failure to provide conditions of reciprocity'. What she actually says is 'Silencing is the process of *depriving* of illocutionary potential' (2011; emphasis added).

24. Saul (2006) is one example of someone who denies that pornography is an illocutionary act of subordination or silencing, although in many respects she is sympathetic to Langton et al.

25. Jacobson (1995; p. 72). Jacobson argues that women *can* refuse, because even if their utterance of words like 'no' fails to count as refusal, they can still do other things, like wriggle (note: not a joke).

26. Jacobson further claims that, by claiming that the raped woman doesn't really refuse, Langton debars herself from describing the rape myth scenario as one of rape. Langton's withering reply is that Jacobson has failed to grasp the distinction between *not refusing* and *consenting* (see her response to Jacobson in Langton [2009]). Though true, this is not the most effective line for Langton to take: Jacobson might reword his objection, accusing Langton of being committed to a view whereby women *positively consent* when they say 'no' (still rendering her unable to recognize rape as rape): if speech conditions can prevent a 'no' being a refusal, they may also make it count as a positive 'yes' (and after all, the 'rape myth' holds that women *mean 'yes'* when they say 'no', not just that they do not mean to refuse). Langton also seems to concede too much by granting that the woman does not refuse. An adequate reply, I think, would have to allow *both* a (distorted) sense in which the woman doesn't refuse— perhaps even consents—*and* a clear sense in which she does refuse, while also acknowledging that the understanding of 'rape' and 'consent' that is appropriate for the purposes of feminist political philosophers may not be the same as the understanding that is appropriate for *legal* purposes. I come back to this in section III.

27. To distinguish this Dworkin from Andrea, of course.

28. In the case I'm imagining, I do actually speak, in the sense of uttering words. But note how natural it is to describe this situation with the phrase I just found myself writing: 'whenever I *try* to say anything'. This seems to me to lend intuitive support to Langton's policy of regarding uptake—or at least the possibility of uptake—as a felicity condition of certain kinds of speech.

29. My view is that the model *could* be helpful to clarify a philosophical point in passing, but that when fixated upon, it may do more harm than good: (i) by distracting us from questions of the reality of rape and of the actual effects of porn (as opposed to questions of what porn *might* do); and (ii) by confining our attention to the *cognitive* aspects of the attitudes which porn may engender in people, and men in particular (how they *understand* or *interpret* women's utterances), rather than on the affective or erotic aspects. Langton has more recently aimed to remedy this (see 'Beyond Belief' in Langton [2009]), although simply revisiting MacKinnon's *Only Words* would also suffice: MacKinnon continually emphasizes that this is an issue of how women are seen and not seen, desired and detested, and focuses on the (presumably non-cognitive) 'eroticization' of hierarchy and violence which she traces to pornography.

30. Green (1998; p. 298). Green concedes that this is an 'important case' nonetheless, but only for the relatively peripheral legal question of what we should say in cases of non-consensual or forced sex where *mens rea* is absent (as occasionally happens with sleepwalkers, for example). I think it's fair to say that this is not the sort of 'importance' Langton is aiming for.

31. Jacobson (1995; p. 77).

32. Langton (2009; p. 58).

33. Ibid., p. 63.

34. This case established the precedent of *mens rea* for rape, such that a man is innocent of rape so long as he *sincerely believes* the woman to have consented. In *DPP v. Morgan*, the defendants were found guilty only because the judge deemed them, despite their claims to the contrary, *not* to have had this belief. This criterion remained in place until the 2003 Sexual Offences Act, which extends the definition of 'rape' to cover those cases where the perpetrator does not '*reasonably* believe' that the other person consents (my emphasis).

35. MacKinnon (2012; p. vii).

36. This has also been couched—misleadingly, as we'll see—as a dispute between 'causal' and 'constitutive' theories—with MacKinnon as arch-'constitutivist' (Maitra and McGowan [2012]).

37. MacKinnon (2012; p. xi).

38. MacKinnon (1994; pp. 86–87, fn. 31).

39. MacKinnon (2012; p. viii, fn. 4).

40. Ibid., p. vii.

41. Ibid., p. xi. Emphasis added.

42. See, for example, Hornsby (2011), Antony (2011).

43. MacKinnon (1994; p. xi).

44. Ibid., p. x.

45. Ibid., p. 20.

46. Ibid., pp. 20–21. Emphasis added.

47. Ibid., p. iv.

48. MacKinnon (2012).

49. Cf. Ibid., p. xvii: 'Why all these topics must be considered within the confines of liberalism is not broached even sideways, leaving liberalism assumed rather than interrogated.'

50. It's important to realize that MacKinnon deliberately focuses on *civil* legal remedies rather than on 'censorship' in the usual sense. The stated aim of her and Andrea Dworkin's Minneapolis Ordinance was to empower victims of pornography to take legal action against the producers of material that had contributed to crimes committed against them.

Chapter Five

Nowhere to Run

The Real World in Political Theory

> The scholars are, among all of humanity, the furthest from politics and its ways. . . . For they are accustomed, in the whole of their enquiry, to mental matters and ideal theorising; they do not know otherwise.
>
> —Ibn Khaldun[1]

One of the more common complaints raised against political philosophy in its dominant mode is that it has become too remote from the 'real world'. A sentiment of this kind unites the otherwise disparate collection of thinkers that have come to be known as political 'realists'. In the last few years particularly, debate over the relative merits and demerits of 'realism'—along with the related question of 'ideal' versus 'non-ideal' theory—has become a prominent theme within mainstream political philosophy. If we are looking for a significant internal challenge to the liberal framework which I've characterized as being centred around the project of 'designing just institutions', this 'realist' movement seems like an obvious contender. Rather than tinkering with the details of particular theories within that basic framework, the 'realist' challenge appears as a challenge to that framework itself. It takes issue with the dominant *methodology* of political philosophy, rather than taking it for granted. This, we might think, is grounds for optimism: even if the consensus is against the 'realists', the prominence of the debate indicates an encouraging willingness on the part of political philosophers to engage in critical reflection on their own fundamental premises. Not so fast: I'll argue, as in the previous chapter, that the impression of an area of thriving dissent

111

against a dominant framework is misleading. In line with the approach taken so far throughout this book, my intention is to take a step back from the existing debate, in order to get a clearer view of its shape, its functions and presuppositions.

None of the terms in this debate—'realism', 'ideal' and 'non-ideal'— admit of any simple or uncontroversial definition. 'Realism' is nothing if not a mixed bag—this is one of the reasons why some thinkers have raised doubts as to the usefulness of the term.[2] Nevertheless, 'realists' share a common emphasis on the idea that political theory should engage more with history and with the contemporary realities of politics. Moreover, as we'll see, there is a fair amount of agreement on the features or aspects of the real world that are of particular importance. 'Non-ideal theory', too, refers to an approach which aims to be more attentive to the real world, shunning the abstraction inherent in much contemporary political philosophy—'relevance' is its watchword. Sometimes, though not always, the term 'non-ideal theory' seems to be used almost interchangeably with 'realism'—and it is certainly true that both are frequently contrasted with 'ideal theory'. One difference is that 'non-ideal theory' is explicitly conceived as a branch of 'normative' political philosophy: it is in the business of telling us what *should* be the case (in this 'non-ideal' world). This need not be so for 'realism'—although, contrary to a common misapprehension, many 'realists' do see their project of engagement with the real world as at least partially one of making value judgements or prescriptions about it. A more significant difference is that the category of 'non-ideal theory' leaves open the question of whether this is something opposed to the methodology of 'ideal theory', or intended to complement it. For some 'non-ideal theorists', the only appropriate methodology for political philosophers is to begin from the conditions that obtain in the real world, and theorize in the light of these.[3] Thus understood, 'non-ideal theory' seems roughly equivalent to 'realism'. But another way to understand 'non-ideal theory' is as the second stage of a two-stage process: stage one, 'ideal theory', discovers the pure principles of justice that would apply under idealized conditions; stage two, 'non-ideal theory', in consultation with the empirical social sciences, adapts these principles for application to the actual world. When understood in this second way, it may be difficult to see what all the fuss is supposed to be about: we don't have to choose between 'ideal' and 'non-ideal', and there is therefore no reason to shun the former.[4] At most—on this reading—the critical force of the advocacy of 'non-ideal' theory is to suggest that political philosophers should do more of this type of theory and less of the other, and not leave it to the social scientists. All can agree on the importance of theorizing in the light of the real world. The only questions are (a) *when?* and (b) *how?*

It is not new to observe that the positions and approaches that are often grouped together under the headings of '(political) realism' and 'non-ideal theory' include elements that are politically more conservative as well as elements which are relatively progressive or radical. But there is, I believe, a lack of clarity as to the relationship between these labels, on the one hand, and the various stances we may adopt relative to the political status quo, on the other. While 'realism' and 'non-ideal theory' tend to be understood first and foremost as *methodological* positions (telling political philosophers to engage more with the real world, rather than telling them anything in particular about what that 'real world' is or should be like), it is striking that many commentators perceive a special tension or difficulty in being *both* 'realistic' (or 'relevant') *and* politically radical, that is, strongly critical of the existing state of things. Or to put it another way, they see a prima facie affinity between 'realism' and a kind of conservatism.[5] The result is that methodological revolt against the dominant framework of liberal theory seems to be incompatible with political radicalism: either you can be an 'ideal theorist', which is supposed to mean being able to entertain wild utopian dreams and to be strongly critical of the status quo (although there are good reasons to be sceptical of this promise),[6] or you can embrace 'realism' (or 'non-ideal theory'), thus claiming the identity of a methodological nonconformist, but only at the cost of a greater political conservatism. For any serious dissenter against the dominant mode of political philosophy, it seems that there is nowhere to run.

This predicament, I'll argue, rests on a deceptive framing of the debate—a setup which turns out already to embody certain political assumptions which militate against deep dissent in advance. In this chapter, I investigate the way in which an ambiguous commitment to 'fact sensitivity' or 'engagement' with the real world, along with a particular kind of pessimism about political possibilities, leads to a position of greater acceptance of the status quo—and I try to show how the ubiquitous trinity of 'realism', pessimism and conservatism might be pulled apart.

I. SOUR GRAPES AND IMPOTENCE

As I observed, we are actually dealing here with *two* debates which, although very closely connected, have recognizably different flavours. 'Ideal theory' may be contrasted either with 'non-ideal theory' or with 'realism', and the latter two are presented in slightly different ways. I want to comment first on the way in which the contrast and debate between 'ideal' and 'non-ideal theory' is set up, before moving in the next section to consider the distinctive tics associated with the label of 'realism'. The task is made more difficult by the fact that 'ideal' and 'non-ideal theory' are terms which themselves get used with a number of divergent senses within the literature on the 'methodology of political philosophy'. Rawls, for example, uses the term 'ideal theory' to refer to theory which proceeds on the assumption of 'full compliance'—that is, we don't have to worry about the enforcement of whatever principles of justice we end up deriving.[7] But this is one among many possible 'idealizing' assumptions that a theorist might make: for example, she might decide to theorize on the assumption of 'perfect information', or on the assumption that everyone is an able-bodied adult. And a theorist might make such a counterfactual assumption in the service of various different ends. The use of a hypothetical device—such as Rawls's 'veil of ignorance' or Dworkin's 'desert island'[8]—might aim to clarify something about the actual world, and what we should do in it, without necessarily implying that we could or should bring the actual world to resemble what this device depicts: for example, a situation in which people are ignorant of their own preferences or capacities. Equally, the term 'ideal theory' may be used to refer to what is sometimes thought to be the main fruit that this kind of technique can yield: a vision of a society as it should be—the sort of project that Marx condemned so vehemently in his attacks on the 'utopian socialists'.[9]

These differences aside, there seems to be general agreement that 'ideal theory' involves a practice of abstraction from the facts, and that this process is meant to yield a purer or more uncompromised insight into a just social order.[10] This way of looking at it is evident in an explanatory diagram offered by Colin Farrelly, which represents the relationship between 'ideal' and 'non-ideal' theory in terms of a mysterious property called 'fact sensitivity':

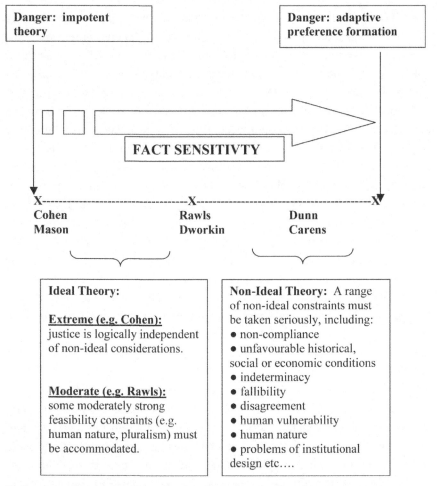

Figure 5.1.   Figure 1 in 'Justice in Ideal Theory: A Refutation' (Farrelly 2007). Copyright © 2007, John Wiley and Sons.

Here, Farrelly has homed in on something like the familiar point that the nature of the world does not always allow the full realization of what we would like—so that when we make demands or suggestions, we have to pay attention not only to what it is that we want, but also to the factors constraining our ability to get it. This, of course, is the source of many a classic political dilemma,[11] as well as a feature of day-to-day life—not to mention game shows ('You can walk away now with £20,000. If you get the next question right, you can walk away with £1,000,000. If you get it wrong, YOU LEAVE WITH NOTHING!'). This sort of decision—'ambition'/'purity'/'principle'/'risk' versus 'compromise'/'practicality'/'safety'—is one which often confronts us when we are trying to decide how to position our political weight: do I join that party, in the hope of having more (or at least *some*) positive impact, even though I cannot identify with all (or even most) of that party's policies? At what point do I judge that enough is enough? When they abolish Clause IV?[12] Or when they invade Iraq? In fact, this sort of choice besets any attempt to act, since to act is always to act both *on* and *with* the world: I can work on a piece of wood so as to shape it according to my will (e.g., to make it part of a table), but at the same time I am constrained by the nature of the tools and materials; and if I impose my vision on the material in a way that is oblivious to its particular nature (e.g., if I insist on trying to bend the piece of wood into a corkscrew shape, because I think corkscrew-shaped table legs would look cool), then I will break things, and possibly injure myself, thus undermining my own project. The task in politics, as in carpentry, is to find a way to act simultaneously on *and* with the world.

All this is, of course, easy to say, but notoriously difficult to know how to implement. There are two obvious but important points here which deserve emphasis. One: there will be no *formula* for such decisions about what counts as 'practical' in the right way (what I called 'working with' the world)—that is partly why it is so difficult. We cannot sensibly argue in any general way about how 'fact sensitive' it is appropriate to be (what would count as an answer . . . *9.5*?), or about what 'fact sensitivity' demands. All we can really do is argue about concrete, local cases: for example, in the recent student protest movement, one issue has been how much to concentrate on opposing higher education fees outright, and how much to focus on mitigating the worst effects of the reforms we have so far been unable to stop. When we argue about that, we must refer to specific factors relevant to the case, and different facts would be relevant to a discussion of 'principle versus practice' in a different context. It might sometimes make sense to say of a person that she is *in general* 'more pragmatic' or 'more principled' than some other, but we could only make such a judgement on the back of knowledge about the line this person has taken in various specific cases.

The second point should be just as obvious: what counts as 'practical', 'pragmatic', 'fact sensitive' (or whatever) must depend on a whole bundle of normative and descriptive judgements we make, about what is the case and about what is to be desired. To return to a point emphasized in previous chapters, whether it is 'realistic' or 'practical' to demand the end of capitalism depends on questions as to how the world works, the answers to which are matters of contention between capitalist and anti-capitalist: according to the anti-capitalist's view of history and economics, the capitalist is the one who is being unrealistic, in thinking that the existing system can be endlessly patched up, or that 'social justice' can be realized under its reign. What counts as 'fact sensitive' depends on what you think the facts *are*. The methodological argument cannot be prior to the political one.

Now let us return to Farrelly and his diagram. He seems to have in mind something like the kind of decision just discussed—a decision to do with how much we feel we must compromise our visions, demands or ideals in the name of 'practicality'—and he is interested in this sort of decision as it confronts political philosophers in particular: on the one hand, we may want to sketch what ought to be, regardless of what is; on the other hand, we might think it appropriate to index our principles to various actually existing constraints. For example, someone might think that 'ideal' justice demands a thorough-going egalitarianism (whatever that means), but that given 'human nature' (whatever *that* means), a more watered-down egalitarianism is in order; then there is a methodological question as to whether it is more appropriate for such a political philosopher to outline the first or the second scheme. Farrelly constructs a rough spectrum according to what (and how much) the political philosopher slots into the space after the 'given . . . ': the 'realist', or 'non-ideal theorist', is someone who slots more in there, not only 'human nature' but things like the contingent course of history thus far, 'pluralism',[13] 'conflict', and so on.[14] As for my two points just mentioned, something like Farrelly's diagram could in principle be proffered in a spirit that respects both of them: he might well acknowledge that the general judgements of 'fact sensitivity' which determine the positioning of different views on his spectrum are rough-and-ready extrapolations from a whole array of more local, particular and concrete decisions that theorists make about what sorts of things to treat as a constraint on their theorizing; and he *could* also present his particular construction of a spectrum and arrangement of figures along it as reflective of a politically non-neutral standpoint—but he doesn't.[15] The result is that a particular setup of the 'ideal'/'non-ideal' opposition is presented as if it were simply a common-sense account of the structure of that opposition, when in fact it rests on a series of presuppositions which shrink the debate before it has even started. It is assumed in advance, for example, that the main task of political philosophy is to describe something better, within tighter or looser empirical constraints, rather than doing anything else (such as offering primarily negative critiques of the existing social order). No space is left for the further question that might be asked as to the *sort of thing* it would be most instructive to describe: a method, a strategy, a set of moral principles guiding political struggles or a stable end point in the form of a set of social institutions. The most 'natural' assumption, in the current political-philosophical climate is, of course, the latter, and by ignoring the question, Farrelly's setup allows that assumption to prevail unchallenged. What Farrelly has done, in effect, is to blot out a whole series of crucial methodological decisions, reducing the choice between 'ideal' and 'non-ideal' to a choice as to how many, out of a series of bullet-pointed factors, to admit as constraints on the project of describing the best social order deemed to be 'feasible'.

This brings us to the main problem with Farrelly's depiction. The problem is that Farrelly seems to conflate *being sensitive to the facts* with *accepting those facts as beyond alteration*: he assumes that working 'with' the world means working with*in* the existing political framework. If that is how being 'fact sensitive' is understood, then to the extent that we are 'sensitive' to the facts, we are also conservative (hence Farrelly's concern that 'extreme non-ideal theory' involves adapting one's aspirations to be too much in line with the status quo), and we can be critical only to the extent that we are 'insensitive' to the facts. On this picture, the 'ideal' versus 'non-ideal' question is a Goldilocks issue: the task is to find the point on the 'fact-sensitivity' spectrum that is 'just right'—not too 'ideal' (*danger: impotence!*), but not too 'fact sensitive' either, because that means reconciling ourselves too much to the state of things (*danger: may contain sour grapes!*).[16] Thus we are sucked into an agonized shuffling between two poles, both of which lie comfortably within the political and philosophical mainstream.

But at what point, we might ask, did this premise sneak in—that being 'sensitive' to the facts means holding them fixed? Must we really regard the goal of paying attention to history and real politics as being in necessary tension with the attempt to be critical of the social world, or to be radical or ambitious in the changes we demand? Farrelly's way of setting up the issue of 'ideal' and 'non-ideal' theory is superficially quite intuitive—partly because it is a familiar way of setting it up, and partly because we obviously *do* sometimes have to decide how much to compromise our ideals in the face of reality. But at a second glance, it seems that something, somewhere along the line, has gone badly wrong. Where would we place someone like Charles Mills on Farrelly's spectrum—a philosopher who objects to 'idealizing assumptions' in political theory on the grounds that they abstract away from the actuality of various systems of oppression and thus prevent theorists from directing the appropriate analytical and critical energy against those systems? Is Mills thereby closer to a whitewashing of the status quo than Rawls is? Where are we supposed to put a critical theorist? Where would we put Marx? If we understand 'being sensitive to facts' as meaning 'starting out from an understanding and an account of those facts', or 'theorizing in a way that is appropriate in the light of those facts', then there is no obvious reason at all why this should be incompatible with radical opposition to the social structures that are part of the object of study—unless, of course, we assume in advance the hyper-conservative position that the appropriate reaction to 'the facts' is always to treat them as unalterable. It is quite coherent to take the contrary view that, *given the nature of the world*, it is necessary to tear down existing political structures and start anew.

At the root of the problem, perhaps, is a way of thinking which owes too much to game theory. In a 'prisoner's dilemma', we have complete and fixed information about the prisoners' preferences: these form a hierarchy, and the task is to maximize expected gain so as to obtain an outcome as close to the top of that hierarchy as possible; but there is no room within the setup of the dilemma for something *even better* to happen—it is not a permitted possibility, for example, that if the prisoner sings a beautiful aria while trying to make his mind up, the guards will come rushing in and award him a Nobel Prize and a private yacht. Nor is it allowed that the outcome of the prisoner's decision might have a transformative effect on his preference hierarchy: for example, that he 'loses' the game and stays in prison for longer, where he falls in love with a fellow jailbird (and comes to value this more highly than a reduction of his sentence); or that he 'wins' the game, becoming a free man and a millionaire, but this brings him so much trouble that he comes to wish that he had ended up with his 'second best' option (of freedom-with-more-modest-means). In the imaginary cases of game theory, the world can at best furnish the agent's top choice, among options already thought of and given a fixed value and ranking: in that sense, there is nothing to gain and everything to lose. The setup is similar in the case of 'fact sensitivity': we work out what would be good, or 'just'; then, if we are at all 'fact sensitive', we will have to look at the world at some point to see what possibilities it affords and hope that it doesn't knock too much of the shine off our initial ideal; the more 'fact sensitive' we are, the more we must be prepared to lose, and the best that can possibly happen is that we don't have to change anything. If we think of it

this way, then it makes sense to see the 'real world' just as a source of more
or less severe constraints on a preexisting vision.

This way of thinking about the relationship between theory and 'the
facts', however, is highly misleading. We do *not* start off with a complete set
of political ideals and values, then turn to the world to see how much of what
we want can be got, any more than we would start off with a fixed vision of
an ideal table, only later looking around to see what materials are available.
On the contrary, we look at the world and detect needs and deficits, potential-
ities and promise, and form our projects and ideals in response; then we look
again, try to implement our ideas, and in the process end up modifying (not
just compromising) those ideas, and ourselves, as well as the world around
us. A defender of Farrelly's spectrum model might retort that this is obvious
and irrelevant. The spectrum of 'fact sensitivity' simply focuses in on a
moment in what is admittedly a dynamic, two-way process: *once you have an
ideal* (whatever its origin and whatever the history of its formation), there
arises a question as to how close the world will allow you to get to that ideal;
and to the extent that (a) you think that this should inform the ideals you hold
and (b) the world falls short of allowing the full realization of your ideal, the
world acts as a constraint. But this is just to point out something which I have
already acknowledged, when I noted that Farrelly's representation is picking
up on something which has great importance in politics, and in life in general—namely, the question of when and how much to compromise in the face
of 'non-ideal' circumstances. The first problem I mentioned with that representation, however, was that it reduces the whole debate over 'ideal' and
'non-ideal' theory—ostensibly a debate over how much notice political philosophers should take of the 'real world', over how 'engaged' and 'relevant'
they should try to be—to this much narrower question of compromise. The
second problem was that 'fact sensitivity' was presented as being proportion-
ate to acceptance of the status quo. What has now emerged is just that the
second problem is a manifestation of the first.

Those discussing 'ideal' and 'non-ideal theory' do not *simply* conflate
'fact sensitivity' with 'fact acceptance'—that would be stupid. But the distinction is set up in a particular and limited way: we start out with a fixed set
of ideals, or hierarchy of principles, and it is an open question whether or not
it will be 'possible' (in the chosen sense of that word) to realize them in the
real world. So to the extent that we deem the possibilities offered by the real
world relevant to the matter of what a political philosopher should be doing—that is, to the extent that we are 'fact sensitive'—our initial ideals and

principles are vulnerable to being eroded by contact with reality. How much they are actually eroded will be a function of the level of 'fact sensitivity' (and the vulnerability that entails) plus the facts about how hospitable to our vision the 'real world' turns out to be—and as we will see in the next section, 'realism' is associated not only with thinking that the actual world is *relevant*, but also that it is *inhospitable* to more ambitious political ideals.

II. 'REALISM' ≠ CONSERVATISM ≠ PESSIMISM[17]

In the last section, I concentrated on the terminology of 'ideal' and 'non-ideal', and I argued that the setup of the debate between these alternative approaches to political theory was not politically neutral or unavoidable but actually rested on some fairly heavy and contestable assumptions. This in itself does not show that this is the *wrong* way to set up the debate, only that the setup stands in need of justification—which means saying something in defence of the assumptions underlying it. And at this point, some may take the view that the task is actually quite straightforward: after all, the real world seems a pretty difficult and recalcitrant place, not always particularly hospitable to our desires or to our efforts at changing it (this is a premise which may easily be shared by some liberals and by their opponents alike); therefore, it makes good sense to regard the world primarily as a source of *constraints* on the realization of political ideals. If some want to insist otherwise, this may be put down to a touching naivety. To complain that the setup is 'conservative' is no objection: it is only as conservative as is warranted by a clear-eyed appreciation of the facts.

A thought of this kind is detectable in the work of certain 'realist' political philosophers (and is perhaps especially prevalent at the level of secondary commentary). Those surveying 'realist' thinkers in political philosophy tend to operate with the assumption that the three positions of 'realism', 'pessimism' and 'conservatism' go hand in hand. They may not often actually use the terms 'conservative' or 'conservatism' (these carrying pejorative overtones in the mainly liberal circles in which most 'realists' move),[18] but 'realism' *is* often associated with being more 'modest' in one's demands and expectations. Hence, we consistently find that the 'realist' emphasis on the permanence of conflict and disagreement (and so on) goes together with a tendency to emphasize 'order' or 'stability'—or the idea of a 'modus vivendi'—as the highest 'realistic' political aspiration, as contrasted with the apparently loftier ideals of 'justice' or 'equality'.[19]

It pays to tread very carefully here, for a number of reasons. First—and most obviously—there is a great deal of variation among 'realists', so that it will not be adequate to brand 'realism' as a simply and purely conservative current.[20] Secondly, the best interpretation of concepts like 'modus vivendi', in particular, is a matter of some controversy (and has generated a sizeable literature which I cannot enter into here). While an emphasis on 'stability' or 'order' or 'modus vivendi' is frequently enough understood as a conservative emphasis—at least relative to the stance of more 'idealist' liberals—this reading is also frequently enough denied by proponents of a 'realist' approach. In principle, anyway, it seems perfectly possible to advocate 'stability' (or some similar ideal) as a central aim of politics, while also holding that the best or only way to achieve that goal is through far-reaching social change and even social revolution. This position, while quite coherent, certainly does not fit my impression of many 'realist' thinkers, the majority of whom can be assimilated to the liberal tradition,[21] and whose most obvious revision of the politics of mainstream 'idealist' liberalism is to remove what are regarded as areas of political over-ambitiousness (such as, for example, the pursuit of 'equality'). But it is not my concern here to demonstrate that the de facto force of 'realism' is a more conservative one than that of the liberal mainstream to which it is a reaction. Which stance is the more conservative depends on how you look at it (and, of course, on what you mean by the term 'conservative'). If my impression is correct, the sort of position that 'realists' tend to hold is less demanding and (at least superficially) less critical of the status quo than that held by more mainstream liberals. But it would be too quick to infer from this that the proponents of liberal 'idealism' or of 'ideal theory' are therefore more 'radical', in any interesting sense of that term, than their 'realist' counterparts: if the 'realists' have a point, when they criticize certain 'ideal theorists' for ignoring various facts about the world which make their particular aspirations to 'equality' and 'fairness' (and so on) unrealizable, then what should we regard as more radical? Advocating the basic framework of liberal capitalism *plus some fantasy of equality of resources or a meaningfully autonomous life for all* (which, we may think, cannot be had—or at least cannot be had within that framework)? Or just the basic framework, without such distracting pretensions?

The answer, I think, could go either way. In some ways or in some contexts, it might be better, from the point of view of bringing about needed social change, for affirmations of the status quo to wear their conservatism on their sleeves, so to speak. A position which combines fundamental affirmation of the status quo with a smattering of empty utopian promises could be much more dangerous. On the other hand, there may be a loss incurred in the move towards a more consistent conservatism. Take, for instance, the idea that there can be meaningful equality (near material equality and substantial equality of opportunity) under capitalism—and let us suppose, with anti-capitalists, that this is unrealistic. This allows us to say, though admittedly in a rather tortured sense, that certain liberals are proposing something 'too radical' (i.e., what they are proposing would require the world to be a radically different sort of place, with different economic, human and social laws or truths holding, than is in fact the case)—we will, of course, simultaneously hold on to a more obvious sense in which the proposal is not radical *enough* (i.e., it holds fixed an economic system which renders the proposal unworkable). Suppose then that a 'realist' reform is carried out on this liberal theory, eliminating the element which calls for an ambitious realization of equality (but not changing much else). It still may make sense to say that there is a loss in terms of the radical and critical force of the theory, even if we also hold (a) that this radical force was already severely limited, and (b) that there is a sense in which the elements eliminated were indeed 'too radical' (qua unrealistic, given the framework within which they were presented), and deserved to be eliminated. There is a loss, all the same, because the notion of a more far-reaching equality might serve to draw our attention, eventually, to the contradiction between this ideal and the framework of liberal capitalism, opening the way for us to question that framework and investigate alternatives. If we believe, then, that liberal theory embodies too fundamentally affirmative a stance towards the status quo, a few elements of (even a misguided) radicalism might—at least in some contexts—serve as a source of welcome dissonance, a reminder of possibilities which the liberal framework may tend to rule out in advance.

The third and final cautionary point to make here is, I hope, as obvious as the first one: it would be a fallacy to draw a simple equation between the 'radical' and the good, the 'conservative' and the bad. Even if there were a straightforward answer to the question of which—the liberal mainstream or the 'realist' camp—is the more conservative, it would not follow that the more radical one was better, the more conservative worse. Even where the demandingness of liberal theory is really that—true demandingness, rather than mere window dressing—it does not follow that the change demanded is a good one. Neoliberalism, after all—the best description of the policies of all major political parties in the United States and United Kingdom at present (including the British 'Conservatives')—is in some ways extremely radical.

The above, I hope, should clarify what I do and do not want to say in this section. What I *do* want to say is that there is a certain current within the diverse movement that is 'realism'—a current which does not exhaust the movement, but which is real enough and strong enough to be worthy of comment—which serves to cancel what radical promise the 'realist' challenge might at first be thought to possess, by concentrating its criticism of the liberal mainstream more or less exclusively on removing areas of perceived utopian overreach (while leaving the basic framework untouched). I am not particularly interested in the question of whether the result is something *more* conservative than mainstream currents, all things considered, or less (or the same)—there may not be an answer to that question, and in any case, I am not too keen on either variety of theory. 'Realism' may in some ways be more *explicitly* or *openly* conservative than liberal 'idealism', but that could be either a good or a bad thing. Radicalness, too, may be either a good or a bad thing. In the present case, as with most of the cases discussed so far in this book, my view is that the conservatism inherent in what we might call 'real existing realism' is a bad thing. But that is not a point I'll try to establish. The main point I want to make—again in line with my analyses in previous chapters—is that the debate over 'realism' is set up in such a way as to make this conservatism seem unavoidable, as though it were a product of the commitment to 'realism' itself. In the space remaining, I want to say a bit more about how that happens.

The basic relationship between the debate over 'ideal' versus 'non-ideal theory' and the debate over 'realism', for my purposes here, is the following: 'non-ideal theory' says that the real world is *relevant* and understands this to mean (only) that it is a potential source of constraints; 'realism' then confirms that the world is indeed a very bad place, and that as the 'non-ideal' theorist had feared, a *lot* of the shine must be knocked off the grand ambitions of the 'ideal theorist'. In this way, the two debates—the connections between which might at first seem befuddlingly complex—work as a simple team, ensuring that departure from liberal 'idealism' ends in little more than compromise and disappointment. Such is life—or so the defender of this framework will say. As I observed at the start of this discussion, the premise that the world is a bad and scary place clearly does a lot of work in shaping the de facto force of 'realism' and 'non-ideal theory' alike, and constitutes the main rationale behind the 'realist' shift to an emphasis on 'stability' or 'modus vivendi' in the place of more usual liberal ideals. That is to say, the move appears to be closely bound up with a certain kind of *pessimism*, evident in the sorts of phenomena on which many 'realists' choose to place emphasis when explaining the importance of the 'real world'. Top choices—as already indicated by Farrelly's list of 'non-ideal' considerations discussed in the previous section—include conflict,[22] human fallibility and irrationality, and the 'passions',[23] all of which are emphasized as fixed facts of life which no amount of liberal idealism can massage away.[24] Simply put: being 'realistic' means looking (an unappealing) reality in the face; looking reality in the face results in pessimism; pessimism brings us to curb our political hopes and ambitions. True, not all 'realists' style themselves as pessimists, and some commentaries acknowledge this.[25] But such thinkers are presented as figures attempting (with an arguable degree of success) not only to buck a trend but to resolve what is at least a prima facie tension. Crucially, even when the attempt is made to break the bond between 'realism' and conservatism, it is still assumed that moving away from conservatism means moving in the direction of greater *optimism*:[26] 'realism' may not mean conservatism, but pessimism does.

This way of thinking is apparent in a recent discussion by Bonnie Honig and Marc Stears, which at one point compares the views of Raymond Geuss, Bernard Williams and James Tully[27] and ends up with something reminiscent of the story of Goldilocks and the three bears.[28] Geuss is Pessimistic Bear, with his bowl of cold porridge: he thinks that the nature of human beings is such that nothing can be or could be much better than it is, and that the most we can ask from politics is to keep people from each other's throats. Tully, on the other hand, is full of 'optimism', 'hope' and even 'gratitude',[29] seeing 'no conflict between realism and some of the bolder ideals of politics'.[30] Williams sits somewhere in the middle, training his sights on lukewarm 'legitimacy'. The more pessimistic the bear, the more conservative; the more optimistic or hopeful, the more radical. (And in the Honig-and-Stears version of the story, all three bears are eventually butchered, put in a blender and turned into a bloody, 'agonistic' gazpacho.) Aside from some straightforward inaccuracies in this portrayal,[31] there also seems to me to be a deep unclarity as to what optimism and pessimism are (and how they affect our political orientations). 'Optimism', of course, can mean various quite different things. For example:

a. thinking that things could be, or could have been, good, or better than they actually are,
b. thinking that things are likely to be good or better in the future,
c. thinking that things *actually are* good, or have been in the past, and
d. demanding that things be good or better, or striving to make them so.

For instance, Tully is taken to be demanding more from politics than Williams or Geuss is, and this is run together with his ability to see 'promise' rather than 'constraint' in history.[32] He emphasizes the element of 'mutuality' in the relations between Euro-Canadians and aboriginals, regarding this as just as 'real' as the domination and genocide, and hopes to inspire efforts to create inter-cultural dialogue by stating that Canada was 'founded on an act of sharing that is almost unimaginable in its generosity'[33] (whose generosity, one wonders?).[34] It's hard to imagine these words having the desired effect: what with all the domination and genocide, Tully's upbeat 'can't we all just get along' message might be found more than slightly offensive. Nor is this sort of line necessary in order to uphold any or all of the other kinds of 'optimism' I just distinguished: the belief in the contingency of evil, the maintenance of hope for the future and the uncompromising insistence on something better. Of course, these things are not completely unconnected either. 'Realists' like Tully[35] may draw their hope for the future by finding the 'bright side' of human history. But that is not the only way to sustain hope, and as Honig and Stears point out, Tully's choice of emphasis in the case of aboriginal-settler relations is not only simplistic but also risks distracting us (against Tully's best intentions) from the sorts of unpalatable facts that 'realists' profess to be eager to confront.

While pessimism is often associated with conservatism, the relationship is not one of simple affinity. We might equally draw an alternative connection, between conservatism and a kind of optimism. There is a sense in which those who deny that it is possible for things to be any less awful than they are, like Dr. Pangloss, view the status quo as the best of all possible worlds. And that, surely, is a kind of affirmation. It doesn't necessarily mean that this sort of 'realist' must *like* the world as she finds it. She may bitterly regret that 'human nature', and whatever other alleged facts about the world, are such as to preclude something less miserable. But sometimes we may be justified in suspecting that 'pessimism' is a more or less cynical mask for a deeper satisfaction with things as they are. It may be more comfortable to occupy the persona of the pessimist than openly to admit that one rather likes the existing setup—especially when there is reason to suspect that this satisfaction is rooted in self-interest. Much easier, though frequently false, to say, 'I don't like it any more than you do, but that's the way of the world. . . . ' Many of those who present themselves as pessimists, then, will turn out to be committed to one or more of the following kinds of optimism: the faith that our existing institutions can be endlessly patched up; the thesis that the world is about as good as it 'realistically' could be; and even the sentiment that things are actually fine, thank you very much.

Conversely, in some ways it is those who are *least* conservative—in the sense of being least keen to keep things as they are, politically speaking— who are the most pessimistic: they typically take a dim view of things as they are; that is why they want to change them. Their attitude is pessimistic, qua 'non-affirmative'—to adopt the terminology associated with Adorno—with respect to the actual state of things. If we assume that their wanting to change things means that they believe that it is in some sense *possible* for things to be otherwise, then we might also say that their attitude towards the world is non-affirmative in a more substantial sense, since it is non-affirmative of it *relative to an alternative way that it could be* (something which the kind of 'realist' I've described here can say only in a more abstruse sense of 'could', indicating, e.g., merely logical or metaphysical possibility): we might be pessimists in the sense of thinking that the world is in a bad state; and—like Adorno—part of what we might mean by saying that it is in a bad state is that it is in such a bad state *unnecessarily*.[36] We might well—again, like Adorno—also be pessimistic about the prospects for improvement, as against continuing and worsening disaster. But we might still throw ourselves into trying to change things against the odds, or into trying to change the odds. Pessimism does not have to mean conservatism any more than 'realism' does.

Even with this disambiguation complete, the attempt to detach pessimism from conservatism may seem somewhat desperate. 'Sure,'—someone might say—'we don't have to have an affirmative view of the social world in order to be radically critical of it (quite the contrary), but nothing that has been said here denies that we will need to affirm the existence of *possibilities*, within that world, for the kind of change that might bring about a world that we *could* affirm.' Perhaps this is correct: in order for our criticisms of the world to be *political* criticisms, and not merely expressions of distaste or existential angst, we need to have some kind of commitment to the possibility of change for the better, even if this is no more than a leap of faith—and even if we judge that the most appropriate course is to be quietists about it. And this kind of possibility—at least as regards certain kinds of radical or 'utopian' change—is precisely what many 'realists' may deny, since they hold the persistence and universality of factors such as human irrationality and conflict to rule it out. At this point, the 'realist' may appear to have the radical critic well and truly cornered: how can anyone deny the reality of these factors, or that they place limits on what is possible politically?

The answer, however, is that there is no need to do anything of the kind. What is difficult to deny is that things like irrationality and conflict are permanent features of the world, which do rule out some forms of social organization and make others difficult—and render absurd the kind of 'ideal theory' which proceeds as if they were not there. But that is not enough to make them 'constraints on political aspiration' in any very salient or interesting sense. We might say, of a person who is starving, that her biological need for sustenance acts as a constraint on her ability to survive and flourish. And that would not be strictly false, but it would be completely inappropriate in most imaginable contexts—what is salient here is the unavailability of food, not the starving person's need for it. Similarly, it is not obviously human irrationality and propensity for conflict that are the salient facts to point to, when thinking about political reality and about the possibilities for political change. Some do take the view that deficiencies of human nature are responsible for war, for economic crises and for the destruction of the planet—think of the tendency for the latest financial crisis to be blamed on 'greed'. But if we are serious about taking a historically informed approach to such questions, we are more likely to see these arguably universal human traits as interacting with highly variable social conditions, political and economic institutions or modes of production, which make a massive difference to the way in which those traits manifest themselves and to the sort of collective existence that is achieved. It may be convenient to pin onto 'human nature' our more catastrophic failures to live together in a way that is minimally humanly acceptable, but it's not terribly plausible, in the face of immense social and historical variation—not to mention certain recalcitrant patterns, such as the recent reluctance of the citizens of Western 'democracies' to countenance the invasion of other countries, a reluctance which necessitates sustained propaganda campaigns in order to whip those populations into a state of fear and paranoia[37] (assuming that they cannot be simply ignored, as the British government ignored the overwhelming popular opposition to the invasion of Iraq and a march of hundreds of thousands of people in London in 2003).

Just as there is a well-known phenomenon of 'victim blaming' in attitudes towards rape, so I noted that a central plank of the realist challenge to the liberal mainstream is to cite the deficiencies of human beings—the large majority of whom are being (and more or less always have been) well and truly screwed by the political structures in which they live—as being at the root of the shortcomings of their political institutions, and hence of the suffering that those institutions cause. It may be true that if people were all impeccably behaved, or perfectly rational, all of the time, then they wouldn't have to face the political conditions they face as a matter of fact—in that case there wouldn't really be any need for politics at all (but then, it may often be true that the behaviour of a woman, including the mistakes and errors of judgement that she makes, plays a causal role in bringing about what subsequently happens to her).

There might seem to be an important disanalogy here: in the case of victim blaming in rape, the problem is that the victim is blamed *rather than the perpetrator*; but on the assumption that the oppressors as well as the oppressed are human beings, the attitude which blames political failure on 'human nature' is one which blames perpetrators and victims alike. But what initially threatens to weaken the analogy turns out to lend it strength. In the first place, when political failures are blamed on 'human' ones, the implication—at least, the conversational implicature[38]—is very often that it is the 'human' failings of the people at large ('the masses') that are explanatorily salient, rather than those of ruling elites. The fact that the deficiencies cited are also held to be common to *all* human beings is perhaps beside the point: if an instance of rape is put down to the victim's alleged inebriation and recklessness, then that is still victim blaming even if it is frankly acknowledged that the rapist was *also* drunk and reckless (because only the *victim's* condition is taken to be relevant)—the only difference this makes is to add a layer of hypocrisy to the evaluation.

When Galston suggests that the imperfections of real politics are due to the fact that people are not as 'principled' as the liberal idealists would like them to be, it seems clear which people he has in mind: 'But the nub of the matter for realists is this: political theory must not assume that the motivation or capacity to act in a principled manner is pervasive among all members of a political community. Some individuals are impaired in their capacity for justice, others lack it outright, a reality that no policies, no institutions, however wise, can change.' If it were the deficiencies of *all* human beings—rulers and ruled, oppressors and oppressed—that were salient here, then the talk of 'a reality that no policies, no institutions, however wise, can change' would seem out of place: the point is not that, given the nature of human beings, policies and institutions will always be exploitative and oppressive (or otherwise 'unjust'); it is that the people who suffer under unjust institutions and policies are deficient—their rulers are too, no doubt, but that is not relevant, because *however* wise they and their policies were, it still wouldn't be enough.[39] This 'pessimism' is not the understandable gloom or anxiety about the fate of human societies, but a mask for a misanthropy so profound that it ultimately threatens to become incompatible with any serious interest in either political philosophy or social change.

III. CONCLUSION

I've now discussed the two closely connected debates over '(non-)ideal theory' and 'realism' at some length. Both 'realism' and the associated critique of 'ideal theory' are presented as serious challenges to the methodology of mainstream liberal political philosophy, and my task in this chapter has been to size up that challenge.

What I've tried to show is that the contrasts involved here are set up in such a way as to place severe limits on the extent to which deviation from dominant modes of political philosophy is even thinkable. A common way of drawing the contrast between 'ideal' and 'non-ideal theory' ends up casting the former as the limit of radical possibility and reducing the latter to a willingness to work within whatever constraints the world seems to impose on political ambition. A complementary emphasis among 'realists' on the intractability of political conditions and the inadequacies of human beings seals the deal.

The combined function of these two debates is to act as a kind of 'political neutralizer' of dissent against mainstream liberal theory. A critic of liberal 'ideal theory', after all, might initially have both methodological *and political* objections to the approach she rejects—perhaps she criticizes liberalism partly on the grounds that its criticisms and proposed reforms of the social world are insufficiently fundamental or far-reaching, and partly on the grounds that it is fatally detached from the same social world—and she may also see these two sets of objections as closely connected.[40] The perception of a tension between 'realism' and the demand for radical social change appears to leave such a critic completely trapped: she can either drop her objections to mainstream liberal theory, reconciling herself to its methodology (and also to any limits which this methodology may place on its politics), or she can embrace the main available alternative, 'realism', coupling a degree of methodological deviance with a more explicit resignation to prevailing political realities than is typical of the liberal mainstream; *or*, at a push, she can 'have it both ways', and be a 'realist' as well as a more severe critic of the status quo—but only at the cost of embracing a rather inane-looking 'optimism' about the history and prevailing politics of the actual world. Moreover, the rhetoric through which the trap is laid has some rather sinister features. At its worst, the 'realist' attitude to citizens is imperious-bordering-on-imperialist, reminiscent not only of rape apologism but also of classic depictions of 'barbarians' and 'savages': passion-driven beasts who, if left unchecked, will stick spears into each other and eat their own babies. All this is particularly regrettable given that the 'realist' critique begins from a genuine insight: the inescapable importance of attention to history and real politics for political theorizing.[41] As it is, this insight is channelled towards what is in effect a *de-politicization* of a 'non-ideal' world—the shortcomings of which are traced to unalterable historical universals and to the deficiencies of human beings—and thus a silencing of demands to change it.

NOTES

1. Ibn Khaldun (2005 [1377]; vol. 3, p. 227).
2. Scheuerman (2008). I tend to agree that 'realism' is a term we would be better off without (although for the moment we seem to be stuck with it). I'll use inverted commas throughout, to emphasize that I am interested above all in the set of people and theories that tend to be labelled in this way (whether or not the label ultimately makes any sense).
3. For example, Mills (2005).
4. See, for example, Swift and White (2008).
5. I use the term 'conservatism' here not to designate a more-or-less definite political position or ideology (as in large-C 'Conservatism'), but simply to indicate the quality of affirmativeness towards the status quo—with 'radical', or 'radically critical', as its contrary. Of course, these terms are relative ones (and hence any given application of them may be contested), but as far as I can see this does not raise any serious problems for what I have to say here.
6. The main reasons for this, in my view, are as follows: first, the social conditions in which we live, and by which we are formed, can be expected to set quite significant limits on the epistemic access we have to a desirable social world—so that attempts to describe such a world are not only likely to fail but are also at risk of transposing into our descriptions of 'utopia' various undesirable features of the status quo; second, by concentrating too much of our energies on describing an ideal system, we risk diverting attention from the arguably more

important task of theorizing real instances of oppression (Mills 2005)—and at worst, sanitizing the status quo by contributing to the impression that these 'non-ideal' phenomena do not exist.

7. He also specifies 'favourable conditions' (whatever that means).

8. Dworkin (2000) imagines a hypothetical auction in which a group of people, survivors washed up on a desert island, bid for 'bundles of resources' with clamshells.

9. See section III of *The Communist Manifesto*, Marx (1998 [1848]); cf. Engels (1989 [1880]).

10. Cf. Rawls (2001; pp. 8, 176), on abstraction and idealization as means of attaining an 'uncluttered view' of justice.

11. The Ken Loach film *The Wind That Shakes the Barley* has some particularly powerful illustrations of this.

12. Clause IV was part of the British Labour Party's constitution from 1918 until its aboli-tion in 1995. Drafted by the Fabian socialist Sidney Webb, it reads, 'To secure for the workers by hand or by brain the full fruits of their industry and the most equitable distribution thereof that may be possible upon the basis of the common ownership of the means of production, distribution and exchange, and the best obtainable system of popular administration and control of each industry or service.'

13. Hence Farrelly's classification of Rawls as only a 'moderate' ideal theorist: Rawls (the later Rawls, anyway) is concerned with crafting principles of justice for a society marked by 'reasonable disagreement'. That's why, in chapter 2, I classed the later Rawls as engaged in 'non-ideal theory', but I attach little importance to the application of that label.

14. I'll discuss the role of these factors in 'realist' thought later in this chapter.

15. One might object that 'fact sensitivity', unlike the more everyday notion of 'practical-ity', is not the obviously partisan matter of *responding adequately to the facts*, but just a matter of how many and what sorts of facts a theorist takes to be *relevant*. To say that Dunn and Carens are more 'fact sensitive' is not to say that they attach the correct significance to factors such as disagreement or fallibility, nor even that they are right in their estimation of the nature and level of these factors in the actual world; the point is just that they consider the levels of disagreement and fallibility to be *relevant* to the task of theorizing, whereas, for example, Cohen would take his theoretical commitments to obtain regardless of what anyone were to discover about such empirical matters. I accept the distinction, but not the conclusion that judgements of 'fact sensitivity' can be completely independent of political disagreements. Suppose that Dunn had said that political theory ought to be more sensitive to the literal truth of the Bible, or to the existence of unicorns, or to the unique destiny of the Aryan race. Then would he be placed on the 'fact sensitive' end? If not, that must be because the spectrum setter judges—plausibly, but not politically neutrally—that those are not (appropriate) *facts*.

16. I am assuming that Farrelly and others see a relatively smooth continuum between 'ideal-critical-irrelevant' and 'non-ideal-conservative-relevant', where critical or radical con-tent is inversely proportional to 'fact sensitivity'. It would be possible to hold, instead, that there is some tipping point or threshold, beyond which 'fact sensitivity' suddenly turns into conservatism, although we would need an explanation of why this is so. Both by omission and by the appearance of his spectrum, Farrelly gives the contrary impression.

17. Some of the material of this section is drawn from the final part of my article entitled 'With Radicals Like These, Who Needs Conservatives? Doom, Gloom and Realism in Political Theory' (published in the *European Journal of Political Theory*, 2015). The full paper provides a more comprehensive discussion of 'realism' than I can offer here.

18. Scruton (2010), by contrast, connects an attitude of pessimism with an *explicit* conserva-tism.

19. Williams (2005) takes issue with Rawls's assertion that 'justice' is the 'first virtue' of a society and suggests replacing this with 'order'. He also criticizes Rawls's use of the phrase 'mere *modus vivendi*', on the grounds that the establishment of a stable collective form of life is already a great achievement: to aim for something more, as Rawls does, equals a 'dangerous utopianism'. Cf. Horton (2010). Geuss, at certain points, also comes close to this sort of view, which may partly explain the tendency for commentators to cast him as either a conservative or a 'liberal of fear' (see Geuss [2008; p. 11] and also Geuss [2011/2012]).

20. As Duncan Bell points out, 'realism' may be found in combination with any number of political positions, 'ranging from conservatism through to radical forms of political critique' (2008; p. 1).

21. Although 'realism' is often presented as a 'challenge to liberalism', it is better thought of in practice as a challenge to a *particular style* of liberal political theory. In fact, most of the names associated with 'realism' self-define—and/or are defined by others—as 'liberal': Bernard Williams; Richard Bellamy; the 'thin liberal' John Gray; the 'liberal of fear' Judith Shklar. Of the fifteen names scattered in the reader's direction at the start of Galston's 2010 survey, all are liberals, with only one exception, Raymond Geuss—although he too is sometimes cast as one (see Honig and Stears 2011, p. 192; Sangiovanni 2009, p. 228, fn. 21).

22. For example, Gray (2007) and cf. Mouffe (2000; 2005a; 2005b). Honig (1993) shares with Mouffe an emphasis on 'agonism'; cf. Honig and Stears (2011; pp. 201–5).

23. Hence, Galston (2010; p. 408) associates 'realism' with the call for a 'more complex moral and political psychology'. Cf. Mouffe (2005a; p. 6): 'The mistake of liberal rationalism is to ignore the affective dimension . . . and to imagine that those supposedly archaic 'passions' are bound to disappear with the advance of individualism and the progress of rationality.'

24. Gray (2007); Mouffe (2000; 2005a; 2005b); Honig (1993); Honig and Stears (2011; pp. 201–5). As Gray (2007; pp. 23–24) puts it, 'Conflict is a universal feature of human life . . . A conflict-free existence is impossible for humans, and whenever it is attempted the result is intolerable to them.'

25. Jonathan Floyd and Marc Stears, for instance, note that some thinkers combine their 'realism' with greater hope and optimism than most, seeing in political reality not only constraints, but also a liberating potential (Floyd and Stears 2011; pp. 7–9). They point to the work of Melissa Lane, who argues that Rawls developed a more sympathetic view of the place of religion in public life after studying its role in the abolitionist movement (see Lane [2011]). Those who had hoped for a politically radical 'realist' alternative to the liberal paradigm will not be able to get very excited about that, but we can still appreciate the recognition by Lane (and by Floyd and Stears) of the fact that taking notice of political reality need not mean treating it as a constraining factor.

26. A similar assumption seems to be at work in an introductory essay by Floyd and Stears (2011), who suggest that 'the demand [of realism] is to situate political philosophy between utopianism and pessimism' (p. 3) and talk about finding 'just the right kind of realism—neither too ambitious nor too pessimistic' (p. 4).

27. Honig and Stears (2011).

28. Pleasingly, for my purposes, in the original version of the Goldilocks story (anonymously published by Robert Southey in 1837), the bears are not a nuclear family, but three bachelors living together in the woods.

29. Honig and Stears (2011; p. 197).

30. Ibid. (p. 181).

31. For example, Honig and Stears repeatedly claim that Geuss reduces everything to power (although they acknowledge that this is not how he sees his own position), and they support this by reference to places where Geuss says that political philosophers cannot afford to lose sight

of power (because it is always a vital dimension of human interactions—moral language, for instance, is always embedded within structures and relations of power). On this basis, Honig and Stears present Geuss as some kind of hideous hybrid of Milton Friedman and the Grinch (who wants to steal Christmas because his heart is 'two sizes too small'): their Geuss is, despite himself, committed to a crude *Realpolitik*, and sees the moral and aspirational aspects of life as offering nothing but hollow 'stories of legitimation' (or 'window dressing', as Friedman would put it). This interpretation seems to me to rest on a basic confusion between 'always' and 'only': the view that power is *always* important is not the same as the view that power is the *only* thing that is important, and the former view in no way implies the latter. I make no judgement here as to whether Honig and Stears are any fairer to Williams or Tully.

32. Honig and Stears (2011; p. 197).

33. Tully (2008; pp. 244–45).

34. Cf. Charles Mills (2010) on 'The Whiteness of John Rawls' (available on YouTube).

35. Tully, as Honig and Stears acknowledge, does not actually describe himself as a 'realist'.

36. As Fabian Freyenhagen (2013; p. 1) puts it: 'Pessimism and optimism often come as a pair. In Adorno's case, his deep pessimism about the contemporary social world is coupled with a strong optimism about human potential. In fact, it is the latter which explains his negative views about the contemporary social world and his demand that we should resist and change it.'

37. See, for example, Chomsky and Herman (1994).

38. I take this term from Grice (1975), who identifies a set of shared rules for efficient communication which govern the way in which we make inferences from the utterances of others in conversation: for example, the utterance 'some athletes smoke' conversationally implies—through what Grice calls the 'maxim of quantity', which requires speakers to be as informative as required—that not all athletes smoke (otherwise the speaker would have said so), even though it is not a logical implication of the statement. Much of what we call 'pedantry' is speech which exploits the difference between logical and conversational implicature, by ignoring the latter.

39. As I acknowledged earlier, we are in the realms of disputable conversational implicature rather than formal proof here—and the single example of Galston cannot prove the general claim. But even if 'realists' in general are better read as blaming human deficiencies as instantiated in *all* social groups—or even these universal deficiencies as instantiated in the powerful in particular (e.g., their 'greed' or 'corruption'), viewed as the realization of a potential lying dormant in the less fortunate—the picture is hardly much more edifying: to explain the incidence of rape by saying that it is just 'human nature' is just one more guise of the same, basically apologist attitude which puts it down to the conduct of the victim.

40. See, for example, Mills (2005).

41. Ironically, some among the 'realist' camp demonstrate the point extremely well, albeit at their own expense. Galston's chosen 'real politics' examples are a case in point. He expresses sympathy for the 'realist' focus on modus vivendi, and adds that 'rough and ready compromise' is the 'only way forward in Iraq'—which might be thought to 'abstract away' from the small matter of what the foreign forces were doing there in the first place. No doubt Galston would insist that he is only being practical—we can't go backwards, after all, only forwards—but no self-respecting 'realist' should deny the importance of attention to historical context to any judgement about political situations. It is not that to assert the necessity of compromise is to assert something strictly false—the need for compromise will apply in almost any complex political situation. But what would you have to think about the situation in Iraq in order to place such exclusive emphasis on 'compromise', as opposed to the entirely warranted antipathy

towards occupying forces and everything they represent, or the continued presence of private security forces to secure the interests of foreign corporations after the 'official' soldiers have withdrawn?

Chapter Six

Small and Unsexy

Political Theory in the Real World

To a question such as 'why still philosophy?'—for the formulation of which I myself am responsible, although its dilettantish tone does not escape me—most people will already guess the answer. They will expect a train of thought that accumulates all kinds of difficulties and reservations in order to lead ultimately, more or less cautiously, to a 'nevertheless' and an affirmation of what at first had been rhetorically cast into doubt. This all too familiar circuit corresponds to a conformist and apologetic attitude that characterizes itself as positive and reckons in advance on consent. And indeed perhaps nothing better can be expected from someone whose job it is to teach philosophy, whose bourgeois existence depends on its continued survival, and who undermines his own immediate interests as soon as he contests it.

—Adorno[1]

Observe yourselves more closely, gentlemen, then you'll see that it's true.

—Dostoevsky ('Notes from the Underground')[2]

The debates over 'realism', 'ideal' and 'non-ideal theory' surveyed in the previous chapter are not only about the question of how political philosophy should be done (e.g., whether it should proceed from the study of the actual world or from the search for 'fact-free' ethical principles). 'Realism', in particular, is also connected with a claim about the *status* of political philosophy: that the latter is not just a bunch of words but is also a kind of political intervention.[3] The political theorist, on this view, is not adequately understood as merely *commenting* on politics; she is a political *actor*—in however

137

small a way, and however non-straightforward the connection between the content of her commentary and the nature of her contribution to real politics. In other words, 'realism' is not only about the place of politics in political philosophy, but also about the place of political philosophy in politics. It is this second aspect, which has been left more or less untouched in my discussion so far, that is addressed in this chapter. My aim is not to defend any particular positive view about what the role of political philosophy is or should be, but instead to examine the way in which political philosophers tend to represent—to others and, above all, to themselves—the role of their discipline within 'real politics'.

It's worth briefly explaining why I've chosen this to be the focus of my last proper chapter. In this second main part of the book, I have been consciously concentrating on what seem to be subversive currents within contemporary political philosophy—hence the focus on 'realism' in the previous chapter. Now, there is nothing necessarily radical or challenging about the idea of looking at philosophy as something which plays some kind of role in the real world—as will be amply illustrated in the course of this chapter. Yet it might be expected, a priori, that a bit of systematic reflection on the question of the place of political philosophy in the actual world is just what is called for by the findings of the past chapters of this book—and that, by the same token, the existence of a flourishing realm of 'methodology of political philosophy', in which theorists address precisely that issue, can be seen as a counterexample to the rather pessimistic thesis that might otherwise be inferred from those earlier chapters. And to that, I want to say the same thing I said in the case of 'realism': *not so fast.* When political philosophers turn to address the question of the 'real-political' significance of their discipline, I'll suggest, the result is a view which manages to be at once depressingly tame and wildly deluded. Far from being a serious challenge to philosophical business-as-usual, much of what political philosophers have to say about their own wider significance seems geared to one objective above all: that of reconciling themselves more thoroughly to the status quo—both within academic political philosophy and in the world outside it.

I. WISDOM TRICKLES DOWN

Political philosophers, like Uriah Heep, are terribly humble. 'I wouldn't dare suggest', says one contributor to a recent volume on the methodology of political theory, 'that the amount of progress made in political philosophy is comparable to that made in science, but I do believe (perhaps naively) that there has been significant progress. I also believe that political philosophers should approach their tasks with the same sense of humility as scientists, and that they should be happy to make a successful contribution, however small and unsexy it may seem, to the overall project of increasing human knowledge.'[4] A further pair of contributors immediately echo the sentiment, asserting that political theorists[5] are 'committed to the pursuit of truth'—the intended contrast class here being politicians—and that as such, they are 'happy (well, prepared) to change their minds, and admit to changing their minds, when someone shows them they were wrong. They don't claim to have all the answers.'[6]

A few words, first of all, on changing (and not changing) your mind. It always seems to me that Foucault makes a sound point when he suggests that if you don't change your mind, you're probably not trying hard enough—what is the point of philosophy, after all, if it does not somehow change the way in which we view the world?[7] So if political philosophers are willing and unashamed to change their minds, then good for them. Unfortunately, though, political philosophers are in my experience perhaps the single group of people most *un*likely to change their minds, at least about any substantial political matter, and this special immovability may be seen as owing to a sedimentation of three thick layers. First, a general human tendency towards intransigence and refusal to change—which hardens with age, but seems to me to be much stronger and to take effect much earlier than is usually recognized. On top of that, the fact that academic philosophers—not just *political* philosophers—generally have a strong (and ever-strengthening) vested interest in *not* changing their minds, partly because of the greater intellectual labour involved in formulating a new position compared with patching up an old one, but also because of the professional advantages accruing to those who have a distinctive piece of the intellectual territory staked out—not having to scrap a large body of writing that you might otherwise publish, having the opportunity to write and publish more of the same, getting invited to speak and to publish on the back of being (for example) 'the autonomy man' or 'the Kant guy'.[8] Lastly, though most controversially, there is the point that political attitudes are particularly clearly bound up with various material interests—and may potentially be seen as forms of 'functionally explained' ideological illusion[9]—so that there is reason to expect such attitudes to be extremely difficult to shift, at least in the absence of certain changes in the underlying political conditions. Contrary to my impression, however—and unsurprisingly enough—the more popular view among political philosophers seems to be that they *are* prepared to change their minds, and that this is one of the things that assists them on their slow trek towards the light.

This image of philosophers valiantly but painstakingly—and above all, *humbly*—picking their way across difficult terrain is then supplemented by a further emphasis on a 'division of labour'.[10] Political philosophers depict themselves as situated within a wider cooperative system dedicated to the pursuit and application of knowledge. For example, Daniel McDermott presents political philosophy as a 'complement to social science':[11] 'Whereas social scientists aim to determine the empirical facts about human behaviour and institutions, political philosophers aim to determine what *ought* to be done in light of that information.'[12] In this way, we are reassured—lest we be alarmed by the thought of too much power concentrated in the hands of political philosophers—that the extent to which they can actually change things, even in the slow-motion manner described, is very limited: philosophers are only one kind of force among many others who exert influence on the political process. In support of this, it is claimed (for example) that '[t]hose who are skilled in conceptual analysis and nice moral distinctions cannot realistically be the same people as those who know how best to research complex empirical phenomena. And neither of them can also be the people who can stir a nation to political action—even to the voting booth—through fine speeches and political leadership.'[13]

The idea of political philosophers as engaged in a 'division of labour' of this kind has certain consequences, which follow almost by definition. First, if there is a division of labour, then all the parties to that division have their particular, specialized roles to play—and in due course, we are given a particular sort of answer as to what this distinctive, specialized task is in the case of political philosophers: in keeping with the thought that the proper objects of philosophical knowledge are facts about the structure of the world or about our concepts, political philosophers are to contribute abstract and normative truths; distinctions (including 'nice moral' ones); and 'conceptual analysis'—others will deal with the rest.

Secondly, the idea of a division of labour presupposes a background of some more or less substantial *consensus* as to the kind of project that is being engaged in and the ends to be furthered by it: 'we are all in it together!'[14] It only really makes sense to see oneself as a political philosopher involved in a division of labour on the condition that one also sees oneself as engaged in a common undertaking with other political philosophers, where the nature of that undertaking can be broadly agreed on by all parties. Participation in such a division of labour is something which is only really possible for those who are operating within a framework that is generally accepted, even dominant.[15]

When we ask more about what this collective enterprise is, which is held to be shared by political philosophers and social scientists and also by politicians,[16] we move from the question of what political philosophy 'is' to a more explicit asking and answering of the question of what political philosophy can *do*—what kind of force, if any, can political philosophy have in politics? The conventional answer, very crudely (but not altogether surprisingly), seems to be that political philosophy contributes to a simultaneous advance towards enlightenment and towards the improvement of the social world. Just as the theoretical progress made by political philosophers is supposed to be real yet tortuous and gradual, so is the process by which they contribute to the reform of society. For example, as Adam Swift and Stuart White see it, 'it took over 100 years for the arguments of Mill's *On Liberty* to find their way into liberal legislation on homosexuality in the UK.' One hundred years—even longer than it took for Mill to put an end to sex inequality (one wonders how long it will take him to find a cure for cancer). But by way of consolation, they add that change 'will not happen at all unless it is argued for'.[17] Political philosophy, then, is a slow burner, but no less indispensable for that (provided that we swallow the rather sizeable assumption that political philosophers are the only people who argue for anything).

How, then, do political philosophers fulfil their noble mission (aside from *slowly* and *with a little help from their friends*)? According to their own assessments, there seem to be three main ways. Political philosophers can exert relatively *direct* influence, by being advisors to government, sitting on committees and 'think tanks', and so on.[18] That, admittedly, is relatively rare. More commonly, they may, through their research, influence current and future 'policy makers'—politicians, business leaders or even future philosophers-who-will-sit-on-committees—even if they never exert direct influence themselves (as is pointed out ad nauseam, everyone in the British Cabinet has probably read both a bit of Mill and a bit of Rawls at some point). Finally, political philosophers may—occasionally directly, through 'pop philosophy' and mainstream media appearances, but more often indirectly, through the other two types of influence mentioned, or just through having their ideas gradually permeate the 'political culture'—have an influence on public opinion:[19] 'public opinion' seems to figure in the story chiefly as a cumbersome constraint on the 'political feasibility set' (albeit a constraint that must be honoured).[20] The image that emerges from all this is one of political philosophers lining up—along with other academics and members of the intellectual elite, such as social and natural scientists, journalists and judges—to feed their specialized insights into one of the waiting apertures of the existing political apparatus.[21]

This sort of function with respect to 'real politics' is typically presented as something which may be an acceptable object of aspiration for any political philosopher who agrees that political philosophy should be in some sense 'practically engaged', pretty much regardless of her first-order political-philosophical commitments, as long as she avows some kind of commitment to democratic politics and due process—that is, no fascists or wannabe dictators.[22] A lot depends, however, on what we mean by a commitment to *democracy* or *due process* or *official channels*. The more restrictive the understanding of those concepts implicit in the model of political philosophy and real politics sketched above, the more problematic the accompanying suggestion of general (i.e., cross-political) acceptability. And the kinds of examples canvassed so far suggest an understanding of 'official channels' that is very restrictive indeed: basically, think tanks, Oxbridge reading lists and a tenuous link to 'public opinion'—read 'upper-middle-class opinion'—operating through a combination of osmosis and BBC Radio 4. The first two of these forms of influence assume that the social change in question will be 'top-down'—it will come from the influence of intellectuals on current politicians or future leaders and 'opinion makers'—and moreover, it is only to be expected that the 'influential' will be selected so as to fit the purposes of the elite that is to be 'influenced'. It is noteworthy that the remaining form of influence—influence on the general public—is often relegated to third place in terms of emphasis or order of mention. It is then construed in a way that subsumes it under the top-down form of social change already noted: political philosophers influence an elite, and then certain elements of this elite transmit this influence to the population more generally. Just as the neoliberal idea is that wealth will 'trickle down' from the top of a society to the bottom, the thought here seems to be that political philosophers' wisdom will percolate through the minds of politicians, through existing political structures, through the public culture and, in diluted form, through the muddled and distractible minds of the masses, who will then send such wisdom as they have absorbed back up into the political machine in the form of a stream of ballot papers. Insight will flow from the places where it is most concentrated, and into emptier vessels. The people, ultimately, will benefit from this process both in that they will gradually become wiser—learning, for example, that homosexuals should not be persecuted—and also in that they will enjoy the benefits of a social order that has been enriched by the infusion of understanding and insight it has received from diverse sources, among which political philosophers, and those whom they help to educate, loom significant (if not exactly large).[23] The influence that 'the people', for their part, are recognized as having on politics is understood almost exclusively in terms of their voting behaviour—the four-or-so-yearly farce in which a dwindling proportion of the population posts its pseudo-choices into one or another of the apertures of a largely oblivious machine.

One reaction, at this point, might be to say, 'So political philosophers are not, on the whole, revolutionaries. Who didn't know that already? It's not as if it can sensibly be maintained that this is a *covert* political commitment on their part. And nor is it a criticism in itself to point out that political philosophers see themselves as endorsing non-revolutionary change. Indeed, there are compelling reasons—for example, invoking the value of peace, democracy or the avoidance of corruption—for favouring this mode of change, much as its pace can be frustrating.'

Once again, however, it all depends on what you mean by the relevant words. For the objection imagined above to be to the point, the term 'revolutionary' would have to stand for any change that is not attained through the official channels of the incumbent political system. It will not always be entirely clear what counts as 'revolutionary' in this sense. Does civil disobedience work through official channels? What about *un*civil disobedience, such as was practiced by the Suffragette movement in the early twentieth century? What about innovative tactics for which there is no real precedent, and where it may therefore be simply indeterminate whether these ways of acting so as to produce change are or are not sanctioned by the set of rules we might normally apply to decide such things?[24]

Although there is no contradiction involved in the idea that we might work *through the existing channels* of some political system so as to change that system's fundamental structure, rather than just the policies which that structure produces and implements,[25] this sort of objective is not what seems to be often on the minds of many political philosophers, who overwhelmingly conceive of things in terms of effecting changes in 'policy' (always code for a decision to limit attention to the *output* of a given political system, leaving aside more fundamentally *political* questions of how that system is structured, who gets to decide what the 'output' of the system should be, and how *this* is decided). To the extent that they conceive of their actual and potential role in the 'real world' in this way, political theorists place the very concerns that are most definitively political beyond the scope of the social change in which they envisage themselves as playing their small and unsexy part.[26]

II. A NARCISSISTIC FALLACY

I've by now offered a sketch of the image that political philosophers meet in the mirror. We have arrived at a pretty late point in the book, and it may be judged that I have allowed myself to get a little carried away. Certainly, it will not have gone unnoticed that I have squeezed a lot of vitriol out of a rather small handful of examples. I should therefore stress that the sketch is not offered as a comprehensive map or survey but—quite consciously—as an illustration and as a caricature. Caricatures, like analogies, may be quite legitimate and efficient vehicles for conveying a truth, and a true concern for 'accuracy', it seems to me, should dictate that a caricature be taken for what it is, and not castigated for not being another thing (a portrait in oils, or an ordnance survey map). As was also the case to some extent with my discussion of the 'realist' movement in the previous chapter, my aim is not to *establish* that the way in which political philosophers in general conceive of their place in politics corresponds to my sketch—not the kind of thing that could admit of a watertight proof, in any case—but rather to draw attention to something which I believe will be instantly recognizable to at least a significant segment of readers (if it turns out not to be, then this is good evidence that I am mistaken, but it seems worth taking the risk that claims of this form inescapably carry).

As well as limiting myself to only a few examples, I have inferred a great deal from what is *not* said. For some, this will also be problematic, since nothing can be strictly deduced—that is, logically inferred—from nothing. For instance, when political philosophers fail to acknowledge the possibility that social change might be brought about through popular uprising rather than through electoral politics-as-usual, or that the change in question might go beyond what normally goes by the name of 'policy', then this is not logically equivalent to *denying* the possibility. Again, however, the claim I'm making should be taken for the kind of claim that it is. To the extent that it is a claim about implicature at all, the implicature in question is firmly conversational rather than logical.[27] There is nothing disreputable about that, nor about the practice of inferring from omissions—our understanding of politics would be seriously deficient if we were to try to do without these kinds of inferences. But perhaps the point is not even best couched in terms of what is 'implied' (or 'meant' or 'intended') by political philosophers. This is not a piece of psychological analysis. In suggesting that political philosophers' conceptions of social change are limited in various ways, I am not making a claim about what is going on in their heads—nor advancing a counterfactual hypothesis as to what they would say, if pressed on the matter. It's quite possible and indeed likely that, if asked whether 'the public' have a role to play in politics beyond participation in general elections, political philosophers would answer in the affirmative; they might affirm, for example, that popular protest is *of course* an important means of bringing about social change—and that philosophers might have a role to play in it.[28] My point, however, has been primarily one about *atmosphere and effect*, rather than about the contents of individual souls. I've tried to give a sense of the way in which political philosophers tend to steer and shape the discourse surrounding the role of philosophy in real politics. And this steering and shaping can happen quite effectively through hints and omissions and telling choices of example, without any need for an explicit commitment to rule out forms of 'impact' less concessive to the political status quo.

The respects in which the self-image I've now sketched and criticized is *delusional* should, I hope, be fairly clear. Assuming for the sake of argument that my general impression of the way in which political philosophers view their place in politics is accurate, and assuming also that the arguments of the chapters leading up to this one are broadly persuasive, then the self-image of political philosophers must be seen as deluded in three main ways.

In the first place, there is what we might think of as a delusion of intellectual virtue. The picture painted by my various case studies so far is of a discipline whose practitioners perpetuate a consistently and radically false impression of the debates in which they are engaged, where that false impression serves to protect the set of assumptions that is currently dominant, by means of tricky devices (such as double standards, distraction from potentially threatening views, and so on) which can hardly be squared with the virtues of rigour, clarity, truth seeking and open-mindedness that figure so strongly in its official self-image.

In the second place, there is a delusion of innocence. The dominant political framework which is the beneficiary of the obfuscatory devices just alluded to is that of liberalism, and a long record of 'liberal' complicity in just about every social evil under the sun should at least make us think twice before falling into line with the prevailing wisdom that Western history is the history of the gradual translation of liberal ideals into the achievement of a freer and more rational world.[29] To the extent that political philosophers can be seen as representing any significant real-political force, it is far from clear that this force is one of which they are entitled to feel at all proud.

Finally, there is a delusion of a certain kind of *grandeur*—the trumpeted modesty and muted conservatism of the vision notwithstanding. The model I've described as belonging to the self-image of political philosophers sometimes seems to treat their input into politics as if it were something generated purely out of themselves, as if the force they exert on the political world were a force exerted on it from a Godlike position outside of the whole system. Again, this can only be an inference from omission—political philosophers are hardly likely to sign up to such an obvious falsehood and conceit in an open and conscious way. But it is significant that they have a lot to say about what their 'impact' might be, but very little about where *they* have come from, about the forces that shape and sustain *them*. The way in which political philosophers answer the question, 'How much effect do we really have?' is not to the point here. However modest their estimation of their degree of impact, there is a delusion of grandeur, so long as the question is asked with the implicit assumption that they somehow stand to politics as First Movers (however small and unsexy).

But the self-image I've described is as restrictive as it is delusory and grandiose. This becomes apparent when we recognize that the *self-image of the self-image*—that is, the way in which this account of the role of political philosophers in real politics presents itself—is also dramatically distorted. The same basic phenomenon identified in the studies of the role of informal methodological norms such as 'constructiveness' and 'charity' in the first and third chapters of this book, and found again in my discussion of the explicitly methodological notions of 'ideal' and 'non-ideal' theory discussed in chapter 5, can once more be detected in the conventional account of the place of political philosophy in politics sketched here. When we are presented with that account, it appears as though we are simply being presented with an array of ways in which philosophers might 'make a difference', within the framework of an innocuous-sounding 'division of labour'. There is no hint that the validity of what I've dubbed the 'trickle-down' model of philosophy and real politics depends on how we resolve various basic questions about politics—and that accepting this model depends on accepting the basic framework of liberal-capitalist politics that is endorsed by dominant approaches to political philosophy. And yet the point is perhaps more obvious here than elsewhere. As soon as we try to substantiate in any detail what it means to say that political philosophy should be 'engaged in real politics', our account will inevitably be informed by our first-order political-philosophical leanings and commitments. Our view as to the sense in which political philosophy can and should be politically engaged will depend on the mixture of descriptive and evaluative judgements we are inclined to make about the workings of the social world. How could this fail to be a *political* matter?

The self-image is tame, then, in that it places strict limits both on the kind of role that the philosopher might play in social change and on the kind of change in which the philosopher might play a role. It is delusory both in that it portrays the actual world and the role of philosophers within it as vastly more admirable than is warranted, and in that it fails to acknowledge the limits it imposes on possible social change, and on the philosopher's relationship to that change, as the politically loaded interventions that they are.

III. CONCLUSION

I've left it slightly ambiguous whether, in describing the image that political philosophers have of themselves and their place in politics, I'm describing what they think their role actually *is*, or what they would *like it to be*. But this reflects my sense that, in this case, there really isn't much of a gap. Political philosophers seem to produce the 'trickle-down' model of philosophy and real politics as *both* a more or less realistic representation of how political philosophers affect politics *and also* as a worthy contribution for them to make. And this gives us a clue as to the *function* of the reflections political philosophers offer as to their *own* 'function'—since the function of those reflections, it seems, cannot be either to represent reality or to encourage any drastic change in professional practice. What actually seems to be going on, I suggest, is a piece of ritualized theatre: an exercise through which political philosophers try to assuage their own and others' worries as to whether there is ultimately any more practical point in doing political philosophy than in doing (for example) formal logic. They ask themselves a rhetorical question:

'Can political philosophy make a difference?' And then, with a sigh of relief, they answer: 'Yes! . . . But only very slowly, only in conjunction with others, only within certain limits, only *a little bit*.' The main point of the exercise: to reconcile political philosophers to their task. The self-image we've encountered attributes to that task a kind of 'modesty to be proud of'—not insignificance or shameful impotence, but a realistic and dutiful appreciation of what is appropriate and realistically possible. As such, it resembles a kind of 'theodicy' for political philosophers (however small . . .): that is to say, it represents their attempt to reconcile themselves with what they do, by giving an account of the purpose and benefits of that activity. [30]

On the face of it, it's not clear that there is anything wrong with this project. Isn't this exactly what we should ask of the study of the 'methodology of political philosophy': that is, an effort, on the part of political philosophers, to reflect on what they are doing and to seek to justify it, rather than merely assuming their approach to be the right and natural one? In a sense, yes. But what I've argued is that the usual efforts of political philosophers *fail* as proper reflection and justification, instead amounting to a lazy and self-serving reaffirmation of their existing position—and of the political order for which, in my view, their activity *also* aims to provide a theodicy.

In addition, it's not clear that *reconciliation* to some way of doing political philosophy is ever quite what we should be aiming at. 'Reconciliation' seems to be something rather stronger than merely offering reasons for what we do, advantages of our way of proceeding, and so on. The kind of attempted theodicy I'm attributing to political philosophers is in fact more or less the *opposite* of the kind of reflexiveness that 'critical theory' aims to embody. The latter crucially incorporates a commitment to reflect critically and continually on itself, its origins, its assumptions and its effects, aiming to avoid various ideological trappings that would be attendant upon a less thoroughly self-conscious practice. That is quite different, it seems to me, from the aim of establishing that one's theory or approach is *satisfactory*. Plausibly, this can never be established—at least, not in any final and stable way. To be 'reconciled' to something is to have seen reason to rest content with it. That is one conceivable outcome of the attempt to stand back from the practice of political philosophy and to offer a justification for it. But it is neither the *only* conceivable outcome nor one that seems particularly appropriate—an attitude of constant uneasy vigilance is perhaps more in order.

We might also doubt whether reconciliation to the practice of political philosophy is even *possible*. Nietzsche thinks that the attempt on the part of human beings to offer a theodicy—if this means a philosophical theory that will satisfy us that life is, despite appearances, worth living—is doomed to failure. If life is not worth living, no *theory* can change this—although *art* may, at least temporarily, seduce us to continue to live. [31] Part of what makes the notion of a theodicy an apt one to apply to the self-image of political philosophers, I think, is that the formulation of this self-image seems to arise out of a felt dissatisfaction or sense of futility, an experienced lack of fit between what political philosophers *at some level* must feel is important and what they actually find themselves doing. Maybe political philosophers *know* at some level that there is something badly wrong. They know that political philosophy does not really make the kind of contribution that their model suggests. This may be what motivates the formulation of the self-image I've described, but it is also, perhaps, what ensures that this self-image can never function as a successful theodicy.

The suggestion I'm making here is ambiguous. I want only to expose the ambiguity now, rather than seeking to resolve it. One reading: political philosophers' practice is unsatisfactory, and they know it; no theory can satisfy them otherwise; to do so, on this view, would be to satisfy them of something *false*; while theories can, of course, sometimes persuade us of falsehoods, the present case is one in which the recipients of the theory could not help but realize ('on some level') that it is inadequate, because they cannot help but be aware ('on some level') of the inadequacy of the practice that such a theory would have to seek to legitimize. Note that it is compatible with this story to add that, for some hypothetical adequate or 'correct' practice of political philosophy, this correctness might not be immediately apparent to the practitioners, and so there might be scope for a successful theodicy to be given— *whereas*, the thought goes, when your *life* is worth living, you don't worry about whether or not it is worth living. A more radical reading, though, would be that the practice of political philosophy is not the kind of thing that can be given a theodicy, even in principle. The point is not that *if* the practice of political philosophy were fine, we would have no need to be shown this by a theory. It is more that there *is* no possible scenario in which the practice of political philosophy is fine: (political) philosophy, or anything that would be recognizable to us as this, is an inescapably problematic, scarred product of unacceptable social circumstances. There may, of course, be better and worse philosophical practices—ones which avoid with greater or lesser degrees of success the trappings to which other practices fall victim—but that is another matter.

Whatever you think of all this, the kind of story that political philosophers tell themselves doesn't look especially capable of reconciling anyone to anything. The prospect of making an incrementally small, 'unsexy' contribution to a project, the promised benefits of which we cannot expect to live to see, is not exactly cheering. One reason for that may be just that we are not persuaded of the worth of the project to which we are supposed to be contributing. After all, the achievement of the vast majority of scientists[32] might be viewed on the incremental-contribution-to-human-knowledge model, and it is not obvious that there is anything regrettable about that, nor that it undermines the value of those contributions.[33] So maybe the ineffectiveness of the small and unsexy theodicy is due not just to its smallness and lack of appeal, but also to the fact that philosophers partly recognize its delusional character in their own case. But there is more to it than that, I think. One of the acknowledged tendencies of the capitalist form of society is to breed a certain kind of competitiveness and ambition in its citizens, a drive to innovate and to 'stand out'. Capitalist society has to carve out a valued role for the *entrepreneur*, and as capitalism develops, it exhibits a growing and self-legitimizing tendency to paint *everyone* as a potential tycoon. Late capitalism may be seen as extending the entrepreneurial mentality to more and more domains of life: going out on the pull is a ('meat-')market; looking for something that we can bear to do with our lives—or just for a means of subsistence—means becoming a 'walking CV' on a job market;[34] making and retaining friends, even as an adult, apparently means having BT wireless internet access to the ready so that everyone can watch the game without glitches.[35] The sickening acme of this is perhaps the advert which shows a father being called into the living room by his two children, who inform him that they are making him redundant (which could have been avoided, the advert implies, if he had bought them a Thompson holiday).[36] Every area of life becomes a matter of 'standing out', 'getting noticed', being a 'big personality', and the appetite for fame and glory is relentlessly whipped up by advertisers in order to get people to buy things which they believe will get them the kind of attention they crave. A dreary Protestant work ethic does not sit particularly well with this—nor, of course, does the reality of life for the vast majority of people. The present point, however, is just that contemporary political philosophers, being products of this late capitalist context like everyone else, are likely to struggle to be able to find the small and unsexy theodicy they craft for themselves either inspiring or entirely satisfactory. At best, that story may function as a partial and temporary analgesic for their occasional bouts of angst and self-doubt.

An application of a more general thought of Adorno's seems appropriate here: so long as political philosophers are sufficiently uncomfortable with their practice to be moved to maintain an illusory self-image (which cannot fully salve this discomfort), there remains—in the gap that is maintained between self-image and reality—a glimmer of hope.[37] It's questionable how uplifting that thought ought to be, though. My instinct is that both Adorno's original point and my partial application of it here should be read negatively—as describing what it would mean for the malevolent phenomenon or process in question to complete itself—rather than as any kind of consolation story, still less a theodicy (considered as which it would be pretty pathetic). In that case, phrasing things in terms of 'hope' is probably a mistake.

Whatever view we take of the origin and prospects of the 'small and unsexy' theodicy, it is clear that the realm of reflection on the role and purpose of political philosophy in the real world cannot be held up as one in which the first-order discipline is made the object of fearless critical scrutiny. The upshot of this chapter and the previous one is that where political philosophers have made a conscious decision to reflect on methodological questions, this has probably made things worse rather than better. Here, the split between first-order and methodological has hardened into a division between disciplines (or subdisciplines, depending on how you look at it): there is political philosophy, and then there is the *methodology* of political philosophy; and if political philosophy is suspect in its informal methodological commitments, what this shows is that it needs an injection of wisdom from the realm of formal methodological reflection. However, far from overcoming the problem, this structure might be expected to compound it by transforming the problematic split into a more rigid division of labour, time and personnel. Moreover, the kind of content that is found within the sphere of formal 'methodology' is perhaps even *worse*—more crudely objectionable, or just more hopelessly confused—than that which is characteristic of the first-order discipline.[38] The realm of 'methodology' tends to be treated as a kind of political philosophers' vomitorium:[39] a space for them to purge themselves of the unwholesome residue of their day job before continuing to gorge themselves on their usual fare. Perhaps there is also an element of the behaviour of the British on a foreign holiday, where whatever minimal standards of decorum and dignity the revellers might generally possess fly out of the window in a haze of cathartic release and arrogant entitlement. The realm

of the formal methodology of political philosophy emerges not as one providing some much-needed critical distance on first-order practice, but rather
as a sphere in which the dominant framework remains largely unchallenged,
and the kinds of dodgy manoeuvres catalogued in the first four chapters of
this book are repeated and entrenched.

NOTES

1. Adorno (2005 [1969]; p. 5).
2. Dostoevsky (2008 [1864]; p. 18).
3. This view of political philosophy has affinities with a view in the philosophy of language emphasizing the 'performative' dimension of speech (see Austin [1962]). As G. J.
Warnock (1973; pp. 69–70) rather tortuously puts it: 'We have to consider, then, first, and if so
when and why, to say something is to do something, in a sense, if there is one, in which to say
something is not always, or even often, to do something, but is so only sometimes, in special
cases.' Cf. also my discussion in chapter 4 of this book.
4. McDermott (2008; p. 28).
5. Swift and White talk about 'political theorists', others in the same volume talk about
'political philosophy'. I won't observe any distinction here.
6. Swift and White (2008; p. 65).
7. 'You see, that's why I really work like a dog and I worked like a dog all my life. I am
not interested in the academic status of what I am doing because my problem is my own
transformation. That's the reason also why, when people say, "Well, you thought this a few
years ago and now you say something else," my answer is, [*Laughter*] "Well, do you think I
have worked like that all those years to say the same thing and not to be changed?"' See 'The
Minimalist Self' in Foucault (1988; p. 14); cf. also Foucault (2002; p. 19).
8. Although not peculiar to political philosophers—or even to philosophers in general—
this is a tendency which must be regarded as *political* to the extent that it is a function of
changes in the way in which academic institutions are internally and externally regulated.
9. I turn to consider this notion of 'ideological explanation' more fully in the conclusion.
10. For example, McDermott: 'In philosophy, as in most intellectual endeavours, progress
depends in part upon a successful division of labour' (2008; p. 15); similarly, Swift and White
call for 'a collaborative division of labour, in which the political theorist has a fundamental, but
precise, role to play' (2008; p. 50).
11. Swift and White build on this view by recommending that political theorists ' . . . look
carefully at what [social scientists] do—*the way concepts are constructed, the particular things
they choose to observe or measure—and one will usually find a host of more specific, often
unconscious, assumptions about what precisely is interesting or significant about their work*'
(2008; p. 61; my emphasis). What is interesting about this is that it is precisely this insight that I
have been arguing should apply to the critical examination of political philosophy, but is in fact
rarely appreciated. Swift and White, in any case, do not transfer the insight from the one
context to the other.
12. McDermott (2008; p. 11). It may also be seen as appropriate for political philosophers to
share their portion of the load among themselves. For example: 'Our "division of labour"
perspective suggests that there is a place for both [ideal and non-ideal theory].' (Swift and
White [2008; p. 60]). This is an instance of a common tendency to offer a quick solution to

worries about whether to do philosophy this way or that, by deciding that in the end everything complements everything else marvellously. The problem with that is that in some cases (such as, e.g., Mills [2005]) an approach to philosophy really is being *opposed*, and it is all too easy to respond to such opposition by ostensibly accepting its content while denying that it is really *opposed* (the familiar 'I think we're really agreeing with each other'), and to pass this off as a *concession* to the opposing view when it is in fact a rejection of it.

13. Swift and White (2008; p. 68). Odd, perhaps, that Swift and White see no need to provide any support for this, given that they have only just finished lamenting another philosopher's failure to back up what seems like a considerably less risky empirical claim—namely that it is unlikely to do wonders for the self-esteem of the unemployed to withhold their benefits, pending proof that they have tried and repeatedly failed to find work. Swift and White's assertion derives some protection, however, from the way in which they conceive of political philosophy, that is, as all about 'conceptual analysis and nice moral distinctions' (delicate work, not suited to dirty or calloused hands). If we go along with that, we are disabled from pointing to some of the figures who might otherwise have served as obvious counterexamples—that is, people like Marx and Lenin, who (whatever one thinks of them) show that it is possible to be not *only* a political philosopher, but simultaneously a social scientist and political presence. We can imagine what sort of face Marx might have pulled at the mention of 'nice moral distinctions'.

14. In this respect, the model is reminiscent of Talcott Parsons's 'functionalist' sociology, according to which individual persons and institutions stand to society at large as the cogs in a smoothly operating machine—see Parsons (1952), cf. Merton (1949). 'We are all in it together' has become a slogan of so-called 'austerity politics', following the financial crises of the early years of the twenty-first century.

15. We can, of course, envisage a network of radical sociologists and political theorists and political movements, held together by some set of common goals and by the rejection of certain mainstream political and academic trends, but there is no indication that this is what the theorists quoted above have in mind. They do nothing to disavow the impression that what is envisaged is a division of labour between political philosophers *in general* (and, by extension, between political philosophers, social scientists and politicians).

16. It's significant that Adam Swift's popular 2006 introduction to political philosophy is subtitled 'A Beginners' Guide for Students *and Politicians*' (my emphasis).

17. Swift and White (2008; p. 67).

18. For example, Wolff (2009), Swift and White (2008; pp. 55–56) and cf. William Galston's role in the Clinton administration. We might also think of Philip Pettit's well-known influence on Zapatero's government in Spain (which, at the time of writing, has been facing protests in every major city).

19. See, for example, Swift and White (2008; p. 67).

20. See Swift and White (2008; p. 63).

21. See, for example, Swift and White (2008; p. 63): 'the theorist is only going to be a useful guide to the practising politician if she is willing to accept the constraints within which contemporary politics operates'. See also pages 49, 56 and 66 of the same and cf. Wolff (2009).

22. For example, Swift and White (2008; p. 66): 'Since the political theorist does not want to set herself up as a philosopher king, she must accept that the only legitimate way for anybody's views about principles or policy to be put into practice is through the dirty and messy business of politics.'

23. To hark back to my comments towards the end of my discussion of Rawlsian 'reasonableness' in chapter 2—about the creepy authoritarianism of the stance which political philosophers sometimes seem to adopt towards citizens—we might envisage this whole trickling-down

process as taking place inside a giant cage, with political-philosophical wisdom flowing into the government and intelligentsia and down to the people in the form of competing cage-improvement plans, designs and proposed accessories (exercise wheels and the like): in what is by far the larger stream, we find *Design 1: 'Justice as Fairness'*, *Design 2: 'Responsibility-Sensitive Egalitarianism'*, *Design 3: 'Autonomy-Minded Liberalism'*, and so on; and then in the direct 'popular philosophy' trickle, *'Consolations of the Cage'*, *'How to Manage Middle-Class Angst in the Cage'*, and so on.

24. I have in mind here, in particular, strategies which make use of relatively new technology, for example, certain uses of the Internet—Wikileaks and so on.

25. Of course, it is also true that many systems will contain a degree of in-built protection against being changed.

26. This general approach can be made fathomable only if we accept a kind of construal of 'real politics' like that employed by Swift and White, who explain it as 'the kind [of politics] that [we] read about in the newspapers and that get debated at election times' (2008; p. 49). To judge by what is most prominent in the U.K. media at the time of writing, 'real politics' must therefore mean the MPs' expenses scandal; the question of whether the Prime Minister is depressed and/or dyslexic; and whether the troops have enough helicopters (the answer being 'no', because they can never have enough to enable them to blow up Afghan civilians from a position of complete safety). The question of the role that political philosophy can play in 'real politics' would not have seemed so interesting in the first place—not to all of us, anyway—if it were made clear from the outset that 'real politics' meant this sort of thing.

27. Grice (1975)—cf. fn. 40 above (chapter 5).

28. As I mentioned in chapter 1 (fn. 30), some have tried to argue that Rawlsian political philosophy could be a useful source of guidance for the 'Occupy' movement.

29. 'Enlightenment, understood in the widest sense as the advance of thought, has always aimed at liberating human beings from fear and installing them as masters. Yet the wholly enlightened earth is radiant with triumphant calamity'—Adorno and Horkheimer (2002; p. 1).

30. Hence the roots of the term 'theodicy' in the idea of 'the trial of God': what is at issue is whether the world is basically ordered in a way which can be shown to be acceptable; to show this—and thus to exonerate God—is to give a theodicy.

31. Nietzsche (1993). We might add—although Nietzsche doesn't—that under circumstances in which life *would* be worth living, we wouldn't need a theory to tell us so.

32. At least, during what Kuhn (1996) calls periods of 'normal science', which make up the larger part of history.

33. In Ian McEwan's 1997 novel *Enduring Love*, the science writer protagonist, Joe, voices regret at his exclusion from what he sees—though with a clearly detectable touch of boredom and reluctance—as the worthier enterprise of academic science: 'I should have been out there myself carrying my own atomic increment to the mountain of human knowledge.'

34. See Nina Power (2009); see also Comité invisible (2007).

35. This is a reference to an advert, popular at the time of writing the first draft of this chapter, but now already a distant memory—which just goes to illustrate the point that the particular manifestations of the tendency I'm talking about here are constantly shifting (while the tendency itself remains and grows in strength).

36. Or whatever the company is.

37. Adorno's point, as expressed at the beginning of the dedication of *Minima Moralia* (1974; p. 15), is actually a different and deeper one: Life has become no more than an 'ephemeral appearance' of production—'Means and ends are inverted'; and insofar as there is hope at all, it lies in the 'dim awareness of this perverse *quid pro quo*', the 'ideology that conceals the fact that there is life no longer'; 'Should the appearance of life, which the sphere of consump-

tion itself defends for such bad reasons, be once entirely effaced, then the monstrosity of absolute production will triumph.'

38. This might be seen as an outrageous, unsupported insult on my part. So it is, but it's interesting to note that unsupported *praise* is generally allowed to pass without so much as a raised eyebrow (see the introduction to chapter 2 above).

39. It is apparently a myth that the Romans would make use of a special room called a '*vomitorium*', in which they could throw up in order to free up some space for further feasting (although they did have *vomitoria*: channels behind or below the seats of an amphitheatre, through which crowds could exit). This is very disappointing—and goes to show that the *Horrible Histories* series cannot be trusted—but it hardly affects the present point.

Conclusion

By now, we've seen six case studies, their subject matter mingling the 'me-thodological' with the 'first-order' political-philosophical. I've aimed to cover quite a wide stretch of ground. In the first half of the book, I focused on cases likely to be recognized as belonging straightforwardly to the current status quo in political philosophy: I looked at the way in which the decks are cleared to leave room only for liberalism; I looked at the later Rawls's use of the categories of 'reasonable' and 'unreasonable' to define legitimate dissent out of existence; and I looked at the way in which the value of 'charity' acts so as to police dissent at the level of philosophical discussion, and to outlaw what I called 'deep dissent' against Rawls in particular. But in the second part of the book, I turned to the apparent exceptions: a discussion which begins when feminist philosophers challenge traditional liberal attitudes to pornography and speech; the 'realist' critique of liberal 'ideal theory'; and an effort among political philosophers to engage in self-reflection and to give an account of their place and purpose in the world.

The results have been somewhat troubling, and would seem so even (or perhaps especially) from the perspective of someone who affirms the dominant framework I've identified; that is, someone who endorses liberal-capitalist politics and an analytic approach centred on the design of 'just institutions', perhaps within the context of 'ideal theory'. It is not only that alternatives to this framework have been in short supply. What has been most striking is a sense that dissent has been kept at bay through philosophically disreputable moves. In several cases, I argued, political content relevant to a given dispute was already implicit in an argument or concept presented as a neutral arbitrator. Frequently, this took the form of an artificial split between the 'political' and the 'methodological'—as if we can generally agree, regardless of our politics, on what counts as 'charitable', 'constructive', or 'reasonable'. So on top of a failure of pluralism—there is less *diversity* in this discipline than many of its practitioners would claim—it seems there is also a failure of transparency (surely an 'analytic' virtue par excellence). Illusions of neutrality or independence are, in the first place, illusions. And if that wasn't bad enough, the analyses presented here have given no indication that the illusions in question are merely incidental ones—that is, inevitable human errors which could easily be rectified. On the contrary, my suggestion has been that they are widespread and systematic, and that they work consistently to the benefit of the broadly liberal-capitalist mode of analytic political philosophy that is currently dominant in (at least) the Anglophone world. In other words, what we have seen looks more like corruption than simple incompetence. But how can that be? Is it a conspiracy? Why would any such conspiracy take hold within a domain of supposedly free and independent intellectual inquiry?

I. PARADIGMS AND PEACOCKS

At this point, there are a range of possible reactions, and the purpose of this conclusion is to say something about the major ones, before advancing a verdict of my own. The first possibility I want to mention is the most subtle. The suggestion is that, contrary to my reaction, there is nothing really sinister going on here: what I have hit upon is not a critique, as such, but a general and well-known thesis (albeit a controversial one) about the structure of claims in political theory.

I have claimed, in effect, that everything is political, including the various methodological devices which political philosophers use to support their positions. Unless I want to suggest that there is, somewhere, some stock of truly politically neutral concepts and values which may be drawn upon instead—in which case, where are they?—then my claim is a very general one indeed, one which applies not only to political philosophy in its dominant mode, but to political theory much more broadly (including, of course, everything that I myself say about politics and political philosophy). The claim seems to mean that there can never be any absolutely independent justification for anything in this area. Either that is a criticism of claims about politics, or it is not (I would be inclined to say that it is not). But either way, it is not a criticism of any particular *mode* of political philosophy, dominant or otherwise.

The immediate response to this is fairly obvious. While I may be committed to the general thesis identified above, a thesis about the structure of claims in this area, that thesis itself was never meant to be a criticism. The critical force of what I have said lies elsewhere, in the specific analyses of my case studies—exemplary debates and arguments drawn from the context of mainstream political philosophy. But this cannot be the last word: particularly given the critical emphasis I have placed on failures of transparency and self-awareness in my object of study, it is worth reflecting a little on the nature and status of my own criticisms. The first thing to acknowledge is that I cannot present those criticisms as exceptions to my own rule: in the sense in which everything is political, those criticisms, too, will be political—in their force and in their underlying presuppositions. That need not be a problem. If the general thesis about the structure of political claims applies to itself, it seems to me, this only shows that it is not falsified as a general thesis. Its self-application can be interpreted as a *reductio* only if we take the non-independence of political claims—that is, the absence of a politically neutral 'foundation' on which they may be rested—as invalidating them: in that case, by the same logic, the thesis which invalidates them is also invalidated, generating an annoying paradox—that is, it is invalid, qua politically non-neutral, to say that claims in political philosophy are non-neutral. But I see no reason for accepting the idea that claims must either be justified by appeal to some independent foundation or not at all. Why assume any such thing? There are plenty of stories we can tell about justification, other than the 'foundationalist' one. I'll say something more about those stories shortly. Before that, though, there is still a worry to address, and this is the worry that my criticisms might, after all—despite my statement to the contrary—boil down to the general thesis just mentioned. I'll now try to set out that worry as clearly as possible.

I have tended to criticize the dominant mode of political philosophy 'internally', for instance by alleging that it 'begs the question' against its opponents, or that it applies 'double standards'—the sorts of things that analytic philosophers, of all people, are not supposed to do. But if the structure of claims in political philosophy is as I suggest, then it seems that these categories—these cardinal sins, from the point of view of the analytic approach—must be recast. What does it mean to apply a 'double standard', for example? The obvious answer is that it is to judge one thing by one principle, and another by another—perhaps in order to get an antecedently desired result. To apply double standards is to cheat in order to win. But a cursory look at the way we actually argue casts this idea into doubt. We all apply different standards to different things, all the time. If you tell me that you heard the voice of God, I will be reluctant to accept this as evidence of God's existence; but if you tell me that our mutual friend has a sister, on the basis that you met her last week, then I am unlikely to question you. I interpret different pieces of sensory information, and different reports of sensory experiences, *differently*, in accordance with my background view as to what kind of place the world is. And in many cases, there seems to be nothing objectionable about this kind of practice. If there is a sin called 'applying a double standard', then, it must be something else. Now take the idea of 'begging the question'—what does *this* mean? Again, there is an easy answer, but it won't get us very far. There is general agreement among philosophers that 'begging the question' refers to an informal fallacy, a species of circular argument, which involves presupposing what you are supposed to be arguing for in the course of arguing for it.[1]

But at second glance, things are not so straightforward. As with the notion of a 'double standard'—as more famously with that of 'pornography'—we often think that we know a question-begging argument when we see one. But in fact, it is not at all obvious what it means for an argument to 'presuppose' or 'contain' its conclusion in the relevant (pejorative) sense. Is it that the argument's premises imply the conclusion, so that if we believe them then we should believe the conclusion too? That would seem only to mean that the argument *works*—hardly a defect.[2] Alternatively, we might follow the suggestion of one commentator, that an argument is question begging if directed to someone who 'would only believe the premise if he already believed the conclusion.'[3] But take the example just given, where someone presents me with the 'evidence' that she hears the voice of God. Does she beg the question against me? Not being a believer, I am not going to accept the premise. Perhaps it is also true to say that I would only accept it if I already believed in God—although perhaps not: who knows what I might be capable of believing, on occasion, depending on my mood or prior thoughts and experiences? We might try replacing the 'would' with a 'should': the point is that I have no *reason* to accept the premise, unless I already accept the conclusion. We might feel more confident in saying *this* about my position relative to a Christian interlocutor—although we should be prepared for her to disagree. Even so, it might seem a bit harsh to say that she has 'begged the question' against me. And what about the case where you are trying to convince me that our friend has a sister (against my prior firmly held opinion that he is an only child)? 'I met her last week', you say, and I (more or less reluctantly) accept that I must have been mistaken; but it seems pretty clear that I should not (and cannot) believe that you have met our friend's sister unless I believe that he has one. So have you begged the question against me? It would seem perverse to accuse you of that. The action must be in the 'already': I don't have to believe *already* that our friend has a sister, in order to have reason to accept the premise that you have seen her (although I will certainly accept the conclusion once I've accepted the premise—in fact, it seems like I'll need to swallow both simultaneously). This, however, is plausible only against a certain background. It matters, for example, that you don't have a history of being a pathological liar. If the Christian, in my other example, is begging the question, it must then be because the premise she is asking me to accept is not one which I have a reason to accept, given my background view (or, perhaps, given the sort of background view which she may reasonably attribute to me).

The problem here is not just that categories like 'question begging' and 'double standard' will turn out, on closer inspection, to make sense only relative to certain background commitments—so that they cannot be expected to act as neutral arbitrators in political disagreements. We were prepared for that. The more worrying thought is that *everything* may turn out to be question begging, or guilty of the application of double standards. In that case, these very categories may collapse. Even if we can continue to use them, the worry is that my accusations of 'question begging' (etc.) will turn out only to hold for the sense of that term which applies to everything—which would seem to cancel any force they might have *as criticisms*. Worse: if that is right, then it looks as though I have been doing the same sort of thing I accuse others of doing—and in the very process of making the accusation: that is, I have been identifying a broad and innocuous sense of terms like 'question begging' with a narrower, pejorative one (carrying undisclosed and possibly controversial political content),[4] and have been trading on the conflation in order to generate the impression that something sinister is going on.

But why would we be led to the conclusion that everything is question begging? The basic thought, I think, is this: the way in which we argue and assess arguments and evidence, and the standards and principles we use to do so, cannot be separated from the views—normative, descriptive or some intermingling of both—that we hold about the world. For example: being a religious believer might motivate the interpretation of certain strange phenomena as supernatural, which from a naturalistic worldview would be interpreted in some other way or dismissed; believing that you are my friend and would not lie to me will influence how I interpret your testimony; being a Marxist may motivate the attachment of a different significance to a piece of 'received wisdom' than a liberal or a self-defined 'apolitical person' would attach. This much, I hope, is obvious. But in that case, it looks as though there is a sense in which 'question begging' is both inevitable and legitimate.

The way in which we argue and evaluate the arguments of others will always be a function of the background views against which we are working. On the hypothesis that there is a deity of a certain (anthropomorphic) kind, a disembodied voice may be interpreted as the voice of God. From the point of view of someone who subscribes to something like the Marxist theory of history, it will make sense to expect the sphere of ideas to arrange itself so as to protect the material interests embedded in the status quo at any given point—and so it will make sense at least to consider an 'ideological' explanation as a possible alternative to the hypothesis that a given consensus reflects the truth. In this sense, the Marxist who performs an 'ideology critique' of a piece of liberal doctrine 'begs the question' against the liberal, who cannot be assumed to believe that ideas shape themselves according to dominant interests. And yet there doesn't seem to be anything obviously disreputable about pointing out that a certain idea, if believed, would be very convenient for certain powerful groups (the rich, the whites, the men . . .), and that this generates an alternative explanation of its being believed. Perhaps something similar might be claimed on behalf of the liberal who attaches a different significance to the failure of nominally socialist regimes than she attaches to the crimes of liberal states: she is working against the background of a certain (complex) hypothesis about the world—as is the socialist who takes the human disasters of liberal capitalism as reason to abandon the latter, without also taking Stalinism to necessitate the abandonment of socialism.

At this point, a quasi-Kuhnian analysis seems to beckon: we might see spheres of discourse such as political philosophy as constituted by rival 'paradigms', self-sustaining and wholly or partially incommensurable bodies of thought and practice, much like those whose succession Kuhn saw as constituting the history of science.[5] We should be wary of getting too carried away with this idea: first, because of the obvious dissimilarities between political thought and the natural sciences (which may make it inappropriate to transfer an account neatly from one context to the other); second, because the Kuh-nian conceptual arsenal is hardly unproblematic—the notion of a 'paradigm' is particularly notorious for its ambiguity.[6] In some ways, I think, we might do better to take our inspiration from Quine, and emphasize above all the web-like interconnectedness of our commitments—including, crucially, the interconnectedness of epistemological tenets with our other views as to the nature of the world. But still, the Kuhnian comparison can be instructive, as far as it goes. Like a Kuhnian paradigm, the dominant mode of political philosophy on which this book has focused is a loose collection of tenets, practices, themes and stock examples; it is practiced by a particular commu-nity of academics, who are introduced to their discipline much as science students are introduced to theirs—not so much through a free-wheeling dis-cussion of the nature, limits and presuppositions of that discipline, but through 'exemplars' and 'puzzles' (in the case of political philosophy, these might include the question of whether 'we' can reconcile 'liberal tolerance' of minority cultures with the imperative to promote women's autonomy and equality, the case of the work-shy 'Malibu surfer', Dworkin's 'clamshell auction', and of course, Rawls's device of the 'Original Position'). And on my account of political philosophy, as in the Kuhnian account of science, there is no completely 'paradigm-neutral' standpoint or set of materials from which we might construct the case for one approach over another.

Both the analogy and the disanalogy between the view of political philos-ophy implied here and the Kuhnian account of science may be of use, I want to suggest now, in responding to the worry that motivated the present discus-sion. That worry, to recall, was that by abandoning the idea of a neutral foundation for political-philosophical claims, I render my own critiques—which frequently appealed to notions such as 'question begging' and 'double standards'—uninteresting and impotent: this is just how paradigms work. The first part of the reply to this, I think, is just an extension of the most appropriate understanding of Kuhnian philosophy of science. Whatever Kuhn is doing, he is *not* trying to argue that, in science, anything goes—that is, that any claim or argument is as good as any other, or even that any paradigm is as good as any other. He is not even abandoning the idea of (degrees of) *truth*—only a particular story that is told as to what it *means* to say that scientific theories are 'true', namely the traditional account which depicts those theories as approximating ever more closely to the mind-inde-pendent reality of the world (a story which Kuhn sometimes indicates with the uppercase: 'Truth'). Clearly, there are better and worse examples of scientific practice, as judged relative to the standards of any particular para-digm—standards which are complex and sometimes partially indeterminate, but not nonexistent or empty. And there can also, I would argue—although this is admittedly more controversial as a reading of Kuhn's account—be better or worse *paradigms* (and better or worse ways of *deciding between* competing paradigms). Paradigm choice is complex, a matter of weighing sets of 'pros' and 'cons'—where there is no single measure which can give us a determinate answer as to which package is better 'overall'. Kuhn some-times describes it as 'non-rational'—at least, relative to the sort of rationality other more conventional accounts might lead us to expect from the sciences, and to the sort of rationality that governs inferences and decisions within 'normal science' (that is, scientific activity conducted within an established paradigm). But he denies that it is *irr*ational, in the sense of actively violating those narrow forms of rationality, and nor does he deny that it could be 'rational' in *some* sense of the term.

To return now to the case of political philosophy, I want to say that there is plenty of room, in my account, for a *pejorative* version of a notion like that of 'question begging', whether within or across 'paradigms'. Nothing that has been said here excludes our making sense of various informal fallacies that might be committed within the general structure I've posited, and which we can recognize as distinct from being 'just the way that structure works'. But we should not expect a neat definition of what, exactly, such a fallacy is, or how to tell when it is being committed. This should not be seen as a cost of adopting a quasi-Kuhnian approach which emphasizes the 'theory-ladenness' of data, however, since no such neat definition of 'question begging' was on the cards in any case. Begging the question, we can all agree, must be a matter of presupposing something relevant to the question *in the wrong kind of way*—but what way is that? Most of those contributing to the analytic literature on question begging—a slightly obscure field, but one which does exist, I discovered—seem to agree that the answer must be a contextualist and pragmatic one: the fallacy is one which takes place within what is at least intended to be an 'epistemically serious argument' (whatever that is),[7] and which violates certain legitimate goals and expectations of the exchange which provide the context of the argument (whatever those are), in such a way as to produce a pragmatic failure of 'probative function', which 'blocks the argument from fulfilling or contributing to the goals of dialogue in which the arguer is supposed to be engaged'.[8] But what are the legitimate goals and expectations of an argumentative exchange, and what counts as failing to fulfil them? In political disagreements, at least, it looks as though this question, too, cannot avoid being a political one. But we already suspected that. The point now is just that the kind of account I've suggested, within what might be described as the 'philosophy of political philosophy', is not so inhospitable to the use of concepts like 'question begging', 'double standards' or 'circularity' as critical categories that my own criticisms, which sometimes appeal to them, are undermined.[9] Whether they ultimate *succeed* is a different question, and one which (obviously) depends on what we decide are proper criteria for success in political-philosophical argument. If we insist on a politically-neutral grounding, then my view is that they will fail (but that so will everything else). An alternative would be to adopt the kind of pragmatic, 'interest-relative' account that Kuhn sometimes applies to science. On this broad account, arguments, claims and positions in political philosophy are successful (and perhaps also to be regarded as *true*) to the extent that they serve certain relevant *interests* we have. In the case of science, the simplest answer to the question 'Which interests?' is: our interests in explaining and predicting the world. In the case of political philosophy, the answer must be slightly different. Prediction, often, seems less to the point—although it clearly played a key role for political theorists like Marx as (in a different way) for liberals thinkers like Daniel Bell and Francis Fukuyama.[10] *Explaining* the world seems a relevant and central end, although the 'world' to be explained will be construed differently: a world of human interactions and organizations and power relations, above all, rather than a world of atoms or planets or organisms (though these things cannot be completely absent from the 'world' of politics). *Prescribing* and *evaluating*, too, have a role in political theory for which there is no straightforward counterpart in science.

My criticisms, like any others, succeed to the extent that they help us to make sense of the relevant aspects of the world in the relevant way—however necessarily vague that may be—and can ultimately be judged only against our attempts to do that. Since what have been presented here are primarily *negative* criticisms of a certain dominant mode (or 'paradigm') of political philosophy, their criterion for success is whether they make that mode of political philosophy make *less* sense—whether, in other words, they make sense of its *not* making sense of the world. This dominant liberal 'paradigm' is a bit like a peacock, performing its courtship display: in political philosophy, it makes a lot of noise and monopolizes onlookers' attention and field of vision. What I've tried to do in this book is to shine an unforgiving light on this performance, to look behind the feathers and to make manifest the difficulty in finding anything to match the promise of fertility. This can never be done from a position of total paradigm-independence—although it should be noted that this is not the same as admitting that my criticisms are made from within a well-defined paradigm of my own (it's not clear to me what that would be)—but this is not to say that it cannot be done at all. [11]

My critique succeeds, then, to the extent that it makes political philosophy in its dominant mode look less attractive, more suspicious than seductive—and there is little more that can be said, on a general level, than that. But there is one important point remaining to be raised, and this is where the disanalogy between political philosophy and natural science comes into its own. An important element of the critique presented in this book has been to allege a kind of *duplicity*: things are not as they are presented as being—in particular, political content and presuppositions are systematically disguised. A possible reaction to this, though, would be to attempt a retort of the same basic type as I considered above: this is just how paradigms (or bodies of belief and practice) work; and there is nothing wrong with that. It may be, for example, that the practitioners of the natural sciences typically labour under illusions as to the kind of activity they are engaged in. Most would not accept a Kuhnian account. But for Kuhn, at least, this is not a problem, either for his account or for the fortunes of science itself: any illusions which scientists may have on this score need not prevent them from being good scientists, that is, from serving the characteristic interests of explanation and prediction; and in fact, it may be the case that certain illusions are helpful or even necessary for the fulfilment of those ends. In the case of the natural sciences, many would argue that these disciplines are 'working' in many cases, relative to ends we would regard as appropriate to them. [12] But it seems difficult to uphold an analogous claim in the case of political philosophy. The idea would be to argue that, while political philosophy might present a false image of itself, this doesn't mean it's not contributing to our understanding of things—and if, as seems to me to be the case, its illusions are not ones which could simply be corrected (perhaps by some kind of 'disclaimer') without this having knock-on effects as regards the way in which the discipline is practiced, perhaps this just shows that these illusions are benign and productive ones. But since political philosophy doesn't yield such tangible benefits as the relief of physical pain or the design of stereos, there is no obvious reason why we should accept this. There are scarcely any ends relative to which political philosophy can uncontroversially be said to be 'working'. It is still churning out books and research programmes and a limited number of jobs, certainly. But I take it that we were looking for something beyond that. Does political philosophy, in its dominant mode, help to transform the world for the better? Does it help us to understand it better? The answer implied by the arguments of this book is a resounding 'no'. But in any case, nobody can pretend that these issues are uncontroversial ones. Rather, they are exactly the issues we are trying to get straight. What is clear is that we cannot argue for the conclusion that political philosophy is 'working', against a set of criticisms that point to its apparent circularity and duplicity and other false moves, by reiterating that it is 'working'—so that none of this apparent bad practice matters. That *is* begging the question.

From this point on, I will work on the assumption that my criticisms are accepted as showing some cause for concern. There is still a good deal of room for disagreement as to what, exactly, has gone wrong. The answer I ultimately want to press, in the next section, emphasizes that the illusions and distortions I've identified in mainstream political philosophy do have functions and do serve certain interests—just not the productive or benign ones often claimed. These functions and interests, I want to suggest, provide the best explanation for the kinds of systematic distortion charted in the course of this book. But since explanations of this kind are currently suffering from something of an image problem, I will have my work cut out. It seems to me, however, that no other available explanation properly accounts for the phenomena. My approach will therefore be to argue that, in the words of the late Mrs. Thatcher, there really is no alternative.

II. WHO'S AFRAID OF THE THEORY OF IDEOLOGY?

Granted that there is a widespread problem in political philosophy, that arguments and concepts are systematically distorted in such a way as to inhibit dissent and deviation from the dominant way of doing things, how is this best to be explained? There are errors and bad arguments in any field, for sure, but what we have in front of us here is too endemic and also too *ordered* to be put down to simple human fallibility: why does the distortion always seem to favour the status quo? Why is it not more haphazard? One option would be to propose a conspiracy theory: political philosophers invested in the dominant liberal framework have made a conscious collective decision to develop and employ a series of obfuscatory devices, in order to safeguard that framework's dominance and deflect opposition. But I assume that nobody believes that. It is at this point that an idea which has so far mostly remained in the background of my discussion offers to come into its own. This is the idea of 'ideology', or 'ideological false consciousness' (note that not all false consciousness is ideological).[13] The core of this idea is that of a particular kind of distortion to which our thought may be subject: a distortion which is explained by its function—in particular, the function of serving certain dominant interests. For Marx—with whom this idea is most strongly associated— the key instance of this phenomenon was the tendency of ideas to arrange themselves in the service of ruling class interests ('The ruling ideas of every epoch are the ideas of the ruling class').[14] But the idea is readily extended to any situation in which the formation of beliefs, attitudes or other facets of consciousness seems to be subservient to particular interests: for example, the belief that women are naturally better suited than men to be homemakers may be understood as a distortion of reality, and one which takes hold not because there is any particularly good evidence for it, but because it is convenient for men. The distortions in question may be local and specific (like the belief that women are naturally suited to be wives and mothers), or much broader (for instance, it might be claimed that the sphere of ideas *as a whole* distorts social reality in key ways). The function may be to serve the interests of a given group (e.g., men, or the ruling class), who occupy a position of material dominance within the social status quo. But in principle, we might also apply the central idea of 'functionally explained false consciousness'[15] at the level of an individual: when someone engages in 'wishful thinking', for example, it seems that her consciousness is shaped—typically in such a way as to distort reality—in accordance with the interest[16] that she has in believing the proposition in question.

It is in just this sort of situation, that is, a situation in which things seem to happen *as if* there were a conspiracy (but where we know that this isn't likely), that an ideological explanation may be applicable. What such an explanation does is account for the appearance without proposing anything so implausible as a secret coven of liberal political philosophers, consciously and cynically manipulating arguments so as to mislead us into letting their particular approach to political philosophy reign unchallenged. The explanation would involve claiming that concepts and arguments are shaped in the way that they are, and take hold or do not take hold, partly according to whether their being accepted will serve to reinforce or threaten the mode of political philosophy enshrined in the current status quo. But it would not claim that this happens because anybody consciously wonders, 'Now, what would secure the continued dominance of the dominant mode of political philosophy?', and then constructs concepts and arguments in the light of the answer. The process happens much more organically and unconsciously than that.

At this point, there are likely to be two main worries—one concerning the 'organically' and the other the 'unconsciously'. To begin with the latter: isn't it even more insulting to portray philosophers as dupes than it is to suggest that they are engaged in a conspiracy? I'm not so much interested in the question of whether it's worse to be a dupe or a conspirator—surely this question cannot be answered in the abstract—but in whether and in what sense an ideological explanation should be seen as 'insulting'. Whether a claim about an object, person or community is 'insulting'—at least, in any sense we should be sorry about—really depends on what the object of the claim is like. And recall that by now, I am working on the assumption that we agree that there is something systematically wrong with the way political philosophy is done. That might also be regarded as 'insulting', but assuming that it is correct, then what we are now trying to explain away is not something that looks particularly good—and so it is perhaps naïve to expect the explanation we eventually hit upon to be a flattering one. True, we may do well to abide by the principle of charity and pick an interpretation of events that maximizes their 'defensibility' within the 'constraints of plausible intent' (although in the light of the discussion in chapter 3, we should be ready for some controversy as to what would count as doing that). Assuming that conspiracy theories fail the test of plausibility, we are left with the question of whether an ideological explanation fails to maximize 'defensibility'. This, of course, will depend on what the other available options are, but in any case it's not clear to me why there should be anything particularly offensive about the suggestion that philosophers are subject to unconscious distortions of thought which occur in the service of certain ends. The reaction might be more understandable if we were singling them out from the rest of humanity. But the idea that certain of the distortions of thought to which we are subject can be functionally explained, including in terms of the interests they further, is a very generally applicable one—as witnessed by a whole range of phenomena from wishful thinking, to the power of advertising, to the power of love.

The second worry I mentioned concerns the idea that functionally explained false consciousness happens 'organically': this might seem to make it rather mysterious—*how*, exactly, does it happen? The suspicion here may be that a theory of ideology avoids being a conspiracy theory only by positing something even more implausible: in the present case, this would be a disembodied ogre called 'the dominant paradigm' (or something), which shapes our consciousness without our even being aware of it. But an ideological explanation need posit nothing of the sort. There doesn't have to be any particular *agent* who masterminds the phenomenon for which we seek to give a functional explanation.

Someone might, at this point, just press the question again: if there is no conspiracy, and no agent who instigates and coordinates the illusion, then how does it happen? There is nothing necessarily wrong with that question, but it should already be clear that there can be no simple or stable answer to it. If 'ideology' is understood as thinly as I understand it here—that is, as 'functionally explained false consciousness'—then *how it happens* will vary enormously, depending on the instance we are talking about. In some instances, we may remain unconvinced that the distortion in question is functionally explained (or that it is explained by the particular function that has been posited), and we may even be unable to see *how* the distortion in question could come to function in that way. And sometimes we will be right to be unconvinced. But this does not show that there is something inherently, unacceptably mysterious about the idea of functionally explained false consciousness per se. And in fact, as I already noted, we seem already to accept plenty of everyday instances of this phenomenon without much trouble at all—as, for example, when we diagnose something as 'wishful thinking', or as a 'convenient excuse'. Ok, in these cases, there does tend to be an easily identifiable agent whose interests are being served: the same individual who labours under the false consciousness or aims to produce it in others (although when this happens at a level that is not fully conscious, it may not be obvious who is 'doing' it). But it is not difficult to point to other cases, where we have little trouble with 'non-agential' explanations for phenomena (including phenomena having to do with features of *consciousness*). Think, for example, of the phenomenon of the 'vicious cycle'—something which may operate both at the level of an individual's consciousness (as in low self-esteem) as well as on a much larger scale (as with periods of hyperinflation, or 'panic buying' during fuel shortages). Or take fashion: at a certain point in the 1980s, the so-called 'mullet' was a popular hairstyle; this, we can now recognize, produced distortions of consciousness which temporarily made this hairstyle appear acceptable and even attractive; yet there was (I assume) no conspiracy that made this happen, and no agent who made it happen; this does not stop us from saying that people saw this hairstyle as attractive primarily *because* it was fashionable.

Now, admittedly, what the last few examples collectively show is only (a) that we don't always have a problem with functional explanations, and (b) that we don't always have a problem with *non-agential* explanations either. It might still be alleged that there is a problem with explanations which are *both* functional and non-agential at the same time. Functional explanations, after all, seem to be in some sense 'teleological': they refer to some end and explain the occurrence of a phenomenon in terms of its bringing that end about. And only agents, we may say, have ends. The fashion for the mullet is not an agent. Therefore, it cannot have ends. And, lo and behold, it does seem very strange to suggest that people found mullets attractive because it perpetuated the mullet fashion for them to do so—they found mullets attractive because of the fashion, certainly, but not because this preference would contribute to this fashion: the causal arrow here goes in only one direction. But there do seem to be plenty of cases—some of which now seem quite uncontroversial—where a distortion of consciousness may be functionally explained, without any suggestion that the distortion has been organized or orchestrated by any particular agent. Take some unambiguous example of a racist distortion: for example, the belief that black people are inferior in intellectual abilities and are therefore fit only to serve white people in various menial capacities (and that it is, in fact, in their own best interests to be made to do so, by force if necessary). An explanation of this distortion which was *not* at least partially a functional one would seem deficient. We might try to say that the idea was *caused by* the interests of white people in subordinating and exploiting black people, while denying that it was believed *because this would then tend to help prop up the racist practices from which whites were benefiting.*[17] But if we denied this, then it would be left mysterious why white people's interest in subordinating black people would cause *this* kind of belief, as opposed to any other. Why does this interest generate beliefs like this—and not, for example, the belief that black humans are equal to white humans in their abilities and needs—or, for that matter, the belief that black people have superpowers, or are especially fit to rule? The obvious answer is that these beliefs would be much less convenient, relative to the immediate interests of the group that happens to be in a position of dominance within the social context in which beliefs about such things are being formed. But that, surely, is to affirm that this is an instance of functionally explained false consciousness par excellence: beliefs and attitudes like this are held, rather than others, *because* they help to sustain the dominance of an oppressive practice by providing it with a veneer of moral acceptability and even benevolence. The micro-processes through which this works will, of course, be extremely complex, and the processes by which a belief in the inferiority of black people is generated and takes hold will differ from the processes at work in other candidate instances of functionally explained false consciousness—such as the 'feminine mystique',[18] the 'American dream', or the 'trickle-down theory of wealth'. But that just means (a) that there are interesting and worthy objects of study here, and (b) that the practical attempt to combat such distortions must be sensitive to these differing realities. What it clearly does *not* mean is that we must abandon the idea that these distortions are functionally explained. In political philosophy, too, there will be a complex story to be told about the micro-processes through which the various distortions I've described come about, and how they serve their functions. I would argue that part of what this book has tried to do, in fact, is to begin to tell exactly such a story.

I hope I have now said enough to show that there is nothing inherently suspicious or unacceptable about explaining certain distortions of thought in terms of what I am calling 'ideology'. In sharp contrast to many of the ideas surveyed in this book—which, I've argued, are wrapped in a cloak of false political neutrality—this is a notion which is *presented* as partisan (a 'Marxist' idea), when in fact, the phenomenon it highlights is one which may be recognized from a whole range of political perspectives. I'll now put my cards on the table and say how I think the findings of this book are best accounted for. The distortions analysed here occur, I suggest, because they are convenient. The notion of ideology that is implicit in this suggestion, on the other hand, is an *inconvenient* idea—that is why it is out of favour, ignored or dismissed for what seem to be transparently poor reasons, such as those mentioned above: it is convenient for it to be distorted and discredited.[19] *For whom* are such distortions convenient? Well, in the first instance, they are convenient for the theorists who are already intellectually invested in the kind of political philosophy that is dominant. Nobody else cares about political philosophy nearly as much as political philosophers do. People inevitably have an interest in continuing to think in the ways they have become accustomed to thinking, an interest which produces a certain distortion of consciousness—sometimes dubbed 'confirmation bias'—in all of us. This universal bias may be greatly amplified when we have invested time and pride in something, and perhaps built a career on it. In that situation, there is a strong incentive to hold firm to our investments, even resorting to trickery and underhand means when necessary—as I've argued is the case on an epidemic scale in contemporary political philosophy. But this is only a proximate explanation. Why is this particular mode of political philosophy dominant, rather than another? It might be argued that it is merely a fashion: although fashions presumably admit of causal explanations, just like other empirical phenomena, there is also a sense in which they 'just happen'. Nobody benefits from a fashion for mullets. It just comes along, stays for a while, and goes. But as we learned in chapter 1, ideas are not like designer dresses. For that matter, I would add, nor are *designer dresses* like designer dresses, if the implication there is that they have no political significance and are in no way subservient to relations of power in society.

So to put it another way, liberal political philosophy is not like the mullet. The kind of political philosophy that is now fashionable did not come out of nowhere; it has shown itself to be much more than a passing fad, and it has a function—though not the function that it would like to attribute to itself. While very visibly challenging some features of the political context within which—in its own small, sheltered corner—it goes about its business, it also reflects and affirms certain key features of the status quo and defends them by any means necessary.

NOTES

1. For example, Sanford suggests that an argument is question begging if directed to someone who would only believe the premise if he already believed the conclusion (1981; p. 150).

2. In fact, given the standard account of logical validity, it is surprisingly difficult to distinguish the condition of a valid argument from the 'fallacy' of question begging. As the *Internet Encyclopaedia of Philosophy* puts it: 'Insofar as the conclusion of a deductively valid argument is "contained" in the premises from which it is deduced, this containing might seem to be a case of presupposing, and thus any deductively valid argument might seem to be begging the question. It is still an open question among logicians as to why some deductively valid arguments are considered to be begging the question and others are not.'

3. Sanford (1981; p. 150).

4. I would say that this is what happens with certain attempts to justify the imposition of demands of 'constructiveness', for example.

5. The original articulation of this view is laid out in Kuhn's highly influential (and equally controversial) 1962 book, *The Structure of Scientific Revolutions*.

6. See Masterman (1970), who identifies twenty-one different uses of the term 'paradigm' in *The Structure of Scientific Revolutions*. Kuhn (1970) concedes the point but ups the count to twenty-two.

7. See Walton (1994; p. 9).

8. Walton (1994; p. 96). Cf. Sanford (1972; p. 198), who characterizes the question-begging fallacy as a failure 'to increase the degree of reasonable confidence which one has in the truth of the conclusion'.

9. Cf. Anderson (2012), who makes the same point in the context of feminist epistemology and philosophy of science: 'It is now generally agreed that the theory-laden character of observations does not threaten their status as evidence for a theory, provided that the theories presupposed in those observations do not immediately include the very theory being tested by those observations. Circularity, at least of a narrow sort, should be avoided. Similarly, the chief danger of value-laden inquiry is a kind of circularity of wishful thinking or dogmatism.'

10. Bell (1960); Fukuyama (c1992).

11. I regard this as an advantage, rather than a weakness, since it may purchase the kind of limited independence that I described in chapter 3.

12. That is, while we might well want to criticize the ends of certain military technologies (although we can acknowledge that these often 'work', relative to those ends), and while we might also want to engage in various political criticisms of the functions and presuppositions of some aspects of medical science (e.g., in relation to gender or mental health), this does not preclude recognition of science's indisputable success in relation to ends that we *would* accept.

13. The term 'ideological false consciousness' might seem like overkill, almost tautological; but I use the phrase to indicate a particular *kind* of (functionally explained) false consciousness. Compare 'syphilitic disease': 'syphilitic' implies disease, but 'disease' does not imply syphilitic.

14. See Marx and Engels (1987 [1848]; part I).

15. I take this definition from Rosen (1996).

16. Note that 'interest' here doesn't have to imply 'objective' or 'true interest'. An interest doesn't have to be 'objective' or 'true' in order to be served and to make itself felt in the world.

17. I hope it is clear that I am applying the past tense here only to this particular manifestation of racism, and not to racism itself, which, in the twenty-first century, shows no sign of abating. I've chosen this example of overt, explicit belief in racial inferiority and fitness for service roles, however, because this *does* tend to be regarded now as obviously unacceptable. The same is true, to some degree, of my earlier example about the fitness of women for a life of homemaking and childcare, but I avoid focusing on that example now because my impression is that it is significantly less firmly established as 'something one does not say anymore'—and I really didn't want to get into a debate with all the people who might say things like, 'Yes, but men can't breastfeed though, can they?'

18. See Friedan (1963).

19. I make the case for an ideological explanation of attitudes towards the theory of ideology elsewhere (see Finlayson 2014).

Afterword

Midnight in the Sausage Factory

But really, gentlemen, who can take pride in his illnesses, even boast about them?

However, what am I saying? Everyone does it; they do take pride in their illnesses, and I perhaps more than most.

—Dostoevsky ('Notes from the Underground')[1]

I've dutifully rounded off the story with a proper conclusion: a little summary of what has been argued, a statement of how the various parts of the account relate to one another, and of the message or imperative that should be drawn from the whole. That is how conclusions tend to go, but much the same points as I made to begin with, against the conventional introduction, apply here too. I don't mean to say that there is no role for summary or for telling people what they should make of an argument: I've done a fair amount of that—possibly a neurotic amount—as I've gone along, and there comes a point where it feels as though the author might reach out of the pages and tie the reader's shoelaces. What I want to do instead now is to say something that will *lead out* of the thoughts that have been put forward here. This seems to me a more fitting complement to an introduction's 'leading *in*' than does the 'closing off' suggested by the etymology of 'conclusion', which suggests in its turn the adding of a protective final coat to an existing piece of work.[2]

When I talk about 'leading out', I *don't* have in mind another common theme of the conclusion, where the author finishes off a negative work with a nod in the direction of something more positive, which she has no intention of taking further, and an 'Over to you!' which dumps on anonymous others some amorphous mammoth of a task (which they can confidently be expected to shun in their turn). It is easy enough to re-express a negative thesis as a positive one. I could spin out a few platitudes now about how political philosophers must search for a way of reflecting on their methodological commitments which *doesn't* just result in more of the same, but constitutes *genuine, critical scrutiny*. The idea is unobjectionable enough, but hardly very instructive, unless the thought is that it is an adequate response simply to vow, like Gordon Brown, 'to do our utmost'—in which case the platitude ceases to be unobjectionable and becomes a dangerous delusion.[3] I could add that the elements of the trichotomy—politics, political philosophy and its methodology—must be 'reunited'. But anyone who has been paying the slightest attention will already know that I must be committed to something of this sort. It's not a significant addition to my negative claims, but a soothing, positive reiteration, which still does not tell us *whether* or *how* the elements of the trichotomy can be brought together so as to make for an acceptable practice of political philosophy. I don't really have any answer to that other than what can be read from my negative statements (or else I would say so). Conclusions that make vague, positive gestures in the direction of unknown better places sometimes seem to me like doorways painted onto stone walls. This is ritual closing off presented as leading out: making the characteristic avenues-for-further-enquiry noises can be a way of sealing a text at its end, a ticking of a box; and whether the avenues are real or imaginary is quite clearly of little interest.

If it really seems that there is nowhere to go, a genuine *leading out* could also be a *closing off* in a different sense: not the placing of a protective seal on what has gone before, but an honest acknowledgement of the predicament.

What I'll set out now are some thoughts about the relation in which philosophy stands to insight. They are not meant to follow from the rest of what has been said in this text, in the sense of being a conclusion that is drawn from it, although I do take them to be in keeping with its basic spirit. They are an attempt at a leading out.

***

There are two very common views about the worth of philosophy, or more particularly, about the worth of the expertise of professional philosophers.

The view that I take to be the most common within the profession, and possibly also among the population at large, is that philosophers, by virtue of their special abilities and training, are better placed than most to get at the truth. There is room for many different shades of this attitude. In the case of political philosophy, for instance, we might distinguish Frank Ramsey's opinion that political matters are strictly for the 'experts'[4] from the 'trickle-down' model discussed in chapter 6, according to which political philosophers' basic task is to help politicians and the public to think more clearly and rationally about the decisions with which they are faced and about the information that stands at their disposal. As I noted there, the expression of this view is usually accompanied by a show of modesty: *Even philosophers make mistakes, and we don't always have our feet on the ground—not like business leaders (business to the rescue!); in any case, everyone should feel able to have a go at this—many of you already think about philosophical issues in your everyday lives, without even realizing it!* etc. etc. But this leaves intact the basic attitude that philosophers are at an advantage.

An opposing attitude, very common outside academia—at least if my own encounters are anything to go by—is that philosophers are frauds, paid over the odds to spout either encoded common sense or encoded nonsense, and that this doesn't require any special expertise but is something which more or less anyone could do.

The two attitudes are often accompanied by superficially similar expressions of admiration for the wisdom of non-experts. The pro-expert view proves itself to be quite compatible with excruciating paeans to the earthy wisdom of the 'common man', tributes which tend to be patronizing, sentimental and fundamentally insincere. The anti-expert view, on the other hand, is correlated with celebrations of 'common sense' and the 'University of Life', which tend to appear bitter, self-righteous and misinformed.

Both views, in any case, strike me as wrong, and there is truth in each; and the truth is inadequately captured by saying merely that there is truth in each. Philosophers tend to be adept and highly trained in an activity that is both very specific and very difficult.[5] It just doesn't obviously have anything to do with *truth*, except insofar as it constitutes an especially sophisticated means of getting in the way of it. That, anyway, is what I'll suggest now.

***

My brother once said to me that the reason why we have better thoughts late at night is that there aren't as many people awake then, 'using up all the ideas'. There is a sense in which this is bollocks, but—as with a lot of things he says—there is more to it, and something kind of magnetic about it. I've remembered it ever since, anyway. What appeals to me is not any thought that other people are out to steal the particular ideas that I think are good ones. This seems not to be the case. And I certainly don't subscribe to any metaphysically weird claim that ideas are actually 'out there', waiting to be 'had'. What I liked about the comment is the way it makes us think of having an idea as like finding a seat on a train, or feeling the jolt of a fish biting on the line. The comparison with fishing also conveys the aspect of thinking that is a kind of active-passive watchful waiting, enhanced by solitude.[6]

This idea subverts, and thereby draws attention to, the more usual way of thinking about thought. The more usual way, I take it, represents thinking as the active *generating* of thought by the thinker. This is not false. Of course thoughts are generated by thinkers. But we also talk about thoughts 'striking' us, or 'occurring to' us. These are two alternative ways of looking at or describing thought; not descriptions of different and mutually exclusive kinds of events. The same goes for descriptions in terms of 'acting' or 'omitting', or more generally, for descriptions couched in positive or negative terms. But that doesn't make the opposition an unimportant or uninteresting one. There may be good reasons, in a given context, to choose one way of looking at things rather than another. To say that the parent 'neglected' the child allows us to express in positive terms that the parent *did not do* various things which we think he or she had a responsibility to do for the child. And by saying that the child 'was neglected'—instead of, for example, that the child 'languished' in misery and solitude—we might emphasize, by the *passive* description, the fact that the child was not in control of or responsible for the situation.

There is a loose family of ideas about inspiration, which emphasizes the negative and passive ways of looking. There is the everyday habit already noted, of speaking of a thought 'striking' us or 'occurring to' us. There is also the anecdotally evidenced phenomenon, reported even by the most narrowly analytic philosophers, that what we take to be our best ideas often seem to arrive without warning, at apparently random moments and in surprising and perhaps unpromising contexts: when we are 'off duty', 'caught off guard', in the shower or on the train; sometimes when we are drunk or otherwise addled, sleep-deprived or grief-stricken. Then there is the emphasis, in Buddhist and Taoist philosophy, on *nothingness*, and on the 'emptying' of the mind so as to put it into a more receptive state. In Western philosophy, on the other hand, Heidegger is an example of someone who emphasizes the negative and the passive, with his idea that thought is a matter of *Gelassenheit* (i.e., of adopting a state of relaxed receptivity) or 'listening to the voice of Being'.[7] And the same theme crops up again and again in the arts,[8] with a tendency for artists to portray themselves as the *conductors* of ideas, rather than as their generators. The most obvious example is probably Romanticism, and in particular Keats's idea of 'negative capability'.[9] But similar ideas appear much more widely.[10]

These thoughts, not all of which can easily be dismissed as bullshit,[11] may be seen as related not only to one another, but also to a kind of shared, underlying *optimism*. The emphasis on relaxation, *non*-doing or non-interference, the *removal* of various obstacles to inspiration, suggests that in some sense the 'default' state of the thinker must be one of *contact* of the right kind with the world, with truth or insight. That does not, of course, mean that this contact is as a matter of fact *common*.[12] But the thought is perhaps that human beings are somehow 'set up' so as to grasp certain important truths about their environment,[13] and will do so unless something goes badly wrong.[14] I'm not concerned here to subject to scrutiny this hypothesis, which will in any case take different forms depending on which member of the family of ideas we look at. A fundamental optimism of this kind may not even be the sort of thesis that can be justified or unjustified, in the conventional sense of finding an evidential or argumentative foundation on which to rest it. Like the principle of charity for Davidson, or the inductive form of inference for Hume, a commitment to this sort of optimism may just be one which we have to make—if only as an act of faith—if we are to get anywhere at all.

It is striking that insofar as the sort of phenomenon I've been talking about is acknowledged among analytic philosophers, it is almost totally relegated to anecdote, put away in a box marked 'context of discovery'; anyone who tries to read too much into what philosophers think about in the shower can only expect to be treated as a cause for concern. This seems to me a mistake. Even if we were to accept—and I don't believe that we should—that the understanding and evaluation of a philosophical position can be completely sealed off from facts about the context in which that position was conceived, it doesn't mean that the phenomenon I'm discussing has no relevance for the methodological question of how we should go about the work of philosophy, or for practical questions as to what might be the most advantageous way to organize academic institutions and events. We might think, for example, that it makes certain practices—such as advising students to 'think of this as a nine-to-five job', or designing working spaces on the model of open plan offices—look bizarrely out of place.

A related phenomenon is that nobody *really* likes going to conferences or reading journal articles, or even finds them very directly helpful (compared with conversations with small numbers of close friends over the right amount of alcohol). I've got over thinking that people's admissions to this effect were just well-meaning attempts to reassure me about what I took to be my own abnormal reactions; it seems to me now that these sentiments are sincere enough, but tend to be expressed only as furtive or guilty asides, due to a (well-founded) fear, lest they be seen as breaches of etiquette or signs of professional flakiness. But thinking about it, why on earth would crowding into a room and sitting still and facing in the same direction for hours on end be a good way to promote either illumination or enjoyment?[15] True, people do claim to 'enjoy' these occasions, but the only explanation I can find for this is that they have invented a special, technical sense of that word.

Why is it that the phenomena I've mentioned are generally accorded no serious significance? It could be that they are exceptional: inevitable moments of dissatisfaction that are easily overemphasized; and occasional flashes of inspiration in unpromising contexts, which are unsurprisingly more memorable and mentionable than the discoveries that are made in the more usual, conventional manner. I don't deny that this is possible. It is a question of which explanation best fits experience. By the nature of that kind of question, I can't prove that my own favoured explanation is the right one, but I can offer it up for consideration and appraisal, and it is this: people are familiar with these phenomena, from experience and from the reports of others, because they are pervasive rather than exceptional; but, partly because we are encouraged to make a strict separation between us-as-philosophers and us-as-private-persons, it does not always occur to us that what we see as merely 'personal' might have any philosophical significance, and we tend therefore to dismiss it. It is at least worth investigating what happens if we resist this tendency.

***

If we emphasize the negative or passive aspects of thought, if we look at thinkers as the conductors rather than the generators of ideas, and if we bring this together with the anecdotal evidence that philosophers are better conductors under what they themselves regard as 'un-philosophical' conditions (that is, *not* in official or professional settings), this raises the possibility that the practices and institutional environments characteristic of academic philosophy might themselves constitute an *impediment* to insight, an artificial obstacle that stands between us and what might otherwise occur to us.

The claim that philosophy is an obstacle to truth can be seen as having an 'internal' and an 'external' (or 'social') aspect. The internal part of the claim would be that academic philosophy imparts to its practitioners a mastery of a very specific technique, along with a conviction that this technique is a complete tool kit for the pursuit of understanding; but the exclusive use of this technique actually serves to prevent us from realizing certain sorts of truths. The kind of thing I have in mind here, for analytic philosophy at least, is the following set of priorities and corresponding aptitudes: an assumption that everything that is true can be stated clearly and explicitly, without ambiguity or self-contradiction; that terms must be defined, and that definition means the provision of necessary and sufficient conditions; the idea that the most purely 'philosophical' part of the philosopher's job can be done a priori—and the rest is just 'application'; that in engaging in this sort of thinking, the philosopher follows rules that are universal, and which for this reason can be accessed and applied by any person in any place and at any time, by the individual in isolation as well as in the context of a particular group. The development and use of this approach might be thought of as the honing and flexing of a particular sort of cognitive 'muscle': some will have greater natural aptitude for it than others; the muscle will be more highly developed in those who have been through a certain process of training; and although it will certainly be useful for some purposes, it by no means follows that it will be *generally* useful, or that the things for which it is useful exhaust the proper objectives of philosophy; and there may well be some worthwhile tasks for which it will be a positive hindrance. It is pleasing to think of analytic philosophers as being in this respect like fiddler crabs, each with one overdeveloped claw, powerful and specialized, but also cumbersome and limited.

As well as this narrow set of abilities and values, academic philosophers absorb a variety of cognitive habits and reflexes—the equivalent of muscular spasms or tics—which act as defence mechanisms against threats to the philosophical positions they hold:[16] for instance, thought-ending clichés, such as that 'events' have discredited all political frameworks but liberal capitalism; glib assimilations of threatening or recalcitrant positions to familiar, easily rebuffed (or easily absorbed) positions—even when these are clearly different, and even explicitly disowned by the theorists in question.[17] The interesting thing here is that at least some of these philosophical mistakes and misdemeanours *could only have been made by a philosopher*. You have to have learned to associate something specific and shrug-offable with terms such as 'political realism', for instance, in order to be ready to use certain stock responses against it.

If these points are at all correct, it makes sense that when the analytic philosopher's cognitive muscle is artificially relaxed, its self-defensive tics suppressed—by exhaustion, inebriation, grief, distraction or whatever else—this moment carries an increased danger of thinking something interesting.

To turn now to the external or social aspect,[18] it is possible to talk about a philosophical 'community', or 'communities': Anglophone philosophers, a particular philosophy department, informal networks of political philosophy graduate students, and so on. The lives of the humans whose specialized task is to do philosophy are often very closely intertwined—sometimes to the near exclusion of interaction with anyone outside of the circle. So if, as seems to me hard to deny, we think that *the interpersonal is philosophical*— in that the social environment of the philosophical community must influence the work and thought of its members—it also seems sensible to say that this effect will be intensified in proportion to the incestuousness of the community.

When we ask about the specific manner of this shaping of the philosophical by the interpersonal, the answer is partly there in the description I've already given of the 'internal' aspect of philosophy-as-obstacle. Being surrounded by philosophers means being surrounded by the sweaty action of cognitive muscles. An ambient buzz of a certain sort of intellectual (hyper-) activity threatens to drown out or distract us from thoughts that are deviant or novel relative to this activity. And the omnipresence of analytic bodybuilding exerts a powerful pressure to emulate this example.

I've drawn attention, throughout this book, to the informal norms that regulate the practice of *political* philosophy in particular. Generalizing from this and building on it, we can note that philosophical *communities* (like all communities) are governed by various norms, and that there will be no sharp cutoff between norms that are 'philosophical' and norms that are 'social'.

Many of the terms that philosophers use to evaluate each other seem to be an inextricable mixture of the two. 'Uncharitable', 'naïve', 'scholarly', 'moderate', 'polemical', 'serious'. These look analogous to what some ethicists call 'thick' moral terms: they are *normative* (to be called 'uncharitable', for example, is to be accused of philosophizing badly), while also having a *descriptive* content which can be readily applied to qualities of mind, habit or personality as well as to academic work.

In that case, the dichotomy between the personal and the philosophical is a misleading one. This dichotomy itself nevertheless figures among the norms that regulate the practice of philosophy and the philosophical community, norms which appear as seamlessly philosophical-and-interpersonal. A particularly powerful kind of informal social-and-philosophical control is exercised by the drawing of the boundaries of 'philosophy' in a given place, so that anything that falls outside of these boundaries may be dismissed without having to be attacked as deficient in itself: it is simply said that such-and-such is 'not a philosophical matter', and hence not to the point. The separation of the personal from the philosophical allows this trump card to be played in the following way: we can say that something is 'merely personal' (and hence not 'philosophical'). At this point, I wonder if there is not a deep-seated hypocrisy in the operation of norms in the philosophical community: these norms are importantly philosophical and personal at the same time, and yet a guiding assumption behind their mode of operating is that the personal is one thing, the philosophical another, and that the former should not be allowed to creep into the latter; so that deviant thinkers can be castigated for being, for example, too 'polemical', where this is a partly-personal criticism of someone for making partly-personal criticisms.

We might add that, insofar as one of the functions of regulative norms is to impose *sanctions*—through philosophically 'thick' terms of disapprobation such as 'polemical', 'hyperbolic', 'uncharitable', 'shrill', and so on—those with relatively lower status within the philosophical community (e.g., women, younger philosophers, 'Continental' philosophers, and holders of left-wing or other unpopular positions) will be less able to afford to deviate from these norms; and so those standpoints that might otherwise be most likely to produce challenges to dominant philosophical dogma are effectively discouraged from doing so. In sum, the personal and interpersonal are philosophical, and both are political.

***

What I've said so far—about philosophy being an obstacle, and about inspiration being correlated with the fleeting moments at which this obstacle is partially removed—might be met with the thought that perhaps the explanation for this latter phenomenon is that if philosophy is an obstacle, it is not so in the usual and straightforward sense of the term, but is in some way an *enabling* obstacle. This would not be so in quite the same sense in which, for Feuerbach, religion stands as an enabling obstacle to human progress: religion fulfils a necessary function for mankind, but there comes a point at which we are ready to cast it off—and *must* do so in order to complete our journey towards self-understanding, happiness and freedom.[19] The thought might be that philosophy is like putting food out for the birds. The birds don't come when you're in the act of putting the food on the bird table. But it's still true that the food is what attracts them, even if the act of placing it there temporarily frightens them off, and it would be an obvious mistake to conclude that the way to make a garden maximally attractive to birds is to avoid feeding them.

In the same way, it might be thought that the internal and external aspects of academic philosophy I've described contribute positively to the genesis of interesting ideas, or are even indispensable to this, while it is also the case that these *relata* do not overlap, temporally and spatially, very much—or at least, not as much as the positive relationship of dependency between them might otherwise lead us to expect.

I don't believe that any such cheerful story applies to the relationship between philosophy and insight, but I do want to acknowledge that the way in which I take philosophy to be an obstacle is not straightforward, and that there is a sense in which philosophy 'enables' valuable insight—although it's not one that shows that institution in a flattering light. We can imagine an abusive relationship, where one or both parties are hindered from seeing clearly the ways in which the other party is mistreating them. If one person treats the other in an unloving way, constantly ridicules him or her, and treats him or her as incapable (which may be self-fulfilling), the person who is treated in that way can come to see him- or herself as hateful, ridiculous and pathetic, and this makes it hard for that person fully to recognize the abuse for what it is: he or she may feel that the treatment is normal or appropriate or deserved; or that he or she cannot trust his or her own perceptions of the situation. In such a case the abuse stands as an obstacle to the abused party's understanding of the abuse. But the abuse is also, in an obvious sense, a precondition of that understanding: without the abuse, there can be no *under-standing* of the abuse (there is nothing to understand). The object of the attempt at understanding, in this case, both makes the understanding possible and also undermines it.

Philosophy does things to us which inhibit our understanding (including our understanding of what it does to us), but it (and what it does to us) is also part of what we are trying to understand. When we change or destroy philosophy as an institution, we are changing the world that exists for us to reflect upon. If we assume that the objects of philosophical enquiry are timeless, unchanging truths, then we might take the claim that the institution of philosophy is an obstacle to truth to mean that if we change or do away with philosophy, this could enable us to reach the same truths which philosophy now prevents us from reaching. What I'm saying is that it is not like that. The effort to change philosophy should not be understood only in terms of an effort to reach more (preexisting) truths. To try to change philosophy must involve a decision about *what truths we want to have around*.

This might push us in the direction of some utopian experimentation with the institution of philosophy, and there is a dangerously short step here to the conclusion that we must all campaign for departmental beanbags and hammocks, smoke a bit more dope, and then we can sit back and congratulate ourselves. Perhaps this would, in fact, produce some philosophical benefits. It would almost certainly be more pleasant. But quite apart from the fact that it's not likely to happen, we should be wary of looking to this sort of innovation as a possible solution. I have the same sort of qualms about this as I have about utopian schemes in general. There may be a role for the setting up of institutions which seek to avoid the faults that are characteristic of the mainstream: progressive schools, for instance, might have various advantages and might help us to see more clearly what is wrong with schooling in general, to realize that conventional approaches to schooling are not the only ones that are possible, and that disaster need not ensue when they are departed from in various ways.[20] But it has to be constantly borne in mind that such schemes do not represent little pieces of utopia at all, but a particular kind of intervention among many other kinds we can make, and which must be seen as part of a wider context which has *not* undergone the kind of transformation which a 'free' school or university aims to effect at a local level. This wider context is like an ecosystem, which always affects the character, consequences and significance that a given utopian project can have in a way that cannot be brought fully (or perhaps much at all) under the control of those engaged in that project. Summerhill will always be 'the school with no rules',[21] despite the manifest inaccuracy of this description, just as Chomsky will always be a 'conspiracy theorist'—and both are cast as examples of *tolerated renegades*,[22] the very possibility of their existence seen as an affirmation of the wider context in which this existence is lived out.[23]

The wider context in which a utopian experiment takes place sets limits both on the extent to which the scheme can enact a practice that is desirable or even satisfactory, and on the kind of force that the scheme can constitute within this wider context. I take this to be a constraint that applies to everything we do. A problem occurs only when we pretend that it is *not* the case. The problem is with the thought that we can make the institution of philosophy—or some little enclave within it—into a sphere within which thinkers can stand in a healthy relationship to truth or enlightenment, that is, that we can realize 'philosophy' in something like the literal and aspirational sense of *love of wisdom*, without also transforming the surrounding social world.[24]

If we were to succeed in bringing about an adequate transformation of the social world, it is deeply uncertain whether this would leave any place for a distinctive institution which we would recognize as philosophy. Assuming that we don't manage this, it will be a mistake to think that we can seal off a space in which to think, which escapes the general abusiveness of the social world and the compromising effect of this on our thought.

If no escape is possible, perhaps all that is open to us is to cultivate survival skills. We should make the most of the enabling side of philosophy-as-obstacle: make its particular style of abuse our subject matter, know that we are up to our necks in it, try to notice and to note the ways in which it constrains our ability to see it and everything else clearly. There may be no stable set of methodological maxims for us to cling to in this task. Certainly, a change in routine or a change of furniture will not be good enough (although, arguably, it couldn't hurt). Perhaps the most we can do is make use of the ineliminable moments of relief and contrast that occur within the social environment of philosophy, cherish the exceptions and flit between this environment and such others as are available to us.

***

If philosophy is an obstacle to insight, I've been suggesting, it is an obstacle which must not merely be *removed* (whether this involves the removal of philosophy itself or its transformation into something that is not an obstacle).

It is an obstacle which must be removed *in the right way*, where that means: *as part of a broader process of social change in the right direction*. What, exactly, that process would be, what its prospects are, and how we ought to react to finding that its prospects are virtually nil—none of these things are clear.

What *is* clear is that the claim that philosophy constitutes an obstacle to insight should not lead us to conclude that the current assault on the subject, on the humanities disproportionately, and on education in general, is anything to be welcomed—even in the heavy-hearted way in which a mercy killing might be welcomed. One of the most important factors rendering contemporary philosophy an environment unconducive to genuine thought is the very process of ever-increasing standardization, instrumentalization and marketization that threatens to destroy its host:[25] the work of students, academics and departments has to be measured more and more by universal, quantifiable criteria;[26] this work is to be conceived as 'output', and judged on its perceived 'impact' on (e.g.) business and 'policy'; and the universities and departments which are not being closed are themselves to be run on a business model—with students initially as clients, and then (when processed) as *products* to be placed, among or along with academics, on a market.[27]

I've so far described the social aspect of academic philosophy as if this were a relatively closed community, operating with an internal system of norms—inextricably philosophical, personal, social and political—which serve to suppress dissent and induce conformity, but unaffected by pressures from without. Philosophy has, of course, never been hermetically sealed off from a larger social context, no matter how insular its community, and no matter how apparently abstract and disconnected its concerns from everyday life.[28] But the tenor of my last observations is that the philosophical community is becoming *less and less* closed—and in an overwhelmingly destructive way.[29] This doesn't at all render obsolete the image of philosophy as deploying norms in order to protect dominant assumptions and to secure conformity. It just notes that those norms and dominant assumptions are becoming ever less distinctively 'philosophical', and ever more identical with the norms and dominant assumptions of the surrounding culture and of business in particular. This can only be expected to make the ideological and conformity-inducing pressures cruder and more intense.[30]

In the current political context, the possibility of satire is forestalled by a reality that matches and seems even to satirize satire in a preemptive attack.[31]

Ten years or so after the conversation about ideas in the night, I'm in the philosophy faculty when my phone rings. My brother wants to know where I am. The signal is dodgy. ' . . . You're in the sausage factory?' he asks, and from then on we have a new piece of half-rhyming slang. The philosophy faculty, like the education system at large, increasingly *is* a sausage factory, smoothly and relentlessly churning out its homogeneous parcels to be packaged, purveyed and consumed.[32]

It seems probable that this will put an end, in the more or less near future, to academic philosophy as we know it. This is so not least because philosophy, understood as a domain of enquiry or even as an interest in a particular kind of question, doesn't obviously make a lot of sense—which is probably why the attempt to characterize it in this way and to distinguish it from other domains and sets of questions is so strikingly unsuccessful.[33] Philosophy as a discipline is a promising candidate for a genealogical analysis of the kind we may associate with Nietzsche and Foucault. A sausage metaphor is apt here once again: a genealogical account is one that shows its object to be constituted by a mishmash of disparate, perhaps unsavoury ingredients that are artificially presented as a unity, as if crammed into a smooth, synthetic skin.[34]

But much as I may cast academic philosophy as being of negative value, a prophylactic against actual inspiration, I've also suggested that if philosophy must be overhauled or destroyed in the interests of greater insight, this is an imperative which must be understood as a commitment to a broader process of the right kind of social change. The transformation of the social world that is currently under way may be confidently expected to destroy philosophy as an institution, but hardly to do so in the service of greater enlightenment. The creatures that inhabit a riverbed may be hideous and slimy, but bringing about their extinction through toxic pollutants does not necessarily make the world a better place.

***

We might distinguish, in what has been said so far, two senses of 'philosophy': the de facto sense, referring to the actual institution of academic philosophy; and an aspirational sense, referring to some ideal of the uninhibited pursuit of truth and understanding for its own sake, the love of wisdom, the attempt to live an examined life or to find a satisfactory way of being in the world (or some similarly important cliché).

My position may then be put this way: while de facto philosophy is destructive of philosophy-in-the-aspirational-sense, so is the *destruction* of de facto philosophy.

Perhaps part of the reason for this is that de facto philosophy harbours, despite everything, some traces of the commitment to philosophy-in-an-aspirational-sense.[35] Something like this idea of a principled and tenacious spirit of truth-seeking was invoked in a 2010 event on the closures of departments at Middlesex and elsewhere, entitled 'Who's afraid of philosophy?' Some commentators there were suggesting that there is something peculiarly *threatening* about philosophy's uncompromising and critical approach to the understanding of the world, which made it a particular target for cuts and other neoliberal attacks.[36] But whether or not philosophy—or the kind of philosophy they had in mind—actually has the character they were suggesting, the thought that this actually scares those in power is surely little more than a comforting delusion.[37] Given the relative political strength of the forces involved, it seems more realistic to ask the question 'Who gives a shit about philosophy?' and to reply, 'No one' or 'No one who counts'. Admittedly, as political sloganeering this would leave something to be desired, but the point stands.

Around about now is the moment at which it would be good manners to proffer some sort of last-minute silver lining, or at least gesture in the vague direction of a place where one might conceivably be found. But it's a bit late for good manners, and anyway I'm suspicious of the tendency for bleak books and papers—not to mention films—to be finished off with the equivalent of an after-dinner mint.

I will now, however, try to say something about what becomes of philosophy-in-the-aspirational-sense, given the need to see the transformation of philosophy as part of the right sort of broader social change, and given also that we appear to be engaged in a battle against social change of the *wrong* sort—a battle which we appear to have little hope of winning (although we must fight it as if this were not the case).[38]

***

There have been perhaps three points in the whole of this text where I've gestured towards a positive programme for philosophy. In the introduction, I mentioned an ideal of philosophy as a restless and insatiable troublemaking. At the end of chapter 6, I raised the idea that an attitude of 'constant vigilance' towards one's own methodology might be more philosophically respectable than an attitude of 'reconciliation'. And earlier in this afterword, I suggested that it would be a mistake to think that we can transform our philosophical practices or institutions into ones which instantiate a satisfactory relationship with truth or insight unless this is done as part of a broader transformation, and that in the absence of such a transformation, the best we can aim at is the cultivation of 'survival skills'—on which point I elaborated only very vaguely, hinting at a combination of self-scrutiny, changes of scene and an eye for unconventional methods and contexts.

A skeletal methodology, advocating restlessness, vigilance and the shunning of comfort, is the positive expression of a commitment *against* various things which it takes to be obstacles to thought: against complacency, against too great a conformity—conformity to the practices of de facto philosophy, and to any methodological programme less skeletal than the one now being described. The programme described is an effort *not* to fall into innumerable and ever-shifting traps (among which one of the most deadly is the trap of thinking that a philosophical programme can take any more positive form than this). It is a kind of theoretical anti-utopianism. To recall my earlier discussion of 'ideal' theory, what is being rejected is the attempt to describe a stable, desirable way of doing philosophy. First, the attempt to give any detailed *description* of the desirable in positive terms is shunned. Of course, the negative account we give will always allow of some positive expression, for example, in terms of 'vigilance' or 'restlessness'. But the matter of what more concrete way of proceeding might answer the demand to be vigilant or restless will constantly be in flux. And second, insofar as the desirable *is* described, there is no pretence to describe a procedure that is 'desirable' *in the sense of being a final, adequate method, which might be an appropriate object of reconciliation.* As soon as we judge of ourselves that we are vigilant enough, that we have reached a satisfactory level of restless discomfort, we thereby falsify that judgement—in much the same way as we sometimes rebuke ourselves for our conduct and then console ourselves with the thought, 'Well, at least I feel guilty about it', where this consolation undermines itself insofar as it works (that is, insofar as it makes us feel less guilty). The enactment of this restless methodology is by definition not something which we can ever be satisfied that we have achieved.[39] It is a perpetual shaking-oneself-awake.

On the face of it, this seems about as far away as you can get from any ideal of Zen-like calm and stillness. But, of course, that sort of ideal is shot through with paradox: it is a matter of *aiming* at a state of complete aimlessness, of *striving* towards the renunciation of striving. The methodology I'm beginning to describe, too, involves constant striving. But in this case it is not only the distractions and other obstacles to thought that are in constant motion (hence the need for constant vigilance), while the wisdom attained is eternal and unchanging;[40] what I'm saying is that at least part of the task and responsibility of philosophy is to grasp with *un*steady mind (*contra* Lucretius)[41] the worldly, changeable things—*including* the world of ideas and its obstructive operations. This cannot be done through calm withdrawal, whether or not such a state is possible, and whatever else it might be able to yield if it is.

The sort of mind-set advocated is instead reminiscent of *angst*, which is defined as a 'nondirectional' emotion—that is, a state of anxiety which (in strong contrast to the concept of a 'phobia') is attached to no particular object. A description of something like perpetual angst—a constant discomfort or restlessness in the face of threats that cannot be located, isolated or made determinate—might be the closest we can get to an account of a state appropriate to a philosopher.[42]

The importance of angst—but also its limitations—may be seen when we look at it in connection with the phase of life with which it is most strongly associated: adolescence.[43] Both elements of this association are commonly sneered at and made the subject of mockery. If we want to talk about regulatory or punitive philosophical norms, calling someone's position 'adolescent' is about as damning as it gets. What is less obvious is which form of disapproval has priority—is angst sneered at because it is 'adolescent', or are adolescents sneered at because they are perceived as being angst-ridden? My impression is that contempt for adolescents is in large part due to the contempt for angst, and not the other way around. Adolescents are threatening for various reasons: besides being likely to outlive their elders, and being suddenly much larger and more powerful than before (and often also suddenly much larger and more physically powerful than those elders), they tend to be in a state of fresh and keenly felt disillusionment. But we do not therefore denigrate *everything* that we associate with this group: their perceived carefree-ness is envied, for instance[44] and their alleged fearlessness and risk-taking behaviour is valued rather highly in a capitalist society. Angst, however, certainly *is* denigrated and contributes to the denigration of adolescents. A plausible thought is that it is adolescents' sudden attitude of unimpressedness towards things they had previously tolerated and even admired that makes them so unacceptable: they threaten to overpower and outlive us, to destroy us and what we stand for.[45] So my claim is that adolescence is denigrated because it is threatening, and it is threatening partly because *angst* is threatening—and the reason why angst is a threat to the social world is that there is *truth* in the radical unimpressed-ness that comes with it. None of this is meant to imply that adolescents in general are undiscovered, unappreciated intellectuals; nor is it meant to deny that adolescent angst and its expression frequently contain unattractive elements of self-righteousness, self-pity, pretentiousness or pseudo-profundity. But the suggestion is that nevertheless there is, as we say, 'something to it'—some insight, or potential for insight; and that the dismissal of it all as 'self-righteous' (etc.) is partially explicable in terms of the social world's fear of being exposed. If we're looking to develop a properly critical approach to philosophy, then this is perhaps not such a bad place to start.

There is another important respect in which I think angst is a promising idea, and this comes out when we ask *why it is* that this mentality is correlated with adolescence. This question can be given a plausible answer in terms of something negative, that is, in terms of what the adolescent is *not* subject to. What I want to suggest is that adolescence produces a fleeting immunity from two main categories of ideological 'disease'—the ideological diseases of childhood and of adulthood; although describing it as a 'period of immunity', however fleeting, is somewhat misleading—the 'immunity' *just is* the changeover between two forms of vulnerability. This can be thought of as being like the moment when a guard changes his grip on the prisoner he is escorting. This is the moment at which the prisoner has his chance of escape (albeit tiny)—at least, it is the moment at which the possibility of escape is likely to strike him with greatest vividness. Likewise, there are two very broad social roles—changing, but doing so stably and smoothly—that we are expected to occupy in our lifetimes: childhood and adulthood.[46] Adolescence may then be seen as a kind of rupture between these two phases, the individual's moment of bumpy transition between secure enclosures, and thus the moment at which the whole situation is at its most volatile. Not only is there the potential for the agent to 'escape'—that is, to avoid being assimilated into the role of 'adult', by turning mad, delinquent or revolutionary—but the danger seems to have a crucial *epistemic* aspect: it is a danger of obtaining insight into something. To switch metaphors momentarily, we all know that the sudden cessation or alteration of a background noise, to which we had adjusted and hence ceased to hear, can make us immediately and acutely aware of it. In the same way, the moment of the guard's change of grip may make the prisoner more aware of the grip in which he has been held, as well as the grip in which he is newly seized. An essential part of that moment's potential for escape is this potential for awareness.

If adolescence is thought of in this way, then rather than sneering at the ideas and sentiments associated with that phase of life, turning our backs on them, and then sneering once again over our shoulders, we should perhaps look at those ideas and sentiments with a special interest and reverence. But if that begins to sound like a positive programme, a second glance at the phenomenon of adolescence should put a stop to it. Whatever danger (i.e., hope) is carried by the transitional moment of adolescence is very effectively neutralized. In the first place, most adolescents are sooner or later absorbed into 'maturity', and part of what that means is that they 'overcome' (i.e., forget)[47] angst—with the earlier noted contempt for this emotion helping to induce the process and to inhibit its possible reversal. Furthermore, there is a powerful tendency for adolescence and its associated attitudes to be trans-formed into something impotent and highly exploitable, and at the same time for adolescence to begin to be eliminated as a distinctive phase. The exten-sion of compulsory education to eighteen, for instance, might be viewed as an attempt to extend the safe enclosure of childhood and eat away at the rocky territory of adolescence; the rise of the 'gap year' as a recognizable and saleable package of tans, backpacks and moral righteousness (and the associated identity of the 'gapper') is an attempt to shape adolescence into an acceptable form. And of course, angst and rebellion too have their associated industries and approved channels, chiefly within music and fashion: you can choose between being an emo kid or a metalhead or a goth (or you could). Finally, and most depressingly of all, there is an increasingly noticeable trend for young people—especially those likely to form future social elites, and in whom persistent angst would be correspondingly the more dangerous—to begin to take an interest in 'maturity' even before adolescence has begun, to skip visible angst altogether and become, to borrow Adorno's words, more insufferably grown-up than their parents ever were.[48] If that is right, we may (now, or soon) only be warranted in consulting the *history* rather than the memory of adolescence.

The case of adolescent angst thus seems to give with one hand and to take away with the other. It offers the glimmerings of an approach to philosophy that is critical and in some sense negatively construed, in that it is presented in terms of the attempt to unmask problematic forms of ideology. Yet reflection on the same case draws us towards a view of ideology as amoeba-like: infinitely supple, constantly in motion and capable of engulfing anything in its path.

***

There is perhaps restlessness and angst in all of us, perhaps in differing forms and strengths[49]—although it can only grow so strong before it makes life unliveable; and perhaps, in the kind of social world in which we find ourselves, this is what constitutes a 'philosophical' attitude, in the aspirational sense of that term.[50] But given the apparently inevitable doomward trajectory of that social world, it is unclear what point there is in the aspiration. Its truth doesn't seem capable of benefiting anyone—least of all the angst-ridden. In that case it is hard to see what differentiates it from a painful disease. We might come to take a keen interest in our condition, to see it as constitutive of our identities, even to take a pride in it. We might feel an evangelical urge to spread it around, or at least to seek out others with similar symptoms. And we may feel it necessary to talk incessantly about it. But if there is anything to justify this enthusiasm, other than its ability to comfort us, it is not the sort of thing that can be established by argument. If there is something valuable here at all, it must be an aesthetic value, or the sort of value that love has. We can't give it a foundation, nor would it make any difference if we could.

Whatever the value of this disease, it cannot be made into a methodological programme. As soon as we set down and advocate a restless- or angst-based approach to philosophy, we alter and undermine the restlessness or angst: we offer rest, or comfort. And as soon as we follow such a methodology or take ourselves to have instantiated it, we *take* this rest or comfort.

Monet is said to have spent many years trying to invent a way to catch sunlight and fling it onto his canvases. The attempt to give an angst-based or otherwise anti-utopian methodology of philosophy is perhaps like that. Of course, we can go through this sort of performance if we wish. We might look on it as a beautiful tribute to the impossible. Or on the other hand, we might think that, like Monet prancing around with a net, it looks a bit ridiculous.

What we shouldn't do is delude ourselves into thinking that we really can fling light onto a canvas. We cannot, by giving a 'methodology-against-methodologies', avoid the kind of dead complacency which refusing to settle on a methodology was meant to avoid. And nor can we escape our enmeshment in an ideological matrix that conditions the force of all our expressions. Sunlight may be pleasant, and angst may have special philosophical value; but there are limits to the use we can make of either. At a certain point, we have to know when to stop.

NOTES

For Baz.

1. Dostoevsky (2008 [1864]; p. 10).

2. To me, this image of *closing off* is reminiscent of sheepdog trials: when the sheep are herded into the pen, you close the gate. It occurs to me now that this is quite a good metaphor both for the coercive aspect of philosophical argumentation that I was trying to capture at the end of my introduction and also for the way in which methodological norms guide and restrict the way philosophy is done.

3. I sometimes think of this as the 'goodwill' response to the phenomenon of ideology-in-a-pejorative-sense—a response that takes the phenomenon sufficiently un-seriously as to be content with a promise to 'try harder' in the future. This reminds me of when I was three or four and insistent that if someone would only buy me a goldfish, I would uncomplainingly spend the whole of each day blowing bubbles into its bowl through a straw, so that there would be no need to buy a special electric filter.

4. Ramsey (1960; pp. 287–88); Chomsky makes a point of opposing something like this attitude and does so in such a way as to suggest that he takes it to be a prevalent one (Chomsky and Foucault [2006]).

5. This is not to say that it is any *more* difficult than plenty of other, less celebrated things—for example, welding—(if that sort of comparison is even possible).

6. Cf. Heidegger's definition of man as the 'shepherd of Being' (*der Hirt des Seins*). As Steiner (1978; p. 123) puts it: 'Man only *is* to the extent that he stands open to Being in what Wordsworth would have called a "wise passiveness"'.

7. Heidegger (1962). It is a matter of some controversy to what extent this particular idea, or Heidegger's ideas in general, can be separated from his Nazism. I am not in a position to speak with any authority on that, although I can say two general things: (i) it is, on the whole, a naïve mistake to think that people's ideas and statements—their meaning and significance—can be understood in isolation from *other* ideas and statements to which they are committed, from their deeds and practical stances, or from the context in which all this occurs; (ii) it is an equally naïve mistake to think that we either can or should confine ourselves to making use of only those ideas whose origins are innocent and pure. Now, there is a rather large gap between being innocent and pure and being a card-carrying Nazi. But there is also a fairly large gap between innocence and the championing of colonialism, racism and sexism (which is something that most of the 'great' philosophers did). To attempt to identify a kind of 'moral reprehensibility bar' (beyond which it is inappropriate to affirm any aspect of the thought of the philosopher in question), seems to me entirely the wrong approach: not least because we end up having to say, in effect, that racism, sexism and colonialism are 'not bad enough' to warrant the full cold-shoulder treatment (or else chuck out pretty much the whole of the 'received' history of philosophy). The judgements we make on this must inevitably be sensitive to context (e.g., the nature and scope of the affirmation, and the intellectual and social background against which the affirmation takes place): for example, I *do* think that there's a problem with worshipping Mill as the godfather of everything good and progressive that ever happened, and doing so

in a climate in which his attitudes on race and British imperialism are far less well known than his more palatable views on women. The case of Heidegger is different, it seems to me, in that his Nazism is one of the most well-known things about him—which does not mean that we have carte blanche to affirm his ideas, free of any worries about legitimizing their context of origin. It all depends on *how* we talk about him (Steiner [1978] seems to me to get it about right). The main point of my own invocation of Heidegger here is just to show how the basic thought I'm interested in (about negative and passive ways of looking) is something which resonates across otherwise disparate traditions—and what could be more disparate than Buddhists and Nazis? Or so you might think (see the 2013 *Vice* article, 'Is Burma's Anti-Muslim Violence Led by "Buddhist Neo-Nazis"?' Downs [2013]).

8. Of course, how much relevance you take observations about art to have to philosophy depends on the relationship that you take to obtain between the two areas. Needless to say, I'm suspicious of the idea of a sharp separation, and I wonder whether it may just be a perversion that is produced by certain academic contexts. When I discussed the point with my father, someone who has had no formal secondary education, he immediately volunteered an intuition that philosophy and art are in some sense continuous. In this, to my mind, he had something right which seems to escape many of those whose job it is to think about such things. Professor Gary Gutting, for example, insisted to me that philosophy must be securely fenced off from literature because the former is obviously about *argument*, while the latter is not. I realize, of course, that Gutting and my father may not be particularly representative of philosophers and non-philosophers respectively. I offer the anecdotes as illustrations of a hypothesis that might be worth further investigation, and to introduce a point to which I return later, relevant to my general interest here in the relative situation of philosophers (as against others) with respect to truth or insight: the thought is that philosophers may be uniquely or especially prone to the making of certain sorts of 'trained mistakes' (cf. again Heidegger [e.g., 1962], who regards the whole of Western philosophy as responsible for a fatal 'forgetting of Being').

9. Keats makes only one explicit reference to this idea, in a letter to his brother, George, dated 21 December 1817, in which he talks about shunning the 'irritable reaching after fact and reason'. See Wu (2005; p. 1351).

10. An arbitrary selection of examples: a sampled voice on DJ Shadow's album, *Entroducing*, says, 'It's not really me that's coming . . . the music's coming through me.' Bob Dylan, in an interview for *Playboy* magazine, says, ' . . . you get the first line and then it's just like riding a bull'. Tom Waits (2006) describes artistic inspiration as a matter of '[making] sure your umbrella is upside down' (p. 66) and says, 'I don't want to sound spiritual, but I try to make an antenna out of myself, a lightning rod out of myself, so whatever is out there can come in. It happens in different places, in hotels, in the car—when someone else is driving' (p. 155).

11. Or, in the words of *South Park*'s Eric Cartman, 'a bunch of tree-hugging hippie crap'. Maybe students should swear on the authority of Cartman instead of Frankfurt (see my introduction, fn. 22).

12. The later Heidegger, in particular, thinks of the poet as the preeminent 'shepherd of Being' and regards 'authentic' poetry as extremely rare—see Steiner (1978; p. 136).

13. Only certain sorts of truth. You wouldn't say, for example, that humans were set up or configured so as to arrive at a true picture of the atomic structure of water, or of how to work a DVD player.

14. Arguably, many invocations of ideological distortion are committed to this sort of optimism. When we say that people only labour under some illusion because it serves the interests of the powerful for them to do so, the implication seems to be that they would get the matter *right* if the illusion did not further the interests of the powerful—or, better, if society were in a condition where the possibility of an illusion furthering the interests of the powerful could not

even arise. One might, of course, make use of an ideological explanation to account for why people think, for example, that their interests are served by buying new cars and hair straighteners *rather than by obeying the Pope*. But it's hard to see how the notion of ideology could have the *emancipatory* potential that, for example, the members of the Frankfurt School take it to have, if there is not also an underlying presumption that human beings have a basic ability to judge correctly what is in their interests—albeit an ability that can be overridden by the pressing of ideas into the service of the powerful (who, of course, share this basic ability to judge their own interests).

15. This is not to deny, of course, that people have other reasons for going to conferences: a sense of obligation; an unreflective attitude that 'this is what academics do'; a desire to impress, 'network', or just to be where one's friends are, get free drink and expenses-paid travel, and so on.

16. This is what my arguments throughout this text have suggested for the particular case of political philosophy, anyway.

17. This was what I suggested was happening in Blackburn's treatment of Marx, and in some reactions to Geuss's attitude to Rawls, and in the liberal appropriation of MacKinnon (see my chapters 3 and 4, and cf. the sort of 'straw realism' highlighted in chapter 5).

18. I should note that the distinction between internal and external dimensions is an artificial, pragmatic one, and that the two are in fact very closely connected—for instance, the set of values outlined above as being instilled in the philosopher included a kind of individualism about the process of philosophizing.

19. It might be tempting to remove the sense of paradox attendant upon the idea of an 'enabling obstacle' here by rendering Feuerbach thus: religion *starts off* as an enabler to progress, then at a certain point becomes an obstacle. But this doesn't capture it adequately. Even at a stage where religion is not yet ripe to be cast off, it will be true to say *both* that religion prevents us from realizing self-knowledge *and* that it is a necessary prerequisite of this realisation. Cf. the situation of a foetus, attached to the umbilical cord, or a kidney patient attached to a dialysis machine: the thing that restricts freedom of movement also, by preserving life, preserves a precondition of any movement at all.

20. Neill: 'Summerhill began as an experimental school. It is no longer such; it is now a demonstration school, for it demonstrates that *freedom works*'(1968; p. 20).

21. As Neill (1968; p. 19) observes: 'Newspapers call it a *Go-as-you-please School* and imply that it is a gathering of wild primitives who know no law and have no manners.' When I talk about Summerhill as the school my brother went to and was expelled from, I almost invariably have to explain to people that Summerhill does have loads of rules—they are determined by the votes of the children and staff—and that it's perfectly possible to be punished and even expelled for violation of these rules—again, according to the outcome of a vote at a school meeting. As it happens, this was not the procedure by which my brother was kicked out—he just received a letter (thus illustrating the tendency for utopian communities to deviate from their ideals).

22. Of course, there are always limits to this tolerance, and the history of Summerhill is in part the history of the numerous attempts to close it down.

23. This is why Illich is good: he emphasizes that the whole of society needs to be 'de-schooled'.

24. Cf. Adorno, *Minima Moralia* §18: *Es gibt kein richtiges Leben im falschen* (loosely translated as 'Wrong life cannot be lived rightly'—see Adorno [1974; p. 39]).

25. The trend is *not* so antithetical, perhaps, to the spirit of what Geuss (2010) calls 'bourgeois philosophy', and the phenomenon of marketization can be seen as a continuation of the Enlightenment process to which bourgeois philosophy has affinities (cf. Adorno and Hork-

heimer [2002]). Put another way, there is an internal tension in the category of 'bourgeois philosophy' in that there is something inherently unphilosophical about the bourgeois.

26. Witness the Dean of Middlesex University Professor Ed Esche's claim, in support of the decision to close philosophy programmes, that the subject makes 'no *measurable* contribution' to the university (my emphasis). The emphasis on measurability was also characteristic, of course, of the Research Assessment Exercise and characterizes the current Research Excellence Framework.

27. For some responses to this widely observed phenomenon, see De Angelis and Harvie (2009).

28. See Akehurst's (2010) study of the importance of prevailing political attitudes (and anti-German sentiment in particular) for the development of analytic philosophy.

29. A recent example would be the appearance of David Cameron's idea of the 'Big Society' in the 'Delivery Plan' of the AHRC.

30. It's interesting to note that, while Foucault (1979—for instance) seems right to portray the development of power as a process of its getting ever more diffuse, refined, sophisticated and invisible, there's also a process—perhaps beginning as recently as the late twentieth century—by which ideology and control seem to get *cruder*, more unmistakeable. My sense is not that this represents a reversal of the kind of process that Foucault identifies (although it may well represent its death throes), but rather that the two processes are simultaneous and even identical—crude somehow becomes 'the new subtle'.

31. Adorno (1974; p. 211): 'There is not a crevice in the cliff of the established order into which the ironist might hook a fingernail.' Cf. the comment attributed to comedian Tom Lehrer: 'Political satire became obsolete when Henry Kissinger was awarded the Nobel Peace Prize.'

32. Anindya Bhattacharya used the same image in an address to members of Essex University during the campaign to save the Middlesex philosophy department, where Bhattacharya was an MA student at the time: Management were 'trying to turn Middlesex into a sausage factory'.

33. See, for example, Glock's (2008) *What is analytic philosophy?*—or any of the innumerable other 'what *is* philosophy?'–themed investigations.

34. Although the skin of a sausage is traditionally made from animal intestine, modern sausage production (conveniently enough for my analogy) replaces this with a synthetic substitute.

35. There are, of course, other places that harbour it too: the independent media, the arts, political movements, perhaps the mind of every individual. Unfortunately, these places are all also under siege, from Rupert Murdoch, funding cuts, police brutality and a stupefying culture respectively.

36. This event took place at the Institute of Contemporary Arts in London, 19 May 2010.

37. My friend Tim Storer helped remove what small danger there was of my enjoying this particular comfort.

38. In Arundhati Roy's *The God of Small Things*, there is a nice line about knowing that someday we will die, but living as if we won't.

39. Heidegger: *Alles ist Weg* (literally, 'All is way')—see Steiner (1978; p. 78). Cf. also Taoism and Buddhism—particularly Mahayana and, even more, Zen.

40. In fact, I'm told that the view of Zen and Taoist doctrine as directed towards understanding of eternal, unchanging truths is at best oversimplified, in that those truths are actually portrayed as 'eternally mutable'. This is not something I know much about but is worth acknowledging. Nothing hangs on it here.

41. See Lucretius (2004; p. 4): 'Then be it ours with steady mind to clasp, / The purport of the skies . . . '.

42. Heidegger places great emphasis on *Angst* as a mark of 'authenticity', and as that which brings us face-to-face with the 'Being question' (*Daseinsfrage*)—see Steiner (1978; pp. 92, 96).

43. See, for example, Hall (1904). Hall connects adolescence with the idea of *Sturm und Drang*, and with Goethe in particular, who 'has exploited all available resources of this genetic period of storm and stress more fully perhaps than any other writer' (pp. 533–34).

44. It's not clear how this fits with the perception of angst-riddenness, but I suppose there is no reason to expect the popular view of adolescents to be internally consistent; in any case, the contempt for and belittling of angst helps, perhaps, to make possible a simultaneous perception of adolescents as carefree—'if they only knew it'.

45. I don't mean to deny, by the way, that there may be other more straightforward (and perhaps sound) reasons for negative attitudes towards adolescents: for example, that they are inconsiderate, bad-tempered and malodorous. I just claim that this is not the full story.

46. Of course, there is a range of different roles for adults, but I suppose the most basic and general is the role of taking part in the prevailing kind of production and consumption.

47. Hall (1904; p. 535): ' . . . it is impossible to remember feelings and emotions with definiteness . . . Hence we are prone to look with some incredulity upon the immediate records of the tragic emotions and experiences typical and normal at this time, because development has scored away their traces from the conscious soul'. He then gives a nice example of a woman who listens to a lecture on adolescence and declares that she must have been abnormal, since none of the phenomena described apply to her adolescent self; at which point, her mother produces her diary.

48. *Minima Moralia*, §2. If Adorno can be interpreted as recognizing the development I am talking about, then of course that suggests that it has actually already been under way for some decades.

49. Cf. Menke's (2011) notion of *Kraft* ('force'), in respect of which he takes us to be *equal*.

50. 'Anyone who cannot cope with life while he is alive needs one hand to ward off a little his despair over his fate . . . but with his other hand he can jot down what he sees among the ruins, for he sees different and more things than others; after all, he is dead in his own lifetime and the real survivor' (Kafka, diary entry of 19 October 1921).

Bibliography

Adorno, Theodor. 1973 [1966]. *Negative Dialectics* (trans. E. B. Ashton). London: Routledge & Kegan Paul.

———. 1974 [1951]. *Minima Moralia* (trans. E. F. N. Jephcott). London: New Left Books.

———. 1984 [1970]. *Aesthetic Theory* (trans. C. Lenhardt). London: Routledge & Kegan Paul.

———. 2005 [1969]. 'Why still philosophy?', in *Critical Models: Interventions and Catchwords*. Henry W. Pickford (trans.). New York: Columbia University Press. Originally published 1969. Frankfurt: Suhrkamp Verlag.

Adorno, Theodor, and Horkheimer, Max. 2002 [1947]. *Dialectic of Enlightenment*. Stanford, CA: Stanford University Press.

Akehurst, Thomas. 2010. *The Cultural Politics of Analytic Philosophy*. London: Continuum.

Almond, Brenda. 2006. *The Fragmenting Family*. Oxford: Oxford University Press.

Alvineri, Shlomo, and de-Shalit, Avner (eds.). 1992. *Communitarianism and Individualism*. Oxford: Oxford University Press.

Anderson, Elizabeth. 2008. 'Expanding the egalitarian toolbox: equality and bureaucracy', talk at the Joint Session of the Aristotelian Society and the Mind Association; cf. her paper of the same name in *Proceedings of the Aristotelian Society Supplementary Volume*, 82, pp. 139–60.

———. 2012. 'Feminist epistemology and philosophy of science', *The Stanford Encyclopedia of Philosophy* (Fall 2012 ed.), Edward N. Zalta (ed.), plato.stanford.edu/archives/fall2012/entries/feminism-epistemology/.

Antony, Louise. 2011. 'Against Langton's illocutionary treatment of pornography'. *Jurisprudence*, 2 (2), pp. 387–401.

Arneson, Richard. 2008. 'Neutrality and political liberalism'. Unpublished paper.

Austin, J. L. 1962. *How to Do Things with Words*. Oxford: Oxford University Press.

Barry, B. 2001. *Culture and Equality*. Cambridge: Polity.

Bell, Daniel. 1960. *The End of Ideology: On the Exhaustion of Political Ideas in the Fifties*. New York: Free Press.

Bell, Duncan. 2008. 'Under an empty sky—realism and political theory', in Bell (ed.) *Political Thought and International Relations*. Oxford: Oxford University Press.

Benn, Claire. 2014. 'What is wrong with promising to supererogate'. *Philosophia* 42 (1), pp. 55–61.

Berlin, Isaiah. 1970 [1958]. 'Two concepts of liberty', in his *Four Essays on Liberty*. Oxford: Oxford University Press.

Blackburn, Simon. 1994. *The Oxford Dictionary of Philosophy*. Oxford: Oxford University Press.

———. 1999. *Think*. New York: Oxford University Press.

Boswell, James. 1986. *The Life of Samuel Johnson* . Hibbert and Christopher (eds.). New York: Penguin Classics.

Brecht, Bertolt. 1953. 'Gleichnis des Buddha vom brennenden Haus', in *Kalendergeschichten von Bertolt Brecht*. Hamburg: Rowohlt Taschenbuch Verlag GmbH.

Caney, Simon. 1995. 'Anti-perfectionism and Rawlsian liberalism', *Political Studies* 43, pp. 248–64.

Celan, Paul. 2003. 'The Meridian', in *Collected Prose* (trans. Rosmarie Waldrop). New York: Routledge.

Chomsky, Noam. 2003. *Hegemony or Survival*. London: Hamish Hamilton.

Chomsky, Noam, and Foucault, Michel. 2006. *The Chomsky-Foucault Debate: On Human Nature*. New York: The New Press.

Chomsky, Noam, and Herman, Edward S. 1994. *Manufacturing Consent*. London: Vintage.

Christiano, Thomas, and Christman, John (eds.). 2009. *Political Philosophy*. London: Wiley-Blackwell.

Cohen, Joshua. 1993. 'Moral pluralism and political consensus', in *The Idea of Democracy*, Copp, Hampton and Roemer (eds.). Cambridge: Cambridge University Press, pp. 270–91.

———. 2011. 'Occupation as fairness: What John Rawls would make of the Occupy Movement'. Interview by Seth Rensler. See www.bostonreview.net/BR36.6/joshua_cohen_seth_resler_john_rawls_occupy_wall_street.php. Or 'Occupy the airwaves, episode 6: Political philosopher John Rawls and Occupy Wall Street: A discussion with Stanford Professor Joshua Cohen', podcast at occupytheairwaves.com/ep6. Both accessed 17 January 2012.

Comité invisible, *L'Insurrection Qui Vient*. 2007. Paris: La Fabrique éditions.

Dahl, Roald. 2008 [1991]. *The Minpins*. London: Puffin.

Davidson, Donald. 1984. *Inquiries into Truth and Interpretation*. Oxford: Oxford University Press.

———. 2001. *Subjective, Intersubjective, Objective*. Oxford: Oxford University Press.

De Angelis, Massimo, and Harvie, David. 2009. '"Cognitive capitalism" and the rat race: how capital measures immaterial labour in British universities'. *Historical Materialism* 17 (3), pp. 3–30.

Dostoevsky, Fyodor. 2008 [1864]. 'Notes from the underground', in *Notes from the Underground and The Gambler*. Jane Kentish (trans.). Oxford: Oxford University Press.

Downs, Ray. 2013. 'Is Burma's anti-Muslim violence led by "Buddhist Neo-Nazis"?' *Vice*. Available at www.vice.com/en_uk/read/is-burmas-anti-muslim-violence-led-by-buddhist-neo-nazis. Accessed 29 October 2014.

Dryzek, J., Honig, B., and Phillips, A. (eds.). 2008. *The Oxford Handbook of Political Theory*. Oxford: Oxford University Press.

Dworkin, Andrea. 1979. *Pornography: Men Possessing Women*. New York: Plume, Penguin Books.

Dworkin, Andrea, and MacKinnon, Catharine. 1998. *In Harm's Way: The Pornography Civil Rights Hearings*. Cambridge, MA: Harvard University Press.

Dworkin, Ronald. October 1993. 'Women and pornography'. *New York Review of Books*.

———. 2000. *Sovereign Virtue: The Theory and Practice of Equality*. Cambridge, MA: Harvard University Press.

Engels, Friedrich. 1883. 'Speech at the grave of Karl Marx'. Highgate Cemetery. www.marxists.org/archive/marx/works/1883/death/burial.htm.

———. 1989 [1880]. *Socialism, Utopian and Scientific*. New York: Pathfinder.

Farrelly, Colin. 2007. 'Justice in ideal theory: A refutation'. *Political Studies* 55, pp. 844–64.

Finlayson, Lorna. 2009. 'Constructiveness in political criticism'. *Studies in Social and Political Thought* 16, pp. 48–63.

———. 2011. 'Death camps and designer dresses: the liberal agenda and the appeal to "real existing socialism"'. *Theoria: A Journal of Social and Political Theory* 126, pp. 1–26.

———. 2015. 'On mountains and molehills: Problems, non-problems, and the ideology of ideology'. *Constellations: An International Journal of Critical and Democratic Theory* 22 (1), pp. 135–46.

———. 2014. 'How to screw things with words'. *Hypatia: A Journal of Feminist Philosophy* 29 (4), pp. 774–89.

———. 2015. 'With radicals like these, who needs conservatives? Doom, gloom and realism in political theory'. *European Journal of Political Theory*. Online for early view. Available at ept.sagepub.com/content/early/2015/01/30/1474885114568815.abstract.

———. forthcoming. 'An Introduction to the introduction', forthcoming in *Think Philosophy for Everyone: A Journal of the Royal Institute of Philosophy*.

———. 2015 (forthcoming). *An Introduction to Feminism*. Cambridge: Cambridge University Press.

Floyd, Jonathan, and Stears, Marc. 2011. 'Introduction', in Floyd and Stears (eds.), *Political Philosophy versus History?* Cambridge: Cambridge University Press.

Foucault, Michel. 1979 [1975]. *Discipline and Punish*. Alan Sheridan (trans.). Harmondsworth: Penguin.

———. 1988. 'The minimalist self', in *Michel Foucault: Politics, Philosophy, Culture (Interviews and Other Writings 1977-1984)*. New York: Routledge.

———. 2002. *The Archaeology of Knowledge*. Oxon: Routledge.

Frankfurt, Harry. 2005. *On Bullshit*. Princeton, NJ: Princeton University Press.

Freyenhagen. 2013. *Adorno's Practical Philosophy: Living Less Wrongly*. Cambridge: Cambridge University Press.

Friedan, Betty. 1963. *The Feminine Mystique*. W. W. Norton & Co.

Fukuyama, Francis. c1992. *The End of History and the Last Man*. London: Hamish Hamilton.

Galston, William. 2010. 'Realism in political theory'. *European Journal of Political Theory* 9 (4), pp. 385–411.

Gauker, Christopher. 1986. 'The principle of charity'. *Synthese* 69, pp. 1–25.

Gaus, Gerald. 1996. *Justificatory Liberalism: An Essay on Epistemology and Political Theory*. New York: Oxford University Press.

Geuss, Raymond. 1981. *The Idea of a Critical Theory: Habermas and the Frankfurt School*. Cambridge: Cambridge University Press.

———. 2005. *Outside Ethics*. Princeton, NJ: Princeton University Press.

———. 2008. *Philosophy and Real Politics*. Princeton, NJ: Princeton University Press.

———. 2009. 'Vix intellegitur'. *Cambridge Literary Review*, vol. 1.

———. 2010. *Politics and the Imagination*. Princeton, NJ: Princeton University Press.

———. December 2011/January 2012. 'Wer das Sagen hat', in *Mittelweg 36*, vol. 6.

Gilligan, Carol. 1982. *In a Different Voice*. Cambridge, MA: Harvard University Press.

Glock, Hans-Johann. 2008. *What Is Analytic Philosophy?* Cambridge: Cambridge University Press.

Gray, John. 2007. *Black Mass: Apocalyptic Religion and the Death of Utopia*. London: Penguin.

Green, Leslie. 1998. 'Pornographizing, subordinating, silencing', in Post (ed.), *Censorship and Silencing: Practices of Cultural Regulation*. Los Angeles, CA: Getty Research Institute.

Greer, Germaine. 2000. *The Whole Woman*. London: Anchor.

Grice, H. P. 1975. 'Logic and conversation', in P. Cole and J. Morgan (eds.), *Syntax and Semantics, 3: Speech Acts*, pp. 41–58, New York: Academic Press. Reprinted in H. P. Grice (ed.), *Studies in the Way of Words*, pp. 22–40, Cambridge, MA: Harvard University Press (1989).

Hall, G. Stanley. 1904. *Adolescence: Its Psychology, and Its Relations to Physiology, Anthropology, Sociology, Sex, Crime, Religion and Education*. New York: D. Appleton & Company.

Hamburger, Michael. 1989. 'An essay on the essay', in *Testimonies: Selected Shorter Prose 1950-1987*. Manchester: Carcanet Press.

Hanisch, Carol. 1970. 'The political is political', *Notes from the Second Year. Women's Liberation*.

Heidegger, Martin. 1962 [1927]. *Being and Time*. Macquarrie and Robinson (trans.). Oxford: Blackwell.

Honig, Bonnie. 1993. *Political Theory and the Displacement of Politics*. New York: Cornell University Press.

Honig, Bonnie, and Stears, Marc. 2011. 'The new realism: from modus vivendi to justice', in Floyd and Stears (eds.), *Political Philosophy versus History?* Cambridge: Cambridge University Press.

Hornsby, Jennifer. 2011. 'Subordination, silencing, and two ideas of illocution'. *Jurisprudence* 2 (2), pp. 379–85.

Horton, John. 2010. 'Realism, liberal moralism and a political theory of modus vivendi'. *European Journal of Political Theory* 9 (4), pp. 431–48.

Ibn Khaldun, Abd Al-Rahman. 2005 [1377]. *Muqaddimah*. A. Al-Shadadi (ed.). Casablanca. See also Franz Rosenthal's 1967 translation: *The Muqaddimah: An Introduction to History*. Princeton, NJ: Princeton University Press.

Illich, Ivan. 1970. *Deschooling Society*. London: Marion Boyars.

Jacobson, Daniel. 1995. 'Freedom of speech acts? A response to Langton'. *Philosophy and Public Affairs*, pp. 64–79.

Jowell, Tessa. 2011. 'To win back power we must stick to the centre ground'. *The Independent*, www.independent.co.uk/opinion/commentators/tessa-jowell-to-win-back-power-we-must-stick-to-the-centre-ground-2175230.html.

Kafka, Franz. 1988. *Diaries 1910-1923*. New York: Schocken Books.

Kelly, Erin, and McPherson, Lionel. 2001. 'On tolerating the unreasonable'. *Journal of Political Philosophy* 9 (1), pp. 38–55.

Kuhn, Thomas. 1970. 'Reflections on My Critics', pp. 231–78 of I. Lakatos and A. Musgrave (eds.), *Criticism and the Growth of Knowledge*. Cambridge: Cambridge University Press.

———. 1996 [1962]. *The Structure of Scientific Revolutions* (3rd ed.). University of Chicago Press.

Lane, Melissa. 2011. 'Constraint, freedom, and exemplar: history and theory without teleology', in Floyd and Stears (eds.), *Political Philosophy versus History?* Cambridge: Cambridge University Press.

Langton, Rae. 1993. 'Speech acts and unspeakable acts'. *Philosophy and Public Affairs* 22 (4), pp. 293–330. Reprinted in Langton, 2009, *Sexual Solipsism* (Oxford University Press).

———. 1999. 'Pornography: a liberal's unfinished business'. *Canadian Journal of Law and Jurisprudence* 109, pp. 109–133.

———. 2009. *Sexual Solipsism*. Oxford: Oxford University Press.

Larmore, Charles. 1990. 'Political liberalism'. *Political Theory* 18 (3), pp. 339–60.

———. 1996. *The Morals of Modernity*. Cambridge: Cambridge University Press.

Leopold, David, and Stears, Marc (eds.). 2008. *Political Theory: Methods and Approaches*. Oxford: Oxford University Press.

Lewis, David. 1986. *On the Plurality of Worlds*. London: Wiley-Blackwell.

Lipton, Peter. 2004. *Inference to the Best Explanation* (2nd ed.). London: Routledge.

Losurdo, Domenico. 2011. *Liberalism: A Counter-History*. London: Verso.

Lucretius Carus, Titus. 2004 [written 50 B.C.E.]. *On the Nature of Things*. New York: Dover.

Lukács, Georg. 1971 [1968]. 'What is orthodox Marxism?' in *History and Class Consciousness*. London: Merlin Press.

Lukes, Steven. 1975. *Power: A Radical View*. London: Macmillan.

MacKinnon, Catharine. 1987. *Feminism Unmodified*. Cambridge, MA: Harvard University Press.

———. 1994. *Only Words*. London: HarperCollins. First published in the United States in 1993 by Harvard University Press.

———. 2012. 'Preface' to Maitra and McGowan (eds.), *Speech and Harm*. Oxford: Oxford University Press.

Maitra, Ishani. 2009. 'Silencing Speech'. *Canadian Journal of Philosophy* 39 (2), pp. 309–38.

Maitra, Ishani, and McGowan, Mary Kate. 2012. 'Introduction', in Maitra and McGowan (eds.), *Speech and Harm*. Oxford: Oxford University Press.

Marx, Karl. 1990. *Capital: Critique of Political Economy*, vol. 1. London: Penguin Books.

Marx, Karl, and Engels, Frederick. 1987 [1848]. *The German Ideology*. London: Lawrence and Wishart.

———. 1998 [1848] *The Communist Manifesto*. London: Verso.

Masterman, Margaret. 1970. 'The nature of a paradigm', pp. 59–89 of I. Lakatos and A. Musgrave (eds.), *Criticism and the Growth of Knowledge*. Cambridge: Cambridge University Press.

Mazie, Steven. 2011. 'Rawls on Wall Street', in 'The Opinionator' section of the *New York Times*. See opinionator.blogs.nytimes.com/2011/10/21/rawls-on-wall-street/.

MacCallum, G. C. Jr. 1967. 'Negative and positive freedom', *Philosophical Review* 76, pp. 312–34.

McDermott, Daniel. 2008. 'Analytical political philosophy', in Leopold and Stears (eds.), *Political Theory: Methods and Approaches*. Oxford: Oxford University Press.

McEwan, Ian. 2004 [1997]. *Enduring Love*. London: Vintage.

McGowan, Mary Kate. 2009. On silencing and sexual refusal', *Journal of Political Philosophy* 17 (4), pp. 487–94.

Mellor, Hugh. 10 October 2008. 'What's wrong with analytic philosophy?' Talk delivered at the 'Moral Sciences Club Retrospective', Cambridge.

Menke, Christoph. 2011. *äesthetik der Gleichheit*. Documenta 13: 100 Notizen—100 Gedanken, No. 010. Hatje Cantz.

Merton, Robert. 1949. *Social Theory and Social Structure* . Glencoe, IL: Free Press.

Mills, Charles W. 2005. '"Ideal Theory" as ideology'. *Hypatia* 20 (3), pp. 165–84.

———. 2010. 'The Whiteness of John Rawls', lecture available to watch on YouTube. www.youtube.com/watch?v=Yfz20ZhOw4Y.

Monbiot, George. 10 May 2000. 'Streets of shame'. *Guardian* ('Society' supplement).

Morris, William. 1970 [1890]. *News from Nowhere*. James Redmond (ed.). London: Routledge & Kegan Paul.

Mouffe, Chantal. 2000. *The Democratic Paradox*. London: Verso.

———. 2005a. *On the Political*. New York: Routledge.

————. 2005b. *The Return of the Political*. London: Verso.

Mulhall, Stephen, and Swift, Adam. 1996. *Liberals and Communitarians*. Oxford: Blackwell.

Neill, A. S. 1968. *Summerhill*. Harmondsworth: Penguin.

Nietzsche, Friedrich. 1993 [1872]. *The Birth of Tragedy Out of the Spirit of Music*. Shaun Whiteside (trans.). Michael Tanner (ed.). London: Penguin.

North, Richard, et al. 2010. Articles in *European Journal of Political Theory* 9 (4): *Special Issue, Realism and Political Theory*.

Nozick, Robert. 1974. *Anarchy, State & Utopia*. New York: Basic Books.

Okin, Susan Moller. 1989. *Justice, Gender, and the Family*. New York: Basic Books.

Parsons, Talcott. 1952. *The Social System*. London: Tavistock.

Pettit, Philip. 2006. 'What are the most important unsolved questions in political philosophy and what are the prospects for progress?', interview in Nielsen (ed.), *5 Questions on Political Philosophy*. London: Automatic Press.

Power, Nina. 2009. *One-Dimensional Woman*. Winchester: 0 [Zero] Books.

Quinn, Ben. 2013. 'MoD study sets out how to sell wars to the public'. *Guardian* (26 September). Available at www.theguardian.com/uk-news/2013/sep/26/mod-study-sell-wars-public.

Quong, Jonathan. 2011. *Liberalism without Perfection*. Oxford: Oxford University Press.

Ramsey, Frank. 1960. *The Foundations of Mathematics*. London: Routledge.

Rawls, John. 1993. *Political Liberalism*. New York: Columbia University Press.

————. 1999. *The Law of Peoples*. Cambridge, MA: Harvard University Press.

————. 2001. *Justice as Fairness: A Restatement* (ed. Erin Kelly). Cambridge, MA: Harvard University Press.

————. 2005 [1971]. *A Theory of Justice*. Cambridge, MA: Harvard University Press.

Raz, Joseph. 1990. 'Facing diversity: the case of epistemic abstinence'. *Philosophy and Public Affairs* 19, pp. 3–46.

Rosen, Michael. 1996. *On Voluntary Servitude*. Cambridge: Polity.

Roy, Arundhati. 1998. *The God of Small Things*. New York: HarperCollins.

Saka, Paul. 2007. 'Spurning charity'. *Axiomathes* 17, pp. 197–208.

Sandel, Michael. 1998. *Liberalism and the Limits of Justice*. Cambridge: Cambridge University Press.

Sanford, David. 1972. 'Begging the question'. *Analysis* 32 (6). 197–99.

————. 1981. 'Superfluous information, epistemic conditions of inference, and begging the question'. *Metaphilosophy* 12 (2), 145–58.

Sangiovanni, Andrea. 2009. 'Normative political philosophy: a flight from reality?', in Leopold and Stears (eds.), *Political Theory: Methods and Approaches*. Oxford: Oxford University Press.

Saul, Jennifer. 2006. 'Pornography, speech acts and context'. *Proceedings of the Aristotelian Society* 106 (1), pp. 229–48.

Scheffler, Samuel. October 1994. 'The appeal of political liberalism'. *Ethics* 105, pp. 4–22.

Scheuerman, William E. 2008. 'A theoretical missed opportunity? Hans J. Morgenthau as critical realist', in Bell (ed.), *Political Thought and International Relations*. Oxford: Oxford University Press.

Scruton, Roger. 2010. *The Uses of Pessimism*. New York: Oxford University Press.

Shklar, Judith. 2001. 'The liberalism of fear', in Rosenblum (ed.), *Liberalism and the Moral Life*. Cambridge, MA: Harvard University Press.

Sirsch, Jürgen. 2012. 'Die Relevanz idealer Theorie bei der Beurteilung praktischer Probleme.' *Zeitschrift für Politische Theorie* 3 (1), pp. 25–41.

Skidelsky, Robert. 15 March 2008. 'Morals and markets'. *Guardian* ('Comment is free' section), www.guardian.co.uk/commentisfree/2008/mar/15/moralsandmarkets.

Steiner, George. 1978. *Heidegger*. London: Fontana.

Swift, Adam. 2006. *Political Philosophy: A Beginners' Guide for Students and Politicians*. Cambridge: Polity.

Swift, Adam, and White, Stuart. 2008. 'Political theory, social science, and real politics', in Leopold and Stears (eds.), *Political Theory: Methods and Approaches*. Oxford: Oxford University Press.

Thatcher, Margaret. 4 May 1979. 'Remarks on becoming Prime Minister (St. Francis's Prayer)', www.margaretthatcher.org/document/104078.

Trotsky, Leon. 1973 [1938]. 'Their morals and ours', Leon Trotsky/John Dewey, George Novack, *Their Morals and Ours: Marxist v. Liberal Views on Morality* (New York: Pathfinder Press).

Tully, James. 2008. *Public Philosophy in a New Key I: Democracy and Civic Freedom*. Cambridge: Cambridge University Press.

Waits, Tom. 2006. *Innocent When You Dream: Tom Waits: The Collected Interviews*. London: Orion.

Waldron, Jeremy. 1989. 'Legislation and moral neutrality', in *Liberal Neutrality*. Goodin and Reeve (eds.). London: Routledge.

Walton, Douglas N. 1994. 'Begging the question as a pragmatic fallacy'. *Synthese* 100 (1), pp. 95–131.

Walzer, Michael. 1993. *Interpretation and Social Criticism*. Cambridge, MA: Harvard University Press.

Warnock, G. J. 1973. 'Some types of performative utterances', in Berlin et al., *Essays on J. L. Austin*. Oxford: Clarendon Press.

Wenar, Leif. 1995. '*Political Liberalism*: an internal critique'. *Ethics* 106 (1), pp. 32–62.

West, Caroline. 2003. 'The free speech argument against pornography'. *Canadian Journal of Philosophy* 33 (3), 391–422.

———. 2012. 'Words that silence? Freedom of expression and racist hate speech', in Maitra and McGowan (eds.), *Speech and Harm*. Oxford: Oxford University Press.

Williams, Bernard. 1981. *Moral Luck*. Cambridge: Cambridge University Press.

———. 2005. *In the Beginning Was the Deed: Realism and Moralism in Political Argument*. Hawthorn (ed.). Princeton, NJ: Princeton University Press.

Wilson, Neil L. 1959. 'Substances without substrata'. *Review of Metaphysics*, XII/4 (48), pp. 521–39.

Wolff, Jonathan. 3 February 2009. 'Political philosophy and public policy'. Talk delivered at the Moral Sciences Club, Cambridge.

Wolff, R. P. 1977. *Understanding Rawls*. Princeton, NJ: Princeton University Press.

Wu, Duncan. 2005. *Romanticism: An Anthology* (3rd ed.). London: Blackwell.

Index

adolescence, 191–194. *See also* angst
Adorno, Theodor, 29, 127, 137, 151, 193,
  197n24, 198n31; and Horkheimer,
  154n29
anarchism, 18
angst, 191–195
Austin, J. L., 92–93, 95, 97, 99, 100,
  102–103, 104, 106, 152n3

beer, 27
Berlin, Isaiah, 57–58, 94–95
Brecht, Bertolt, 34n38

capitalism, 18–19, 27, 28–29, 48, 122–123,
  150, 158, 162, 182, 191
caricature, 83, 99, 144
charity, 3–4, 65–84; concept of, 66–67,
  68–69; formal principle of, 68, 179;
  incompleteness of norm, 72–73; as
  political, 66, 73–75, 78–79, 82;
  rationale for, 69–71; role of norm, 39,
  67, 82–84, 89, 146–147, 157
common sense, 34n37, 39, 55, 177
conservatism, 113, 121–131
constructiveness, 24–31, 66, 67, 81, 82,
  105, 146, 158; fact and foil, 26–27,
  34n32
critical theory, 2, 148

Dahl, Road. *See The Minpins*

democracy, 21, 52, 142–143; paradox of,
  48
depoliticization, 4–5, 131; of dissent,
  39–40, 106–107
division of labour, 140–141, 146–147
double standard, 21, 145, 159–165
Dworkin, Andrea. *See* MacKinnon,
  Catharine A.

education, 10; neoliberal reform of, 10,
  116, 187–188. *See also* school
end of history. *See* ideology, end of

fact sensitivity, 114, 115, 116–121,
  132n15–132n16
feminism, 2–3, 32n8, 33n12, 89–107, 157,
  174n9
Feuerbach, Ludwig, 184
forest of sin. *See The Minpins*: Austinian,
  106; Rawlsian, 40
Foucault, Michel, 58n2, 139–140, 152n7,
  188, 198n30
freedom of speech, 90–91, 93–94, 95–96,
  98, 104–105

Goldilocks, 125; Goldilocks issue, 118

Heidegger, Martin, 179, 195n6–196n8,
  196n12, 198n39, 199n42
Horkheimer, Max. *See* Adorno, Theodor

Made in the USA
Las Vegas, NV
09 December 2023

82405147R00132